About The Beijer International Institute of Ecological Economics

The Beijer Institute was established in 1991 as one of the research institutes of the Royal Swedish Academy of Sciences, to promote interdisciplinary research between ecologists and economists. The objective is to improve understanding of the links between economic and ecological systems, in order to ameliorate the management of these interconnected systems. The Institute brings together leading scholars from economics, ecology, and related disciplines in a number of research programs. The Institute works through extensive networks with scientists from all over the world, who are involved in the Institute's research programs, projects, or teaching and training activities.

Beijer Reprint Series and Beijer Discussion Paper Series are produced by the Institute. The Annual Report and Beijer Institute Newsletter, published twice a year, are available on request.

For more information please contact:

The Beijer International Institute of Ecological Economics
The Royal Swedish Academy of Sciences
Box 50005
S-104 05 Stockholm
Sweden

Rights to Nature

Rights to Nature

*Ecological, Economic,
Cultural, and Political
Principles of Institutions
for the Environment*

Edited by
Susan Hanna
Carl Folke
Karl-Göran Mäler

Technical Editor:
Åsa Jansson

Beijer International Institute
of Ecological Economics,
The Royal Swedish Academy
of Sciences, Stockholm, Sweden

ISLAND PRESS
Washington, D.C. • Covelo, California

Library of Congress Cataloging in Publication Data

Rights to nature : cultural, economic, political, and economic
   principles of institutions for the environment / edited by Susan S.
   Hanna, Carl Folke, and Karl-Goran Maler.
       p.   cm.
   Includes bibliographical references and index.
   ISBN 1-55963-490-1 (pbk.)
       1. Conservation of natural resources—Law and legislation.
   2. Right of property.   3. Environmental policy.   I. Hanna, Susan.
   II. Folke, Carl.   III. Mäler, Karl-Göran.
   K3478.Z9R54   1996
   333.7′2—dc20
                                                    96-31798
                                                       CIP

10   9   8   7   6   5   4   3   2   1

Contents

About the Contributors

Scott Barrett is Associate Professor of Economics at London Business School, a graduate school of the University of London, and Research Director at the Centre for Social and Economics Research on the Global Environment, University College London. His research focuses on economic issues of international environmental agreements and transboundary resources.

Fikret Berkes is Professor and Director of the Natural Resources Institute at the University of Manitoba. His research focuses on the interface between social systems and ecological systems, investigating in a variety of geographic and cultural settings (Northern Canada, Turkey, India, the Caribbean) the conditions under which the "tragedy of the commons" may be avoided.

Robert Costanza is Director of the Institute for Ecological Economics and Professor at the Center for Environmental and Estuarine Studies at the University of Maryland. He is cofounder and past president of the International Society for Ecological Economics (ISEE) and Chief Editor of *Ecological Economics*. Costanza's research focuses on the interface between ecological and economic systems, particularly at larger temporal and spatial scales.

Thráinn Eggertsson is a native of Iceland and Professor of Economics at the University of Iceland in Reykjavik. He has been a visiting faculty member at several U.S. universities and the University of Hong Kong, and is currently a Visiting Fellow of the Hoover Institution of Stanford University. Eggertsson's recent field of interest is the economics of institutions. He is the author of *Economic Behavior and Institutions* (1990).

Jean Ensminger is Associate Professor of Anthropology at Washington University. She is the author of *Making a Market: The Institutional Transformation of African Society* (1992). Ensminger's research focuses on applications of rational choice theory to anthropological questions, specifically on the uses of new institutional economics to understand the interaction between property rights and economic performance.

Carl Folke is Deputy Director of the Beijer International Institute of Ecological Economics, the Royal Swedish Academy of Sciences, and Associate Professor in the Department of Systems Ecology at Stockholm University. His research interests are in the transdisciplinary field of ecological economics, related in particular to the role of ecosystems and biological diversity as life-support systems for social and economic development.

Susan Hanna is Professor of Marine Economics at Oregon State University, and Director of the research program Property Rights and the Performance of Natural Resource Systems at the Beijer International Institute of Ecological Economics, the Royal Swedish Academy of Sciences. Her research focuses on fishery economics and management, the economics of common-pool resources, and the economic history of natural resource use.

Crawford S. Holling holds the Arthur R. Marshall Jr. Chair in Ecological Sciences at the University of Florida and is a Fellow of the Royal Society of Canada. His current research focus is a comparative assessment of the structure and dynamics of the Boreal forest and Everglades ecosystems. The key questions are how these systems are organized across spatial and temporal scales and how they might respond to global and climate change.

Svein Jentoft is Professor of Sociology at the University of Tromsö, Norway. He is the author of several books and journal articles on fishery issues. His most recent publication is *Dangling Lines: The Fisheries and the Future of Coastal Communities: The Norwegian Experience* (1993). He is also coeditor of *Aquaculture Development: The Social Dimensions of an Emerging Industry* (1996).

Narpat S. Jodha is with the Social Policy and Resettlement Division of the Environment Division of the World Bank, Washington, D.C. His research interests include agriculture and natural resource management in fragile areas. He has held positions at the International Crop Research Institute for Semi-Arid Areas (ICRISAT), the International Institute for Tropical Agriculture (IITA), and the International Center for Integrated Mountain Development (ICIMOD).

Karl-Göran Mäler is Director of the Beijer International Institute of Ecological Economics, The Royal Swedish Academy of Sciences, and Professor of Economics at the Stockholm School of Economics. He has published a number of books and articles on environmental economics. His current research interests are national income accounts and environmental resources, valuation of environmental resources, transboundary environmental problems, and problems of development and the environment.

Bonnie J. McCay is Professor of Anthropology in the Department of Human Ecology, Rutgers University. Her research is in fisheries and coastal communities of the North Atlantic, focusing on how people—as individuals and as members of different social units—respond to and affect marine ecological change. She has served on committees of the National Research Council and the Mid-Atlantic Fisheries Management Council, and is a Fellow of the American Association for the Advancement of Science.

Margaret A. McKean is with the Department of Political Science at Duke University and President of the International Association for the Study of Common Property. Her teaching and research interests lie in Japanese politics, environmental politics, property rights, and environmental policy.

Elinor Ostrom is Arthur F. Bentley Professor of Political Science and Co-Director of the Workshop in Political Theory and Policy Analysis at Indiana University. She is the author of *Governing the Commons* (1990), *Crafting Institutions for Self-Governing Irrigation Systems* (1992), and coauthor of *Local Commons and Global Interdependence* (with R. Keohane, 1995); *Rules, Games and Common Pool Resources* (with R. Gardner and J. Walker, 1994); and *Institutional Incentives and Sustainable Development* (with L. Schroeder and S. Wynne, 1993).

Steven Sanderson is Chair of the Department of Political Science and Co-Director of the Tropical Conservation and Development Program at the University of Florida. His current research interests include the role of property rights in biodiversity conservation. Sanderson's most recent book is *The Politics of Trade in Latin American Development* (1992).

Edella Schlager is Assistant Professor in the School of Public Administration and Policy at the University of Arizona. Her research explores institutional arrangements that local communities devise to address and resolve problems associated with natural resource use and conflicts.

Oran R. Young is a political scientist and Director of the Institute of Arctic Studies and the Institute on International Environmental Governance at Dartmouth College. He serves as the U.S. Delegate to the International Arctic Science Committee (IASC) and is a member of the Scientific Steering Committee of the Human Dimensions Program (HDP). His most recent book is *International Governance: Protecting the Environment in a Stateless Society* (1994).

Foreword

Every species above the most primitive draws resources for its sustenance from other forms of life. Species compete with each other for the scarce resources. But no other species has achieved anything remotely like the dominance of *Homo sapiens* over the food chain. Already this control has led to the extinction of many other species, some even during periods of very low human technological capacities. Here is a form of resource allocation, the allocation of living organisms, plant and animal, that seems to involve far more than the traditional considerations of economists, yet certainly requires their tools as well as others and also certainly influences the economic development of humanity.

The competitive economy, as usually analyzed, is a marvel of adaptation. Under the conditions of private property, resources are used efficiently in all the technical senses that economic analysis has brought to bear. The use of inputs needed to achieve a given output, say of food, is minimized. Retention of necessary resources for the future is provided by capital markets, which make it individually desirable to refrain from excessive consumption today, thereby freeing resources for the future. For example, when egrets or elephant tusks grow scarce because of hunting for profit, their prices will rise and induce consumers to shift to other, more abundant, resources.

Though the story is clear enough and has certainly worked in part, there is abundant evidence that the private property system is frequently not working as it is supposed to. Indeed, with regard to many branches of life, the very idea of property in the ordinary sense is practically and conceptually difficult. Fish and wild animals are mobile; they do not well accord with ordinary property concepts, for they cannot be identified with property rights defined, for example, by locality. They fall to some extent into the category of free-access goods, and both theory and practice show the dangers of over-utilization. The nineteenth century showed the possibilities of extinction of some aquatic mammals and near-extinction of others, such as sea-otters. These extinctions were not even in the long-run interests of the human predators, let alone of human beings as a whole, even if one granted no rights to the animals themselves.

Our modern understanding of ecological interconnections shows that the analysis of the effects on a given species is only the beginning of the story. Biological activity is an interconnected web, a complex dynamic system, in which attempts to exploit one resource may lead to effects in quite different domains. Hence, the concept of systems resilience comes to the fore. It is hard to see that any system of property rights could account for the ultimate effects, which sometimes transcend national boundaries and operate over very long distances.

The traditional economic analysis of production thus fails to be rich enough to encompass the actual links observed in the use of natural living systems as resources. But it is also true that economic analysis is not rich enough in its understanding of alternative social arrangements. When private individual property fails, economists usually think of state intervention, in the form of regulations or substitutes for prices (taxes and subsidies, for example). But human societies have long faced the problems of free access and frequently have created social institutions that regulate them. The "tragedy of the commons" is not based on the actual use of common lands. These had a long history of self-regulation. Social institutions of all kinds emerge to meet social needs; private property rights, frequently hard to define, on the one hand, and the supervision of the state, on the other, only begin to exhaust the list of social devices to balance individual initiative with prevention of injury to others.

The chapters contained in this volume give ample evidence of the complexities of both the natural and the social systems. The nature and magnitude of the pressure of human society upon the natural ecology, the great variety of existing property rights and social controls, the interactions among population, institutions, and economic development, and the lessons to be learned for the design of norms and institutions to meet the strains imposed today at the global level are all here addressed. Both future research and future policy and attitudes should profit from this work.

Kenneth J. Arrow
Stanford University

CHAPTER I

Property Rights and
the Natural Environment

SUSAN HANNA, CARL FOLKE,
AND KARL-GÖRAN MÄLER

Introduction

This book is about the human use of nature. More specifically, it is
about the systems of rights, rules, and responsibilities that guide and
control the human use of the natural environment. As we near the
end of the twentieth century, the challenge of using and sustaining
the capacity of the environment to generate a continuous flow of
resources and services becomes ever more difficult. The globalization
of human activities and large-scale movements of people have created an era of co-evolution of ecological, social, and economic systems at regional and even planetary scales. These have become so
interwoven that actions which are taken locally may accumulate and
spill over into regional and global effects.

One of the ways people are connected to their natural environment
is through the system of property rights. Regimes of property rights—
the structure of rights to resources and the rules under which those
rights are exercised—are mechanisms people use to control their use
of the environment and their behavior toward each other (Bromley
1991). Property-rights systems are a part of society's institutions: the
norms and rules of the game, the humanly devised constraints that
shape human interaction (North 1990). The way institutions are
designed will strongly influence the interaction between people and
the natural environment.

When we think about the way people interact with the environment, the following questions naturally arise. Who has rights to
nature? Is it possible to define rights that exclude some from the use
of nature? How are the rights specified, what are the rules under
which rights are exercised, and what are the duties and responsibilities that accompany those rights? How are rights allocated among

competing interests? To what extent are they connected spatially and temporally, and how do they evolve? Are they in tune with the dynamics of resource stocks, and processes and functions of ecosystems? What are the characteristics of successful property rights systems, how can they be designed for flexibility and adaptability, and redirected so that instead of causing overexploitation and environmental degradation, they contribute to a sustainable management of the natural environment? Issues like these are analyzed in this book, and from a diversity of perspectives.

In this introductory chapter we discuss the relationship between property rights and the natural environment and present the design of the book. We believe that it is through a deeper understanding of the role of institutions such as property-rights regimes, that environmental sustainability and social efficiency can be achieved.

Property Rights and the Natural Environment

The outcome of the human–environment interaction affects both the quantity and quality of environmental resources. Were property rights well defined, decisionmakers would take all consequences of their decisions into account. However, this is rarely the case with the natural environment. It is difficult, if not impossible, to establish well-defined property rights for "public goods" such as the atmosphere, climate, or migrating fish populations. These are also often poorly enforced, leading to the pattern of unconstrained resource use that Garrett Hardin has called "the tragedy of the commons."

> Each man is locked into a system that compels him to increase his herd without limit—in a world that is limited. Ruin is the destination toward which all men rush, each pursuing his own best interest in a society that believes in the freedom of the commons. Freedom of the commons brings ruin to all (Hardin 1968).

Hardin's famous parable conveys the important message that property rights matter. On Hardin's "commons," herdsmen can bring any number of animals to graze because the pasture is open to all. Since the right to graze is unspecified and unlimited, herdsman continue to add more animals, taking only their own benefits and costs into account and ignoring the collective effect of their actions. The pasture becomes overgrazed, because there is no system of rights and responsibilities that describes how grazing is to take place and how it is to be sustained.

It is of course possible to structure rights to the pasture in ways that are different from what Hardin describes. The pasture land can be owned as private property with grazing rights tied to land ownership, where individual owners use the land themselves, lease grazing rights to others, or sell the land. Alternatively, property rights to the pasture may be specified in a way that is not private but is nevertheless limited. One possibility is for a village to own the grazing land as community property, restricting use to village members, and regulating their use. Another possibility is for all citizens of the state to own the grazing lands, with a state management agency making decisions about pasture management and setting limits on grazing which are consistent with social goals for the environment. In either case of public ownership, rights to the natural environment are specified and allocated by collective decisionmaking.

In both private and public ownership of the grazing land, circumstances may exist which lead to overuse. Private owners may decide to mine the benefits of the land quickly to earn cash for investments that have higher rates of return. Village owners may find that expanding employment opportunities elsewhere lower the importance of the future productivity of the ecosystem, and so lower enforcement efforts or loosen the rules of access. State owners may succumb to political pressures exerted by some interests, allowing higher levels of short-term use. Uncertainties caused by political upheaval, health risks, or financial variability may create incentives to focus on current consumption at the expense of future productivity. Information critical for efficient management may be hard to centralize, or be asymmetric (people have different information), leading to inefficient management. Broadly viewed, environmental problems are problems arising from incomplete and asymmetric information combined with incomplete, inconsistent, or unenforced property rights.

Without a solution to the property rights problem, the environmental problem will remain. Economic development and sustainable resource use ultimately depend on institutions that can protect and maintain the environment's carrying capacity and resilience (Arrow et al. 1995). The knowledge of how property-rights regimes, as particularly important types of institutions, function in relation to humans and their use of the natural environment is critical to the design and implementation of effective environmental management and conservation. In the case of both public and private ownership of the natural environment, and the resources and services it generates, what matters is that property rights are well defined, that they reflect the social goals of use of the environmental resource-base, and that they are enforced.

Types of property-rights regimes comprise an almost infinite spectrum from open access to private property (Table 1.1). As our understanding of common property regimes and combined state/common property regimes has increased, it has become clear that no single type can be prescribed as a remedy for all problems of resource overuse and environmental degradation. In some contexts collective ownership is more appropriate for management of the natural environment than private ownership (cf. McCay and Acheson 1987; Berkes 1989; Feeny et al. 1990; Ostrom 1990; Bromley 1992). In addressing environmental problems, policy must focus on establishing property-rights regimes that are designed to fit the cultural, economic, geographic, and ecological context in which they are to function. Although general design principles are applicable in different contexts, their specific details must be determined by a particular context (Hanna and Munasinghe 1995a,b).

Property-rights regimes are only a beginning in the quest for efficient use of the natural environment. The basic functions of resource management—coordinating users, enforcing rules, and adapting to changing environmental conditions—cannot be fostered without a specified system of property rights. Resource management, in turn, cannot be maintained unless management costs are kept within bounds. These coordinating, enforcing, and adapting functions are associated with costs that are influenced by the particular structure and context of the property-rights regime and by the condition of the ecological system (Eggertsson 1990). As resources become depleted or as demand increases, property-rights regimes must account for more tradeoffs and spillover effects, increasing the cost of program design and regulatory enforcement. It is possible to create a system which is so costly to implement that it overwhelms the potential benefits to be gained from control. Movements to alter property-rights regimes are often driven by attempts to reduce management costs.

Many property-rights regimes have failed in the past and continue to fail, overwhelmed with pressure in the form of human population growth and increased per capita demand for resources. Patterns of resource use that are maintained in relatively stable situations may be disrupted under conditions of technological, economic, or environmental change. For example, the introduction of new technology,

TABLE 1.1

Types of Property-Rights Regimes with Owners,
Rights, and Duties

Regime type	Owner	Owner rights	Owner duties
Private property	Individual	Socially acceptable uses; control of access	Avoidance of socially unacceptable uses
Common property	Collective	Exclusion of nonowners	Maintenance; constrain rates of use
State property	Citizens	Determine rules	Maintain social objectives
Open access (nonproperty)	None	Capture	None

development of wider market areas, or changes in ambient weather conditions may all lead to changes in behavior that alter the property-rights regimes and change the rates of resource use. Groups may not be flexible enough to adapt rules to guide appropriate behavior. On the other hand, the markets may respond too quickly for protective regulations to adapt as well as take advantage of short-term profit opportunities.

Clearly, property rights must be designed appropriately and must also be robust. If the property-rights regime coordinates the human and natural systems in a complementary way, and if it contains feed-backs through which they interact, the result can be the maintenance of both ecological and human long-term objectives. Where natural and human systems conflict, or when feedbacks between them are absent, the resulting pattern of resource use can only accidentally achieve both ecological and human objectives. The more likely out-come is the short-term realization of human objectives, and the long-term realization of neither.

Design of the Book

Property-rights research has developed around the general question of how incentives are shaped by systems of property rights (Alchian and Demsetz 1972), and how those incentives lead to particular patterns of environmental use (Stevenson 1991). Its diversity is reflected in the variety of disciplines under which research is conducted: anthropology, economics, law, political science, and sociology. Each discipline frames its members' world views by its theory, its methodology, and its terminology. This disciplinary diversity provides simultaneously a richness of knowledge and a confusion of meaning. The confusion is most apparent in the terminology of property rights, where different terms are applied to a single concept. Perhaps the most frequent example is the term "common property," which is variously applied to resources which have unlimited access, resources which have restricted but collective access, and property-rights regimes in which rights are assigned to a group or community of people. To avoid the confusion caused by this particular example of multiple terminologies, we restrict the use of "common property" in this book to regimes in which rights are assigned to a specified group of people, and use the term "common pool" to represent those resources which have multiple users and for which individual ownership is difficult. In other cases where terms may have multiple meanings, we have asked authors to define them either directly or by example.

The chapters in this book comprise products of the research program "Property Rights and the Performance of Natural Resource Systems" conducted at the Beijer International Institute of Ecological Economics, The Royal Swedish Academy of Sciences, Stockholm, Sweden. The program began in 1993 with support from the World Environment and Resources Program of the John D. and Catherine T. MacArthur Foundation and the Environment Department of the World Bank. Its goal is to further the scientific understanding of ways humans relate to their natural environments through the structure, function, and context of property-rights regimes.

A major objective of the program is to expand the scope of property rights research through collaborations of social scientists and natural scientists. The benefit of such collaborations is that research problems are addressed in their full social and ecological dimensions. Traditionally, the field of property rights research has been the domain of social scientists. The focus has been on humans as "managers" of natural systems, disregarding the environmental feedbacks that management may generate (Gunderson et al. 1995). The natural system itself has been left in the background as the provider of resources and the recipient of impacts. Similarly, the field of natural resource management has been dominated by biological scientists. Their focus has been on various species of concern, usually a single species at a time. Humans are viewed as intruders, peripheral to the system's functions. The failure of research to account for the full spectrum of natural system functions and human system complexity has often hindered its ability to produce realistic results that lead to informed policies. Social scientists working with natural scientists, however, have a unique opportunity to contribute to the solution of pressing scientific and policy problems associated with human interaction with natural systems through property-rights regimes.

The papers that were the foundation for the chapters in this book were originally written to provide background to participants in the Beijer Institute's research program on the different dimensions of property rights and the environment: the interface between social and ecological systems, the structure and formation of property rights, culture and economic development, and property rights at different scales. The book is therefore divided into four sections reflecting these same categories.

Part I (The Interface Between Social and Ecological Systems) considers the basic attributes of the human–environment interaction. In Chapter 2, Robert Costanza and Carl Folke examine the structural and functional properties of ecological systems that affect the way they provide natural resources and ecosystem services. They argue that well functioning ecosystems are models of sustainable systems that offer design principles for institutions that respond to changes in essential ecological features. In Chapter 3, Susan Hanna and Svein Jentoft examine the social and economic properties of human behavior in interaction with the natural environment, looking at how culture, values, economics and social organization influence the use of environmental resources. Although important, these influences are often unrecognized in policies of resource management. In Chapter 4, C.S. Holling and Steven Sanderson examine what natural and social systems have in common. They focus on the need for adaptive management of natural resources to accommodate the complex dynamics of ecosystems, and argue that the social dynamics of the reconfiguration of institutions needs to be understood. The success of adaptive management hinges on the degree to which the human institutional timeframe can be made to reflect the cycles of natural systems. In Chapter 5, Fikret Berkes extends the discussion of ecological and human systems into the realm of property rights. He describes the major issue as being the crafting of the appropriate mix of property-rights regime and ecological system, citing the need for diverse, flexible property-rights systems that effectively link ecological and social systems.

Part II (The Structure and Formation of Property Rights) addresses the way property-rights regimes are conceptualized, the way they form, and their associated costs In Chapter 6, Bonnie McCay discusses a number of concepts related to property-rights regimes, clarifying their meaning and raising issues that contribute to the further development of theory related to property rights and the environmental resource base. In Chapter 7, Elinor Ostrom and Edella Schlager review property rights to common pool resources where exclusion is costly, and harvest by one diminishes the total available to others. They present a general theory of how property rights are established, how they are affected by social and physical factors, and how they are organized at different scales. In Chapter 8, Thráinn Eggertsson looks at the costs of developing and maintaining property-rights regimes as systems of control over resource use. These costs are incurred to gather information, develop rules of governance, and coordinate exclusion.

Part III (Culture, Economic Development, and Property Rights) examines the influence of the cultural context on the functioning of a property-rights system and on its link to economic development. In Chapter 9, Jean Ensminger illustrates the relationship between culture and property rights in the context of attempts by African governments to change property rights for land. Many top-down approaches to establish private-property regimes for environmental resources have failed not only because they have imposed high transaction costs, but also, and perhaps more importantly, because they are ill-adapted to the specific cultural context in which they are developed. In Chapter 10, Narpat Jodha looks at the process of rural development and its relation to local resource practices and customary arrangements in the dry tropical regions of India, where, in the interest of promoting economic development, a state can impose a property-rights regime over the natural environment that is ill adapted to traditional practices and creates the very environmental destruction it was designed to prevent.

Part IV (Property Rights at Different Scales) examines the coordination of property-rights regimes across boundaries of geography and jurisdictional authority. In Chapter 11, Margaret McKean addresses the problems of scale and linkage that create potential advantages for common-property regimes over common-pool resources through lowered monitoring and enforcement costs, improved fit between institutions and ecological systems, and internalized ecosystem effects. The advantages of common-property regimes in performing these functions are illustrated by a case study of Japanese communities that settled their competing claims to resources through the development of common property. In Chapter 12, Oran Young discusses the international coordination of the use of the natural environment, looking at the conditions under which "governance without government" can succeed in solving problems with the use of resources and ecosystems at the international level. He compares international governance to governance problems faced by common-property regimes in small-scale societies. In Chapter 13, Scott Barrett looks at the problems inherent in trying to manage resources that cross political boundaries. Such problems are difficult to solve because the initial allocation of rights to resources may not be well defined and because agreements between the countries are self-enforced.

Concluding Remarks

Institutional change shapes the way societies evolve through time. A society's evolution is ultimately dependent on a finite capacity of ecosystems to support it with essential resources and ecosystem services. To secure human well-being, there is an urgent need to design institutions that safeguard this dynamic capacity of the natural environment.

Property-rights regimes are critical institutions in this regard. They link society to nature and have the potential to coordinate human and natural systems in a complementary way for both ecological and human long-term objectives. In the past, proposals have often been made to transform the environmental resource-base into private property to remedy environmental problems. The theory behind such proposals was that under private ownership the incongruence of private and social costs and benefits would be removed, and private owners would have the incentive to protect the productivity of resources. However, ample evidence of resource overuse even under regimes of private ownership, and a large body of research on successful collective, decentralized regimes undermines this theory.

The issue at stake is not whether there should be private, or communal, or state-owned rights to the natural environment. The issue is how the bundles of different rights, from private to communal to national to international, and from local to regional to global, relate to each other, relate people to each other, and relate people to their natural environment on which social and economic development depend. Although the challenge of designing property-rights systems that fulfill the goal of sustainability, equity, and efficiency may seem overwhelming, it is our hope that this book will provide valuable insights of the important role that property-rights regimes play in achieving these goals.

ACKNOWLEDGMENTS

The editors acknowledge and thank Åsa Jansson for her diligent expertise as a technical editor. We also thank Christina Leijonhufvud and Astrid Auraldsson for their skillful coordination of the Property Rights Program workshops.

REFERENCES

Alchian, A. and H. Demsetz. 1972. Production, information costs, and economic organization. *American Economic Review* 62:777–795.

Arrow, K., B. Bolin, R. Costanza, P. Dasgupta, C. Folke, C.S. Holling, B.-O. Jansson, S. Levin, K.-G. Mäler, C. Perrings, and D. Pimentel. 1995. Economic growth, carrying capacity, and the environment. *Science* 268:520–521.

Berkes, F., ed. 1989. *Common Property Resources: Ecology of Community-Based Sustainable Development.* Belhaven Press, London, UK.

Bromley, D. W. 1991. *Environment and Economy: Property Rights and Public Policy.* Basil Blackwell, Oxford, UK.

Bromley, D., ed. 1992. *Making the Commons Work: Theory, Practice, and Policy.* ICS Press, San Francisco.

Eggertsson, T. 1990. *Economic Behavior and Institutions.* Cambridge University Press, Cambridge, UK.

Feeny, D., F. Berkes, B. J. McCay, and J. M. Acheson. 1990. The tragedy of the commons: Twenty-two years later. *Human Ecology* 18:1–19.

Gunderson, L. H., C. S. Holling, and S. S. Lights, eds. 1995. *Barriers and Bridges to the Renewal of Ecosystems and Institutions.* Columbia University Press, New York.

Hanna, S. and M. Munasinghe, eds. 1995a. *Property Rights and the Environment: Social and Ecological Issues.* The Beijer International Institute of Ecological Economics and The World Bank, Washington, D.C.

Hanna, S. and M. Munasinghe, eds. 1995b. *Property Rights in a Social and Ecological Context: Case Studies and Design Applications.* The Beijer International Institute of Ecological Economics and The World Bank, Washington, D.C.

Hardin, G. 1968. The tragedy of the commons. *Science* 162:1243–1248.

McCay, B. J. and J. M. Acheson, eds. 1987. *The Question of the Commons: The Culture and Ecology of Communal Resources.* University of Arizona Press, Tuscon.

North, D. C. 1990. *Institutions, Institutional Change and Economic Performance.* Cambridge University Press, Cambridge, UK.

Ostrom, E. 1990. *Governing the Commons: The Evolution of Institutions for Collective Actions.* Cambridge University Press, Cambridge, UK.

Stevenson, G. G. 1991. *Common Property Economics: A General Theory and Land Use Applications.* Cambridge University Press, Cambridge, UK.

PART I

The Interface Between Social and Ecological Systems

CHAPTER 2

The Structure and Function of Ecological Systems in Relation to Property-Rights Regimes

ROBERT COSTANZA AND CARL FOLKE

Introduction

Ecological systems consist of interconnected biotic and abiotic components at a range of scales from microcosms to the entire biosphere. They are complex systems that exhibit a diversity of structural and functional characteristics that affect both their sustainability and their relationship to property-rights regimes. Well-functioning ecosystems are a prerequisite for economic and other human activity. They are also models of sustainable systems from which we can learn in order to design more efficient and adaptive human institutions. This chapter describes some basic features of ecological systems of relevance for the design of property rights, and it discusses linkages between ecological systems, property-rights regimes, and other human institutions. The chapter begins with a description of the nature of ecological systems and their generation of essential ecosystem services. In the next section we discuss some problems and constraints of evolution in ecological and economic systems. In the final section we relate the properties of ecological systems to property-rights regimes and conclude that, in order to be sustainable, social systems and property-rights regimes need to be concordant with the characteristics of the ecological systems they refer to and at the proper scales.

Ecosystems, Biodiversity, and Ecological Services

An ecosystem consists of plants, animals, and microorganisms which live in biological communities and which interact with each other and with the physical and chemical environment, with adjacent ecosystems, and with the atmosphere. The structure and functioning of an ecosystem is sustained by synergistic feedbacks between organisms and their environment. For example, the physical environment puts constraints on the growth and development of biological subsystems which, in turn, modify their physical environment.

Solar energy is the driving force of ecosystems, enabling the cyclic use of materials and compounds required for system organization and maintenance. Ecosystems capture solar energy through photosynthesis by plants. This is necessary for the conversion, cycling, and transfer to other systems of materials and critical chemicals that affect growth and production (i.e., biogeochemical cycling). Energy flow and biogeochemical cycling set an upper limit on the quantity and number of organisms, and on the number of trophic levels that can exist in an ecosystem (Odum 1989).

Holling (1986) has described ecosystem behavior as the dynamic sequential interaction between four basic system functions: exploitation, conservation, release, and reorganization. The first two are similar to traditional ecological succession. Exploitation is represented by those ecosystem processes that are responsible for rapid colonization of disturbed ecosystems during which organisms capture easily accessible resources. Conservation occurs when the slow resource accumulation builds and stores increasingly complex structures. Connectedness and stability increase during the slow sequence from exploitation to conservation, and a "capital" of biomass is slowly accumulated. Release or creative destruction takes place when the conservation phase has built elaborate and tightly bound structures that have become "overconnected," so that a rapid change is triggered. The system has become brittle. The stored capital is then suddenly released and the tight organization is lost. The abrupt destruction is created internally but caused by an external disturbance such as fire, disease, or grazing pressure. This process of change creates opportunity for the fourth stage, reorganization, where released materials are mobilized to become available for the next exploitive phase.

The stability and productivity of the system are determined by the slow exploitation and conservation sequence. Resilience, that is, the system's capacity to recover after disturbance, its capacity to absorb stress, is determined by the effectiveness of the last two system functions. The self-organizing ability of the system, or more particularly the resilience of that self-organization, determines its capacity to respond to the stresses and shocks imposed by predation or pollution from external sources.

Some natural disturbances, such as fire, wind, and herbivores, are an inherent part of the internal dynamics of ecosystems and in many cases set the timing of successional cycles (Holling et al. 1995b). Natural perturbations are part of ecosystem development and evolution, and seem to be crucial for ecosystem resilience and integrity. If they are not allowed to enter the ecosystem, it will become even more brittle and thereby even larger perturbations will be invited with the risk of massive and widespread destruction. For example, small fires in a forest ecosystem release nutrients stored in the trees and support a spurt of new growth without destroying all the old growth. Subsystems in the forest are affected, but the forest remains. If small fires are blocked out from a forest ecosystem, forest biomass will build up to high levels, and when the fire does come it will wipe out the whole forest. Such events may flip the system to a totally new state that will not generate the same level of ecological functions and services as before (Holling et al. 1995b). These sorts of flips may occur in many ecosystems. For example, savannah ecosystems (Perrings and Walker 1995), coral reef systems (Knowlton 1992), and shallow lakes (Scheffer et al. 1993) all can exhibit this kind of behavior. The flip from one state to another is often induced by human activity. For example, cattle ranching in savannah systems can lead to completely different grass species assemblages; nutrient enrichment and physical disturbance around coral reefs can lead to replacement with algae-dominated systems; and nutrient additions can lead to eutrophication of lakes.

Natural ecosystems, including human-dominated systems, have been called "complex adaptive systems." Because these systems are evolutionary rather than mechanistic, they exhibit a limited degree of predictability. Understanding the problems and constraints which these evolutionary dynamics pose for ecosystems is a key component in managing them sustainably (Costanza et al. 1993).

Biodiversity and Ecosystems

Species diversity appears to have two major roles in the self-organization of large-scale ecosystems. First, it provides the units through which energy and materials flow, giving the system its functional properties. There is some experimental evidence (Naeem et al. 1994; Tilman and Downing 1994) that species diversity increases the productivity of ecosystems by utilizing more of the possible pathways for energy flow and nutrient cycling. Diversity also provides the ecosystem with the resilience to respond to unpredictable surprises (Solbrig 1993; Holling et al. 1995b; Folke et al. in press).

"Keystone process" species are those that control the system during the exploitation and conservation phases. The species that keep the system resilient in the sense of absorbing perturbation are those that are important in the release and reorganization phases. The latter group can be thought of as a form of ecosystem "insurance" (Barbier et al. 1994). The insurance aspect includes the reservoirs of genetic material necessary for the evolution of microbial, plant, animal, and human life. Genes preserve information about what works and what does not. Genes thereby constrain the self-organization process to those options which have a higher probability of succeeding. They are the record of successful self-organization (Schneider and Kay 1994). Günther and Folke (1993) distinguish between working and latent information in terms of the function of genes. The organisms or groups of organisms that are controlling the ecosystem during the exploitation and conservation phases can be looked upon as working information, and those with the ability to take over the system during the release and reorganization phases (those that keep the system resilient) as latent information. Both are part of functional diversity.

Hence, it is the number of organisms involved in the structuring set of processes during the different stages of ecosystem development, and at different spatial and temporal scales, that determines functional diversity. This number is not necessarily the same as the number of all organisms in the system (Holling et al. 1995b). Therefore, it is not simply the diversity of species that is important, it is how that diversity is organized into a coherent whole system. The degree of organization of a system is contained in the network of interactions between the component parts (see Ulanowicz 1980, 1986), and it is this organization, along with system resilience and productivity (or vigor), which jointly determine the overall health of the system (Mageau et al. 1995).

Ecosystems and Ecological Services

Ecological systems play a fundamental role in supporting life on earth at all hierarchical scales. They form the life-support system without which economic activity would not be possible. They are essential in global material cycles like the carbon and water cycles. Ecosystems produce renewable resources and ecological services. For example, a fish in the sea is produced by several other "ecological sectors" in the food web of the sea. The fish is a part of the ecological system in which it is produced, and the interactions that produce and sustain the fish are inherently complex.

Ecological services are those ecosystem functions that are currently perceived to support and protect human activities or affect human well-being (Barbier et al. 1994). They include maintenance of the composition of the atmosphere; amelioration of climate, flood controls, and drinking water supply; waste assimilation; recycling of nutrients; generation of soils; pollination of crops; provision of food; maintenance of species and a vast genetic library; and also maintenance of the scenery of the landscape, recreational sites, and aesthetic and amenity values. Ecosystems generate and sustain natural resources and ecological services, and also maintain nature in a condition attractive to humans. Some natural resources are priced in society. Most ecological services are unpriced and even unperceived, and lack effective property-rights regimes for their conservation. Preference-based valuation is often related to aesthetical and recreational aspects of nature, or specific resources such as fish, taken out of context of the fundamental value of functional ecosystems. (Table 2.1) (Ehrlich and Mooney 1983; Folke 1991; Ehrlich and Ehrlich 1992; de Groot 1992). Biodiversity at all levels (genetic, species, population, and ecosystem) contributes to maintaining these functions and services. Cairns and Pratt (1995) argue that if a society were highly environmentally literate, it would probably accept the assertion that most if not all ecosystem functions are, in the long term, beneficial to it.

The work of ecosystems and the services that they generate are seldom reflected in resource prices or taken into account by existing institutions. Many current societies employ social norms and rules which: (1) bank on future technological fixes and assume that it is possible to find technical substitutes for the loss of ecosystem goods and services; (2) use narrow indicators of welfare; and (3) employ world views which alienate people from their dependence on healthy ecosystems. But as the scale of human activity continues to increase, environmental damage begins to occur not only in local ecosystems, but regionally and globally as well. Humanity now faces a novel situation of jointly determined ecological and economic systems. This means that as economies grow relative to their life-supporting ecosystems, the dynamics of both become more tightly connected. In addition, the joint system dynamics can become increasingly discontinuous the closer the economic systems get to the carrying capacity of ecosystems (Costanza et al. 1993; Perrings et al. 1995).

The support capacity of ecosystems in producing renewable

TABLE 2.1
Natural Resources and Ecological Services
Generated and Sustained by Ecosystems

Natural resources

Oxygen

Water for drinking, irrigation, industry

Crops, fruits, vegetables, meat, fish and shellfish, other food and nutritious
   drinks

Fodder and fertilizer

Genetic resources

Medicinal resources and other biochemicals

Fuel and energy

Raw materials for clothing and household fabrics

Raw materials for building, construction, and industrial use

Ecological services

Fixation of solar energy

Protection against harmful cosmic influences

Regulation of the chemical composition of the atmosphere and oceans

Operation of the hydrological cycle, including regulation of floods and
   runoff

Water catchment and groundwater recharge

Regulation of local and global climate and energy balance

Formation of topsoil and maintenance of soil fertility

Prevention of soil erosion and sediment control

Food production by food webs

Biomass production

Storage and recycling of nutrients and organic matter

Assimilation, storage, and recycling of waste

Maintenance of biological (including genetic) diversity

Maintenance of habitats for migration and nursery

Maintenance of the scenery of the landscape and recreational sites

Provision of historic, spiritual, religious, aesthetic, educational, and scientific information and of cultural and artistic inspiration

---

Source: Modified from de Groot 1992.

resources and ecological services has only recently begun to receive
attention, despite the fact that this "factor of production" has always
been a prerequisite for economic development. In the long run a
healthy economy can only exist in symbiosis with a healthy ecology.
The two are so interdependent that their isolation for academic purposes has led to distortions and poor management.

Defining and Predicting Sustainability in Ecological Terms

Defining sustainability is actually quite easy (Costanza and Patten 1995)—*a sustainable system is one which survives or persists.* Biologically, this means avoiding extinction, and living to survive and reproduce. Economically, it means avoiding major disruptions and collapses, hedging against instabilities and discontinuities. Sustainability, at its base, always concerns temporality and, in particular, longevity.

The problem with this definition is that, like "fitness" in evolutionary biology, determinations can only be made after the fact. An organism alive right now is fit to the extent that its progeny survives and contributes to the gene pool of future generations. The assessment of fitness today must wait until tomorrow. The assessment of sustainability must also wait until after the fact.

What often pass as definitions of sustainability are therefore usually predictions of actions taken today that one hopes will lead to sustainability. For example, keeping harvest rates of a resource system below rates of natural renewal should, one could argue, lead to a sustainable extraction system—but that is a prediction, not a definition. It is, in fact, the foundation of maximum sustainable yield theory, for many years the basis for management of exploited wildlife and fisheries populations (Roedel 1975). As learned in these fields, a system can only be known to be sustainable after there has been time to observe if the prediction holds true. Usually there is so much uncertainty in estimating natural rates of renewal, and observing and regulating harvest rates, that a simple prediction such as this, as Ludwig et al. (1993) correctly observe, is always highly suspect, especially if it is erroneously thought of as a definition.

The second problem is that when one says a system has achieved sustainability, one does not mean an infinite lifespan, but rather a lifespan that is consistent with its time-and-space scale. Figure 2.1 indicates this relationship by plotting a hypothetical curve of system life expectancy on the *y* axis versus time and space scale on the *x* axis.

We expect a cell in an organism to have a relatively short lifespan, the organism to have a longer lifespan, the species to have an even longer lifespan, and the planet to have a longer lifespan. But no system (even the universe itself in the extreme case) is expected to have an infinite lifespan. A sustainable system in this context is thus one that attains its full expected lifespan.

Individual humans are sustainable in this context if they achieve their "normal" maximum lifespan. At the population level, average life expectancy is often used as an indicator of health and well-being

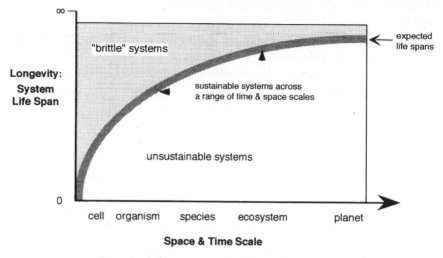

FIGURE 2.1. Sustainability as a scale-dependent (time and space) concept. *Source:* Costanza and Patten (1995).

of the population, but the population itself is expected to have a much longer lifespan than any individual and would not be considered to be sustainable if it were to crash prematurely, even if all the individuals in the population were living out their full "sustainable" lifespans.

Since ecosystems experience succession as a result of changing climactic conditions and internal developmental changes, they have a limited (albeit fairly long) lifespan. The key is differentiating between changes due to normal lifespan limits and changes that cut short the lifespan of the system. Things that cut short the lifespan of humans are obviously contributors to poor health. Cancer, AIDS, and a host of other ailments do just this. Human-induced eutrophication in aquatic ecosystems causes a radical change in the nature of the system (ending the lifespan of the more oligotrophic system while beginning the lifespan of a more eutrophic system). We would have to call this process "unsustainable" using the above definitions since the lifespan of the first system was cut "unnaturally" short. It may have gone eutrophic eventually, but the anthropogenic stress caused this transition to occur prematurely.

More formally, this aspect of sustainability can be thought of in terms of the system and its component parts' longevity (Patten and Costanza in preparation):

(1) A system is sustainable if and only if it persists in nominal behavioral states as long as, or longer than, its expected natural longevity or existence time; and

(2) Neither component- nor system-level sustainability, as assessed by the longevity criterion, confers sustainability to the other level.

Within this context, one can begin to see the subtle balance between longevity and evolutionary adaptation across a range of scales that is necessary for overall sustainability. Evolution cannot occur unless there is limited longevity of the component parts so that new alternatives can be selected. And this longevity has to be increasing hierarchically with scale as shown schematically in Figure 2.1. Larger systems can attain longer lifespans because their component parts have shorter lifespans and can adapt to changing conditions. Systems with an improper balance of longevity across scales can become either "brittle" when their parts last too long and cannot adapt fast enough (Holling 1986) or "unsustainable" when their parts do not last long enough and the higher level system's longevity is cut unnecessarily short.

Ecosystems As Sustainable Systems

Ecological systems are our best current models of sustainable systems. Better understanding of ecological systems and how they function and maintain themselves can thus yield insights into designing and managing sustainable economic systems. For example, in mature ecosystems all waste and by-products are recycled and used somewhere in the system or are fully dissipated. This implies that a characteristic of sustainable economic systems should be a similar "closing the cycle" by finding productive uses for and recycling of currently discarded energy and material, rather than simply storing it, diluting it or changing its state, and allowing it to disrupt other existing ecosystems and economic systems that cannot effectively use it.

Ecosystems have had countless eons of trial and error to evolve these closed loops of recycling of organic matter, nutrients, and other materials. A general characteristic of closing the loops and building organized nonpolluting natural systems is that the process can take a significant amount of time. The connections, the feedback mechanisms in the system, must evolve and there are characteristics of systems that enhance and retard evolutionary change. Humans have the special ability to perceive this process and potentially to enhance and accelerate it. The economic system should reinvent the "decomposer" function of ecological systems.

The first by-product, or pollutant, of the activity of one part of a system that had a disruptive effect on another part of the system was probably oxygen, an unintentional by-product of photosynthesis that was very disruptive to anaerobic respiration. There was so much of this "pollution" that the earth's atmosphere eventually became saturated with it and new species evolved that could use this by-product as a productive input in aerobic respiration. The current biosphere represents a balance between these processes that have evolved over millions of years to insure that the formerly unintentional by-product is now an absolutely integral component process in the system.

Eutrophication and toxic stress are two current forms of by-products that can be seen as resulting from the inability of the affected systems to evolve fast enough to convert the "pollution" into useful products and processes. Eutrophication is the introduction of high levels of nutrients into formerly lower nutrient systems. The species of primary producers (and the assemblages of animals that depend on them) that were adapted to the lower nutrient conditions are outcompeted by faster growing species adapted to the higher nutrient conditions. But the shift in nutrient regime is so sudden that only the primary producers are changed and the result is a disorganized collection of species with much internal disruption (i.e., plankton blooms, fish kills) that can rightly be called pollution. The introduction of high levels of nutrients into a system not adapted to them causes pollution (called eutrophication in this case) whereas the introduction of the same nutrients into a system that *is* adapted to them (i.e., marshes and swamps) would be a positive input. We can minimize the effects of such by-products by finding the places in the ecosystem where they represent a positive input and placing them there. In many cases, what we think of as waste are resources in the wrong place.

Toxic chemicals represent a form of pollution because there are *no* existing natural systems that have ever experienced them and so there are no existing systems to which they represent a positive input. The places where toxic chemicals can most readily find a productive use are probably in other industrial processes, not in natural ecosystems. The solution in this case is to encourage the evolution of industrial processes that can use toxic wastes as productive inputs or to encourage alternative production process which do not produce the wastes in the first place.

Energy and Organization

Economists often think of energy as a *commodity* (i.e., oil, gas, coal) rather than as a *property* (the ability to do work) that is a characteristic of all commodities. Discussing the substitutability of energy for other factors of production makes sense if energy is a commodity, but not if it is a property of all commodities (Odum 1971).

The first law of thermodynamics tells us that energy and matter are conserved. But this refers to all energy regardless of its degree of organization. The ability to do work is in general related to the degree of *organization* or order of a thing, the amount of information stored in it, not its raw energy content. Heat must be organized as a temperature gradient between a high-temperature source and a low-temperature sink in order for useful work to be possible. Likewise, complex organized structures like cars or books have an ability to do work that is not related to their raw energy content but is related to their degree of organization. Pollution, too, has an ability to do work (albeit unwanted destructive work) that is proportional to its degree of organization.

The second law of thermodynamics tells us that useful energy (organization) always dissipates (entropy or disorder always increases) in a materially closed system and in order to maintain organized structures (like trees, cars, books and, in general, natural and human-made capital) one must constantly add energy from outside the system. Planet Earth is a materially closed system and solar energy is constantly added.

But how does one measure the degree of organization of complex structures? Information theory holds some promise in this regard, but it has yet to live up to its potential. One way to *approximate* the degree of organization of complex structures is to calculate the amount of energy it takes, directly and indirectly, to build and maintain them. To do this one must look at the complex web of interconnected production processes that are ecological and economic systems.

As previously discussed, ecology is often defined as the study of the relationships between organisms and their environment. The quantitative analysis of interconnections between species and their abiotic environment has therefore been a central issue. The mathematical analysis of interconnections is also important in several other fields. Practical quantitative analysis of interconnections in complex systems began with the economist Wassily Leontief (1941) using what has come to be called "Input–Output (I–O) Analysis." More recently, these concepts, sometimes called the materials balance approach or flow analysis, have been applied to the study of interconnections in ecosystems (Hannon 1973, 1976, 1979; Costanza and Neill 1984; Finn 1976). Related ideas were developed from a different perspective in ecology, under the heading of "Compartmental Analysis" (Barber et al. 1979; Funderlic and Heath 1971; Patten and Jørgensen 1995). Isard (1972) was the first to attempt combined ecological economic system analysis using input–output methods. We refer to the total of all variations of the analysis of ecological or economic networks as "Network Analysis."

Network analysis holds the promise of allowing an integrated quantitative treatment of combined ecological economic systems. One promising route is the use of "ascendancy" (Ulanowicz 1980, 1986) and related indices (Wulff et al. 1989) to measure the degree of organization in ecological, economic, or any other networks. Measures like ascendancy go several steps beyond the traditional diversity indices used in ecology. They estimate not only how many different species there are in a system but, more importantly, how those species are organized. This kind of measure may provide the basis for a quantitative and general index of system organization applicable to both ecological and economic systems.

Ecological networks evolve to utilize the low entropy, high embodied energy by-products of processes in positive, productive ways. Economic systems may also evolve in this general direction, but we may wish to accelerate the evolutionary process in order to minimize the costs and disruptions inherent in trial and error. In addition, some of the possible "trials" could lead to destruction of our species and we would not want to risk that. There are several problems and constraints that limit this accelerated but informed economic evolution. To develop sustainable, nonpolluting ecological economic systems we need to understand and remove these constraints. Institutions, such as property-rights regimes, play an important role in this context.

Scale and Hierarchy

In modeling complex systems, the issues of scale and hierarchy are central (O'Neill et al. 1986). Some claim that the natural world, the human species included, contains a convenient hierarchy of scales based on interaction-minimizing boundaries—scales ranging from atoms to molecules to cells to organs to organisms to populations to communities to ecosystems (including economic, and/or human dominated ecosystems) to bioregions to the global system and beyond

(Allen and Starr 1982; O'Neill et al. 1986). By studying the similarities and differences among different kinds of systems at different scales and resolutions, one might develop hypotheses and test them against other systems to explore their degree of generality and predictability. According to hierarchy theory, nature can be partitioned into "naturally occurring" levels that share similar time and space scales, and that interact with higher and lower levels in systematic ways. Each level in the hierarchy sees the higher levels as constraints and the lower levels as noise. For example, individual organisms see the ecosystem they inhabit as a slowly changing set of constraints and the operation of their component cells and organs is what matters most to them. However, Norton and Ulanowicz (1992) suggest that what appears to be "noise" at a lower level could be turned into significant perturbations on the higher level. This can happen when a critical mass of components participate in a "trend," a behavioral pattern, which affects the slower processes at the higher level. The rapid and extensive human uses of fossil fuels could be seen as such a trend, causing perturbations at the global atmospheric level, which might feed back and radically alter the framework of action at the lower level.

Shugart (1989) explains the relationship between scales: "Clearly, natural patterns in environmental constraints contribute substantially to the spatial pattern and temporal dynamics of particular ecosystems . . . these patterns, especially temporal ones, may resonate with natural frequencies of plant growth forms (i.e., phenology and longevity) to amplify environmental patterns." The simplifying assumptions of hierarchy theory may ease the problem of scaling by providing a common (but somewhat generalized) set of rules that could be applied at any scale in the hierarchy.

Ecological and economic links between hierarchical levels and spatial and temporal scales can be illustrated by the relationship between migratory insectivorous bird populations and changes in insect outbreaks in the Boreal regions of Canada. A set of insectivorous birds is one of the controlling factors of the forest renewal patterns produced by budworm population cycles. Their existence contributes to the resilience of the boreal forest. Simulations based on long-term studies of budworm/forest systems dynamics indicate that the total bird population would have to be reduced by about 75% before the system would flip to a different pattern of behavior (Holling 1988). A large proportion of the bird species spend the winter in Central America and parts of South America. Radar images of flights of migratory birds across the Gulf of Mexico over a roughly 20-year period have revealed that the frequency of trans-Gulf flights has in fact declined by almost 50%, approaching the range of uncertainty in the simulation estimate above. Hence, in addition to regional forest fragmentation and its negative effects on nesting success of migratory birds (Robinson et al. 1995), Canadian Boreal forests and the economic activities dependent upon their functioning, are threatened by increasing land-use pressures in neotropical countries and along the migration paths of insectivorous birds (Holling 1994).

Another example of scale and hierarchy concerns the widespread cutting of mangrove ecosystems in Southeast Asia and South America for shrimp farming. This behavior causes the loss of spawning and nursery grounds for fish and shellfish. Occasional and local cutting of mangroves will not cause severe effects. But continuous and widespread cutting causes spillover effects on higher spatial and temporal scales. In this case the degradation takes place in the coastal area of one country, but causes reduced or lost yields of adult fish harvested in feeding grounds that belong to other countries. Land and water uses that reduce the diversity of the landscape, and with it communities, populations, and species, are likely to be less resilient to change in the long run.

The hierarchical approach in ecology makes it possible to shift the focus from preservation of single organisms or management of single resources to protecting the resilience of socially important ecological processes and the services they generate. It recognizes spatial and temporal scale interdependencies or cross-scale interactions.

Ecological Systems and Property-Rights Regimes

What can be said about property rights—given true uncertainty, the necessity of sustaining ecosystem functions and processes, and the challenge of managing cross-scale interactions among resources, ecosystems, and human uses? It is fairly easy to assign property rights to some resources and ecosystems such as trees or a lake. However, it is much more difficult to assign property rights to resources such as migrating fish populations and in particular to many ecological services such as the role of biological diversity in running nutrient cycles and water cycles in a forest. The reason is that these resources and ecological services are connected to other ecosystems than the forest, and thereby transcend several property-rights regimes. There is a major challenge in designing institutions and property-rights regimes that are in tune with the functions of ecosystems and the goods and services that they generate. A way to achieve such a synergy between ecosystems and institutions would be to look at whole drainage basins, and clarify the interconnections of the various ecosystems and land uses within the drainage basin, when it comes to generating ecosystem services and natural resources. How do we design institutions and property-rights regimes that account for the flows and feedback between systems and that maintain the buffer capacity to ensure a continuation of these flows? Luckily, there are design principles derived from studies of long-enduring institutions that have, at least to some extent, been successful in managing resources in a sustainable fashion (see Chapter 7). The design principles include: clearly defined boundaries for the use of a forest or of groundwater, as well as clearly defined individuals or households with rights to harvest the resources; rules specifying the amount of harvest by users related to local conditions and to rules requiring labor, materials, and/or money inputs; collective-choice arrangements; monitoring of resource conditions and user behavior; graduated sanctions when rules are violated; conflict-resolution mechanisms; long-term tenure rights to the resource, and rights of users to devise their own institutions without being undermined by governmental authorities; and, for resources that are parts of larger systems, appropriation, provision, monitoring, enforcement, conflict resolution, and governance activities need to be organized in multiple layers of nested enterprises (Becker and Ostrom 1995).

Some of the most sophisticated property rights institutions are found in areas in which these systems have developed over a long period of time, on the order of hundreds of years. Examples include Spanish *huertas* for irrigation, Swiss grazing commons, and marine resource tenure systems in Oceania (see Chapter 5). Yet other systems have collapsed and recovered over a period of time, sometimes more than once. In contrast, many traditional local communities have recognized the necessity of the coexistence of gradual and rapid change as described above for the forest fires in ecosystems. In their institutions they have accumulated a knowledge base for how to respond to feedbacks from the ecosystem. Holling et al. (1995a) argue that they have developed social mechanisms that interpret the signals of creative destruction and renewal of ecosystems and cope with them before they accumulate and challenge the existence of the whole local community. Disturbance has been allowed to enter at smaller scales, instead of being blocked out as is often the case in contemporary society. There is a culturally evolved 'monitoring' system that reads the signals, the disturbances, and thereby is more successful in avoiding the build up of an internal structure that will become brittle and invite large-scale collapse. The local institutions have evolved so that renewal occurs internally while overall structure is maintained. The accumulation and transfer of this knowledge between generations has made it possible to be alert to changes and continuously adapt to them in an active way. It has been a means of survival (Holling et al. 1995a).

We should learn from those local institutions that do not undermine their existence by degrading their ecological life-support system, thereby losing ecological and institutional resilience. A major task for modern society is to find similar ways of responding to changes in ecosystems. At present, there is a pervasive lack of social mechanisms for dealing with changing environmental conditions.

Human–Ecosystem Relationships: A Framework

To help us understand and model the relationships between ecosystems and human systems, we need a common language and an adequate conceptual framework within which to work. The lack of this framework has hindered communication between the relevant disciplines and has limited progress on sharing data, concepts, models, and results. One cannot develop a common theoretical structure and tie work relevant to the behavior of an ecosystem to the behavior of human systems unless a shared language exists. Developing a lexicon of key terms is an essential part of our task since many of the important concepts used in the diverse, relevant sciences are not known and understood in different disciplines. If there is to be a serious joint effort by scholars from diverse disciplines that goes beyond working on different parts of a large project, those participating have to start using concepts in a broadly similar way.

Figure 2.2 represents a general schema of parallels between human and ecological systems, and the nature of their interactions which has been worked out by an interdisciplinary team of natural and social scientists (Cleveland et al. 1996). Both ecological and social systems have "stocks," "flows" among those stocks, and "controls" of those flows. Both systems also have attributes of stocks, flows, and their interactions even though particulars differ. In an ecosystem, the biomass of, for example, fish comprises one stock. Stock can flow from the fish population into a fisheries catch, a flow that can be predictable or unpredictable. In such an example, the human systems and ecosystems interact, and all such interactions also have flows, controls, and attributes. By structuring the human and ecological systems, and their interactions, in parallel forms, we hope to facilitate comparisons of multiple levels.

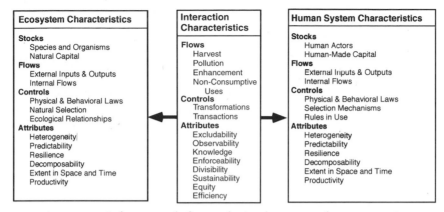

FIGURE 2.2. A framework for analyzing human and ecosystem interactions. *Source:* Cleveland et al. (1996).

A generalized interactive simulation game based on the general framework described above has also been developed in order to help understand the dynamics of linked ecological economic systems, including natural capital depletion, property-rights regimes, and trade-offs between economic efficiency, equitable distribution, and ecological sustainability (Costanza et al. in preparation). The model consists of a unit model containing two state variables—natural capital and human-made capital—which is replicated for each of three spatial cells meant to represent areas of land or water. A second scale is included as "higher level capital" meant to represent a generalized governance function—either a formal government or a less formal governance system. A complete description of the model and its behaviors is given in Costanza et al. (in preparation).

Even though the model is fairly simple, it produces a very rich array of behaviors that cover many of the general situations encountered in natural resource management. For example, there are three basic cases that the model can deal with:

(1) *Isolated systems*—When transfers (externalities) between cells are small the three cells operate as relatively independent systems. In this case, the maximum sustainable harvest rate in each cell depends completely on the local conditions in that cell's ecosystem. Three separate property-rights regimes (one for each cell) are appropriate in this case.

(2) *Large externalities and no higher level control*—This corresponds to an open access resource where free-riding and over-exploitation are possible. If a shared property regime can be developed and enforced covering all three cells, this is the most

simultaneously efficient, equitable, and sustainable way to manage this case.

(3) *Large externalities and no shared property*—If shared property cannot be implemented, then to avoid crashing the resource there must be effort to control flows between cells (externalities) using higher level (government) enforcement. This is costly and can be inequitable, sacrificing the efficiency and equity goals for sustainability. If control is insufficient in the interest of maximizing efficiency, the system will not be sustainable.

The model can also be played as an interactive game so that users can experiment with the various trade-offs themselves. It can also be used as an experimental system and statistically analyzed to assess the causes of variance in the system. The results of this analysis show that because the model (like the real world) has discontinuities and thresholds, it is very difficult to predict sustainability from the model's parameter settings (the "independent" variables in the statistical analysis of the model). The best guarantee of obtaining a sustainable run is to have all harvest limits in the model adequately below a safe threshold.

Conclusions

Sustainability requires that human social systems and property-rights regimes are adequately related to the larger ecosystems in which they are embedded. Understanding the complex evolutionary dynamics of these ecosystems is essential, but we must acknowledge and deal with the inherently limited predictability of complex systems. Because our knowledge of the structure and function of ecological systems is limited, and because we *do* know that sustainability depends on these systems, we must take a precautionary approach to their management (O'Riordan and Jordan 1995). Complex adaptive systems require "adaptive management" (Holling 1978). This means that we need to view the implementation of policy prescriptions in a different, more adaptive way that acknowledges the ever-present uncertainty and allows participation by all the various stakeholder groups. Adaptive management views regional development policy and management as "experiments"—wherein interventions at several scales are made to achieve understanding and to identify and test policy options (Holling 1978; Walters 1986; Lee 1993; Gunderson et al. 1995)— rather than as "solutions."

We have briefly discussed here some of the general characteristics of ecological systems as they relate to property-rights regimes and other human institutions. This work is only beginning and will require the continuing interaction and dialogue of natural and social scientists as described in the remaining chapters of this book.

REFERENCES

Allen, T. F. H. and T. B. Starr. 1982. *Hierarchy: Perspectives for Ecological Complexity*. University of Chicago Press, Chicago.

Barber, M., B. Patten, and J. Finn. 1979. Review and evaluation of I-O flow analysis for ecological applications. *In* J. Matis, B. Patten, and G. White, eds. *Compartmental Analysis of Ecosystem Models,* Vol. 10 of "Statistical Ecology." International Cooperative Publishing House, Bertonsville, MD.

Barbier, E. B., J. Burgess, and C. Folke. 1994. *Paradise Lost? The Ecological Economics of Biodiversity*. Earthscan, London, UK.

Becker, C. D. and E. Ostrom. 1995. Human ecology and resource sustainability: the importance of institutional diversity. *Annual Review of Ecology and Systematics* 26:113–133.

Cairns, J. and J. R. Pratt. 1995. The relationship between ecosystem health and delivery of ecosystem services. Pages 63–93 *in* D.J. Rapport, C.L. Gaudet, and P. Calow, eds. *Evaluating and Monitoring the Health of Large-Scale Ecosystems*. Springer-Verlag, New York.

Cleveland, C. J., R. Costanza, T. Eggertsson, L. Fortmann, B. Low, M. McKean, E. Ostrom, J. Wilson, and O. Young. 1996 Beijer Discussion Papers 76. Beijer International Institute of Ecological Economics, Stockholm, Sweden.

Costanza, R. and B. M. Hannon. 1989. Dealing with the "mixed units" problem in ecosystem network analysis. Pages 90–115 *in* F. Wulff, J. G. Field, and K. H. Mann, eds. *Network Analysis of Marine Ecosystems: Methods and Applications*. Springer-Verlag, Heidelberg, Germany.

Costanza, R. and C. Neill. 1984. Energy intensities, interdependence, and value in ecological systems: A linear programming approach. *Journal of Theoretical Biology* 106:41–57.

Costanza, R. and B. C. Patten. 1995. Defining and predicting sustainability. *Ecological Economics* 15:193–196.

Costanza, R., L. Waigner, C. Folke, and K.-G. Mäler. 1993. Modeling complex ecological economic systems: Toward an evolutionary, dynamic understanding of people and nature. *BioScience* 43:545–555.

Costanza, R., B. Low, E. Ostrom, and J. Wilson. In preparation. *Beijer World 1: A Dynamic, Spatial, Multiscale Integrated Model of a Linked Ecological Economic System*. Forthcoming in the Beijer Discussion Papers, Beijer International Institute of Ecological Economics, Stockholm, Sweden.

de Groot, R. S. 1992. *Functions of Nature*. Wolters Noordhoff BV, Groningen, the Netherlands.

Ehrlich, P. R. and A. E. Ehrlich. 1992. The value of biodiversity. *Ambio* 21:219–226.

Ehrlich, P. R. and H. A. Mooney. 1983. Extinction, substitution and ecosystem services. *BioScience* 33:248–254.

Finn, J. 1976. The cycling index. *Journal of Theoretical Biology* 56:363–373.

Folke, C. 1991. Socioeconomic dependence on the life-supporting environment. Pages 77–94 *in* C. Folke and T. Kåberger, eds. *Linking the Natural Environment and the Economy: Essays from the Eco-Eco Group*. Kluwer Academic Publishers, Dordrecht, the Netherlands.

Folke, C., C. S. Holling, and C. Perrings. In press. Biological diversity, ecosystems and the human scale. *Ecological Applications*.

Funderlic, R. and M. Heath. 1971. *Linear Compartmental Analysis of Ecosystems*. Oak Ridge National Laboratory, ORNL-IBP-71-4.

Gunderson, L., C. S. Holling, and S. Light, eds. 1995. *Barriers and Bridges to the Renewal of Ecosystems and Institutions*. Columbia University Press, New York.

Günther, F. and C. Folke. 1993. Characteristics of nested living systems. *Journal of Biological Systems* 1:257–274.

Hannon, B. 1973. The structure of ecosystems. *Journal of Theoretical Biology* 41:535–546.

Hannon, B. 1976. Marginal product pricing in the ecosystem. *Journal of Theoretical Biology* 56:256–267.

Hannon, B. 1979. Total energy costs in ecosystems. *Journal of Theoretical Biology* 80:271–293.

Holling, C. S., ed. 1978. *Adaptive Environmental Assessment and Management*. Wiley, London.

Holling, C. S. 1986. Resilience of ecosystems: Local surprise and global change. Pages 292–317 *in* E. C. Clark and R. E. Munn, eds. *Sustainable Development of the Biosphere*. Cambridge University Press, Cambridge, UK.

Holling, C. S. 1988. Temperate forest insect outbreaks, tropical deforestation and migratory birds. *Memoirs of the Entomological Society of Canada* 146:21–32.

Holling, C. S. 1994. An ecologist's view of the Malthusian conflict. Pages 79–103 *in* K. Lindahl-Kiessling and H. Landberg, eds. *Population, Economic Development, and the Environment*. Oxford University Press, Oxford, UK.

Holling, C. S., F. Berkes, and C. Folke. 1995a. *Science, Sustainability and Resource Management*. Beijer Discussion Papers 68. Beijer International Institute of Ecological Economics, Stockholm, Sweden.

Holling, C. S., D. W. Schindler, B. H. Walker, and J. Roughgarden. 1995b. Biodiversity in the functioning of ecosystems: An ecological synthesis. Pages 44–83 *in* C. A. Perrings, K.-G. Mäler, C. Folke, C. S. Holling, and

B.-O. Jansson, eds. *Biodiversity Loss: Ecological and Economic Issues.* Cambridge University Press, Cambridge, UK.

Isard, W. 1972. *Ecologic-Economic Analysis for Regional Development.* The Free Press, New York.

Knowlton, N. 1992. Thresholds and multiple stable states in coral reef community dynamics. *American Zoologist* 32:674–682.

Lee, K. 1993. *Compass and Gyroscope.* Island Press, Washington, D.C.

Leontief, W. 1941. *The Structure of American Economy, 1919–1939.* Oxford University Press, New York.

Ludwig, D., R. Hilborn, and C. Walters. 1993. Uncertainty, resource exploitation, and conservation: lessons from history. *Science* 260:17–36.

Mageau, M., R. Costanza, and R. E. Ulanowicz. 1995. The development, testing, and application of a quantitative assessment of ecosystem health. *Ecosystem Health* 1:201–213.

Naeem, S., L. J. Thompson, S. P. Lawler, J. H. Lawton, and R. M. Woodfin. 1994. Declining biodiversity can alter the performance of ecosystems. *Nature* 368:734–737.

Norton, B. G. and R. E. Ulanowicz. 1992. Scale and biodiversity policy: A hierarchical approach. *Ambio* 21:244–249.

O'Neill, R. V., D. L. DeAngelis, J. B. Waide, and T. F. H. Allen. 1986. *A Hierarchical Concept of Ecosystems.* Princeton University Press, Princeton, NJ.

O'Riordan, T. and A. Jordan. 1995. The precautionary principle in contemporary environmental politics. *Environmental Values* 4:191–212.

Odum, E. P. 1989. *Ecology and Our Endangered Life-Support Systems.* Sinauer Associates, Sunderland, MA.

Odum, H. T. 1971. *Environment, Power and Society.* John Wiley, New York.

Ostrom, E. 1990. *Governing the Commons: The Evolution of Institutions for Collective Action.* Cambridge University Press, Cambridge, UK.

Patten, B. C. and R. Costanza. In preparation. *A Rigorous Definition of Sustainability.*

Patten, B. C. and S. E. Jørgensen, eds. 1995. *Complex Ecology: The Part-Whole Relation in Ecosystems.* Prentice-Hall, Englewood Cliffs, NJ.

Perrings, C. and B. H. Walker. 1995. Biodiversity loss and the economics of discontinuous change in semi-arid rangelands. Pages 190–210 *in* C.A. Perrings, K.-G. Mäler, C. Folke, C. S. Holling, and B.-O. Jansson, eds. *Biodiversity Loss: Ecological and Economic Issues.* Cambridge University Press, Cambridge, UK.

Perrings, C. A., K.-G. Mäler, C. Folke, C. S. Holling, and B.-O. Jansson, eds. 1995. *Biodiversity Loss: Ecological and Economic Issues.* Cambridge University Press, Cambridge, UK.

Robinson, S. K., F. R. Thompson III, T. M. Donovan, D. R. Whitehead, and J. Faaborg. 1995. Regional forest fragmentation and the nesting success of migratory birds. *Science* 267:1987–1990.

Roedel, P. M., ed. 1975. *Optimum Sustainable Yield as a Concept in Fisheries Management*. Special Publication No. 9, American Fisheries Society, Washington, D.C.

Scheffer, M., S. H. Hosper, M.-L. Meyjer, B. Moss, and E. Jeppsen. 1993. Alternative equilibria in shallow lakes. *Trends in Ecology and Evolution* 8:275–279.

Schneider, E. and J. J. Kay. 1994. Complexity and thermodynamics: Towards a new ecology. *Futures* 24:626–647.

Shugart, H. H. 1989. The role of ecological models in long-term ecological studies. Pages 90–109 *in* G. E. Likens, ed. *Long-Term Studies in Ecology: Approaches and Alternatives*. Springer-Verlag, New York.

Solbrig, O. T. 1993. Plant traits and adaptive strategies: Their role in ecosystem function. Pages 97–116 *in* E. D. Schulze and H. A. Mooney, eds. *Biodiversity and Ecosystem Function*. Springer-Verlag, Heidelberg, Germany.

Tilman, D. and J. A. Downing. 1994. Biodiversity and stability in grasslands. *Nature* 367:363–365.

Turner, B. L., W. C. Clark, and W. C. Kates, eds. 1990. *The Earth as Transformed by Human Action: Global and Regional Changes in the Biosphere Over the Past 300 Years*. Cambridge University Press, Cambridge, UK.

Ulanowicz, R. E. 1986. *Growth and Development: Ecosystems Phenomenology*. Springer-Verlag, New York.

Ulanowicz, R. E. 1980. An hypothesis on the development of natural communities. *Journal of Theoretical Biology* 85: 223–245.

Walters, C. J. 1986. *Adaptive Management of Renewable Resources*. McGraw Hill, New York.

Westoby, M., B. H. Walker, and I. Noy-Meir. 1989. Opportunistic management for rangelands not at equilibrium. *Journal of Rangeland Management* 42:266–274.

Wulff, F., J. G. Field, and K. H. Mann, eds. 1989. *Network Analysis of Marine Ecosystems: Methods and Applications*. Springer-Verlag, Heidelberg, Germany.

CHAPTER 3

Human Use of the Natural Environment: An Overview of Social and Economic Dimensions

SUSAN HANNA AND SVEIN JENTOFT

Introduction

Across cultures and time, the natural world has shaped and been shaped by the way people think, act, and live. Beliefs and ideology have framed the relationship between people and nature, social and economic groupings have formed human behavior, and ecological variability has influenced styles of living. People interact with nature through the technology they use, the labor they perform, and, in particular, their institutions—the rules and conventions for coordinating behavior. In the context of the human–nature interaction, institutions represent the arrangements which people devise to control their use of the natural environment (Bromley 1989). These arrangements are called property-rights regimes, and include two components: *property rights*, the bundles of entitlements defining rights and duties in the use of natural resources, and *property rules*, the rules under which those rights and duties are exercised (Bromley 1991). Rights, obligations, and rules embody people's expectations about their claims on the environment, and in this way link humans to nature (Bromley 1989; North 1990).

This chapter is about the human use of nature. Just as the previous chapter summarized the properties of ecological systems, we summarize the social and economic properties of human behavior in the use of ecological systems, drawing concepts and perspectives from various disciplines. We describe some of the important links that exist between people and nature and discuss the analytical concepts that are frequently used to identify key issues and problems in resource use and conservation. Human behavior has many social and economic dimensions, reflecting views of nature, individual and social

35

incentives, the transformation of nature into resources, and levels of human organization. Views of nature are based in culture, resource dependence, and economic systems. People transform pieces of the natural environment into resources according to their values, goals and objectives, and the adaptations they make to an uncertain environment. In making this transformation, human behavior reflects the dual influences of individual and social objectives. Perhaps most importantly, human behavior in the use of ecological systems is influenced by the different dimensions in which people are organized as individuals, communities, and states. The tension and interplay between these organizational dimensions have an important influence on environmental outcomes.

Views of Nature

People see nature as both partner and property. Views of nature vary with context, influenced by culture, ethics, religion, economic condition, and climate. The landscape we live in, the resources we live from, and the tools we employ are reservoirs of meaning and identity. The human–nature relationship embodies various ideas about the meaning of ownership and property. It also reflects the degree to which people see themselves as individuals as opposed to members of groups, their perceptions of interdependence, and their expectations about the level of control they can exert over place. Humans live in two realities: the earth and the world. The earth is the physical/biological system that we call "nature" in this book. The world is the earth including and influenced by human society (Caldwell 1990) as, for example, through social institutions such as property-rights regimes.

The way humans organize their relationships with each other and with nature varies widely across cultures, particularly with regard to notions of property. In western societies, ownership signals possession and control, but in other cultures ownership has broader meanings. Ownership means shared identity for the Pintupi of Australia (Pálsson 1991). It means allegiance ("We belong to the land") to nature for the Naskapi Indians of Labrador (Henriksen 1986), and also to the Sami people of northern Norway (Gaski 1993). A respect for the animal as a fellow being was common to nineteenth century Native Americans, to whom the large-scale slaughter of buffalo by white frontiersmen was a sacrilege (Campbell 1988). In some hunting groups, ownership means social obligations, sharing, and reciprocity instead of individual retention and control (Pálsson 1991). The Cree fishermen of James Bay approach fishing with humility and modesty, limiting their catch to what is needed for food (Berkes 1989b).

The definition of property often has its basis in the extent of integration between humans and nature. In harsh climates, where a respectful relationship between people and their environment is essential for survival, the oneness between nature and humans is emphasized. This oneness reflects a bond with the environment that is based on dependence. The dependence is illustrated by the detailed knowledge of plants and animals held by the Inuit and other northern peoples, as well as by the ritual acts used to kill animals by the Bushmen of Australia (Campbell 1988). These groups kill animals to survive, and to them their dependence means that animals are not property but are rather the spiritual equals of humans. To the native peoples of north-central British Columbia, the human–animal relationship is a complex partnership, in which all species have an important role to play. Animals have intelligence, power, and spirit as do humans, and the partnership functions smoothly as long as all parties perform their roles properly (Morrell 1989). In some northern myths, humans transform into animals and back. "The grass and trees are our flesh, the animals are our flesh" (Brody 1987). Sometimes nature is given a status superior to property through religious sanction. "Sacred groves," for example, establish natural areas protected from human use through divine intervention (Gadgil and Guha 1992; Hughes 1994).

As economies develop and the nature of the human dependence on nature evolves, views of the human–nature balance tend to change (Gadgil 1991). The view of nature as a partner or as sacred gives way to the secularized view of nature as property. The development of specialized markets transforms the view of nature from a partner to a production input. In eighteenth-century Europe, for example, where a belief in the divine sanction of human dominance over nature enabled the rapid expansion of industrial development, nature was seen as a collection of goods and services under human power and control (Merchant 1980; Cartmill 1993). Human exploitation was justified because nature's value was primarily mechanical, lying in its contribution to human well-being (Ponting 1993). Even the scientific understanding of nature at the time was shaped by the hierarchy of the Linnéan system of classification (Viner 1972; Thomas 1983).

Views of nature can come into conflict when different cultures interact. When early American colonists emigrated from the resource-stressed areas of eighteenth-century Europe, they brought specialist "commodity" views of resources which were in direct contrast to those of the subsistence-based Native Americans. To Native Americans, nature was more a general ecosystem portfolio of goods and services (Cronon 1983). The ensuing struggle over resources on the North American continent and the eventual dominance of the commodity view over the ecosystem portfolio view is similar to conflicts that have played out in many resource settings worldwide.

Human Behavior: Individual and Social

Despite the many human views of nature, the human use of nature illustrates a universal theme: the potential conflict between the individual and social sides of human behavior. Individual behavior is often self-centered and short-sighted. Left to the devices of unregulated individuals, natural environments tend to become overused and degraded even in cases where they have been conferred sacred status (Gadgil and Guha 1992; Hughes 1994). But social behavior takes a broader and longer perspective. Society needs to maintain the productivity of the natural environment, and this collective goal may lead to coordinated long-term actions which place social necessity above individual desires. Both as individuals and as members of social groups, human behavior is a response to particular institutional incentives. When people act in self-centered ways, it is because the social, economic, or regulatory environment promotes such behavior. And correspondingly, people act collectively when there are positive incentives to do so.

A frequent representation of human behavior toward nature is that of individual shortsightedness and greed. Completely individualistic behavior that leads to resource overexploitation has been called "the tragedy of the commons" (Hardin 1968). Hardin's parable of the tragedy of the commons describes herdsmen sharing a common pasture, each of whom, in the pursuit of profits, increases his herd size. The herdsmen do this because the private gain from owning more cattle is greater than the private cost. The gains from each additional animal go to the individual owner, while the costs of having additional animals on the pasture are shared among all pasture owners. Eventually, increased grazing results in lower fodder production and malnourished animals. Even though the herdsmen read the environmental signals of an overgrazing problem, they don't change their behavior because each acting alone cannot solve the problem.

The "tragedy of the commons" is a caricature of individual human behavior responding to the incentives of open-access resources. The herdsmen are single-minded in their pursuit of higher earnings.

Because they don't know how other herdsmen will behave, they make decisions about the size of their herds without regard to fellow users, the carrying capacity of the environment, or requirements for long-term sustainability of the pasture. They are self-centered and short-sighted, unrestricted by collective strategies and responsibilities. "Herders have the right to pasture their cattle in the commons, but this right is unmatched by a corresponding responsibility. . ." (Hardin 1977). The parable suggests that humans require regulation by some external authority (Bjørklund 1990).

In any situation of natural resource use the individual and social sides of human behavior compete for ascendancy, with the environmental outcome depending in many instances on which side dominates. The tragedy of the commons models purely individualistic behavior and ignores social behavior. In practice, most herders faced with overgrazing would eventually recognize the futility of uncoordinated use and act to change the property rights or property rules under which the pasture is used. Users add responsibilities to rights once they organize around the collective need to maintain resources. Norms, standards, behavioral rules, and sanctions are developed to manage and limit the effects of human use of the environment. History tells us that social organization has countered some of the more destructive tendencies of individualistic behavior toward nature, because people have realized that degraded environments cannot robustly support human life.

The "tragedy" parable uses the term "commons" to mean everybody's, and therefore nobody's, property. But, in fact, resources managed as common property are not everyone's property but are "property in common," in which property rights are assigned to a community or a social group rather than to private individuals or to the state (Ciriacy-Wantrup and Bishop 1975; Davis and Kasdan 1984; McCay and Acheson 1987; Berkes et al.1989). Communities develop rules about using natural resources, and they also develop social values and norms, many of them informal and noncontractual, that may stress moderation and prudence rather than excessiveness and recklessness (Durkheim 1964). Management of common resources may take place through completely self-regulated systems or through "comanagement" arrangements in which a group of users shares authority with governments (Jentoft 1989; Jentoft and Kristoffersen 1989; Pinkerton 1989; Ruddle 1989; Pomeroy 1994). Rules are developed through cooperation among users, a tendency that has been demonstrated by both simulations (Axelrod, 1984; Feeny, 1992) and empirical research (McCay and Acheson 1987; Berkes 1989a;

Ostrom 1990; Bromley 1992; Runge 1992). The necessary conditions to ensure that communities are able to manage resources by themselves include the ability to make collective decisions, define the rightful users, establish use rules, monitor use, sanction improper use, and resolve conflicts (cf. Ostrom 1993).

Turning Nature into a Resource

When people use nature's goods and services, they transform nature into a resource. The parts of nature that are valued as resources are relative to a particular culture or period of time. For example, while in the past peat was valued as fuel, today it has been supplanted by petroleum fuel sources. And while past resource-use behavior has tended not to consider the indirect services of individual species to ecosystem function, those services are now becoming more frequently recognized as resources. For both the direct and indirect services of nature, human use is affected by information on location and use, the technology of production, the costs of extraction, and the number and type of available substitutes.

As nature enters the human sphere as resources, it takes on attributes of capital and is influenced by goals, values, and uncertainty. Ecosystems are natural capital because they are stocks of natural assets producing flows of goods and services. Goals and values indirectly shape the stock of natural assets and the flow of goods and services through the preferences of living generations for their own consumption and for their bequest to future generations. Decisions take place in an environment of uncertainty. This section presents a brief discussion of the role played by capital, goals, values, and uncertainty in the use of nature as a resource.

Capital

Plants and animals, water and minerals have been described as natural capital (Costanza et al. 1991). As capital, these resources embody value in the stock of natural assets and the flow of goods and services produced by those assets. Services such as reproduction and genetic diversity and goods such as food for wildlife and humans are all drawn from the stocks. Overall, humans have been more successful in designing incentives to capture the flow of ecosystem goods than in protecting either the capital stock or the flow of ecosystem services. Our failure to protect these productive capacities of natural capital has in many cases eroded its ability to function effectively as an asset.

To transform natural goods and services into resources, people apply other types of capital to natural capital. Physical capital in the form of tools and technology is used to extract resources. Financial capital is garnered to purchase physical capital. Cultural capital—the norms, values, and rules which lead to human adaptation and modification of the natural environment—provides the social milieu in which the human–ecosystem interaction takes place (Berkes and Folke 1994). Institutional capital, a subset of cultural capital, embodies the stock of rules and underlying human organizational skills which coordinate human behavior in its use of natural resources (Hanna 1996). The value embedded in these additional types of capital lies in the ways they produce flows of services to either the ecosystem or the human system through mechanical assistance, investment, ethical guidance, and the regulation of behavior. The many origins of capital mean that ecosystem use is strongly influenced by conditions of economics, culture, and politics. Through human action, physical, cultural, and institutional capital are linked to natural capital and to each other to produce particular environmental effects. For example, increases in the amount of available financial capital or in the efficiency and sophistication of physical capital can strain the ability of a property-rights regime to protect natural capital. A classic example of the effect of capital on environmental outcomes is found in the world's marine fisheries, where financial capital (government subsidies) has been combined with sophisticated physical capital (fishing technology) and inadequate institutional capital (regulation and enforcement), leading to chronic and large-scale overcapitalization and resource depletion (Weber 1994).

Goals

People in different settings develop a variety of different goals for the ecosystems in which they live, goals that are reflected in property-rights regimes. Goals for natural resource use are based in the desire to sustain human life, enhance standards of living, maintain a culture, and protect environmental quality for generations to follow. The range of possible ecosystem goals leads to different expectations as to which goal should have priority. All use involves tradeoffs, so achieving all goals to the maximum effect is impossible. We end up with mixed outcomes which approach some goals more closely than others. People have conflicting ideas about the appropriate balance between goals, because human values are not homogeneous with regard to the appropriate resource mix to sustain.

Experience indicates that there are specific conditions which are necessary goals for any natural system if its productivity is to be maintained over time. These conditions are resilience, management efficiency, and equity. Resilience is the capacity to absorb perturbations and is dependent on flexibility and adaptation (Holling 1973). Ecological resilience is fostered by use levels which maintain enough surplus to allow response and adaptation to changing environmental conditions. It requires stewardship practices that successfully promote social behavior over individual behavior. To achieve resource stewardship, decisions must be made over a longer time horizon than would be used by individuals acting alone, and regulations must be monitored and enforced. Institutional resilience is fostered by management flexibility that allows adaptation to ecological and economic changes.

The efficiency of resource management can be defined as the cost-effectiveness with which the property rights and rules are implemented; that is, the ratio between the effectiveness of the outcome and the effort required to achieve it. Management requires, among other activities, information gathering, coordination of resource users, monitoring of behavior, and enforcement of rules. The costs of time and money engendered by these activities are called transactions costs (Dahlman 1979; Matthews 1986; Eggertsson 1990), and because time and money are limited, a management process is most efficient when it reduces transactions costs to their lowest possible level for a given level of benefits. That is, when the management goals are met with the minimum amount of arranging, coordinating, monitoring, and enforcing. Keeping transactions costs low is made easier when a resource management process is perceived to be equitable. Equity does not necessarily mean that resource users get equal shares, but it does mean that resource management is consistent with social standards for representation, distribution, openness, and conflict resolution.

Values

The goals set for natural systems are based not only on the values people place on their goods and services but also on wider individual and social values. We imbue natural resources with value because of their potential to contribute to other things we value, such as economic production, social identification, cultural symbolism, aesthetic appreciation, evolutionary potential, and biodiversity. Social considerations also inform the way we organize harvesting systems to capture these goods and services. For example, we do or do not do certain things in the harvest of resources because we are concerned about maintaining communities and preventing the erosion of social networks.

The value of a natural resource has different components that are based in both use and nonuse. Use value has three parts: direct value (e.g., harvesting for food) indirect value (e.g., contributing genetic diversity to reproduction), and option value (e.g., the potential for future contribution). Nonuse value derives from a resource's existence and intrinsic value as a source of aesthetic pleasure, a bequest to future generations, or a contributor to the general feeling about the environment (Norton 1987; Pearce and Turner 1990; Pearce 1993). Direct use values are easiest to observe and measure because they are expressed in monetary terms. Indirect, option, and existence values are equally important but are usually less obvious since their value lies in their more diffuse contribution to genetic diversity, ecosystem health, future options, and aesthetic pleasure. The measurement difficulties magnify when we consider the combination of services and functions at the ecosystem level.

But the fact that indirect, option, and existence values are difficult to measure and to systematically understand does not mean that they are any less real. What it does mean is that these ecosystem values are seldom bought or sold, and are often underrepresented in resource management decisions. Because values unexpressed in prices are at a comparative disadvantage in a market economy, the ecosystem components containing them can often be undervalued and overused. A further complication is posed by environmental values that are distributed between current and future generations. People's willingness to pay to protect resource values is an expression of living generations, and it is natural for members of the current generation to place greater value on present benefits than expected future benefits. A common response to the difficulty of long-term protection is to take a "warehouse" approach of protecting environmental resources by removing them to protective custody, away from human activity, in marine sanctuaries, wildlife refuges, or biosphere reserves (Norton 1987).

Uncertainty

Uncertainty is endemic to natural systems. It underlies human views and actions toward the natural world, and it exists whenever the likelihood of some occurrence is unknown and information is scarce. Uncertainty takes a toll on the sustainability of the natural world. Uncertainty has many manifestations but includes most importantly a lack of knowledge, a lack of assurance about others' actions, and impatience about the future. In natural systems, variations in weather, climate, and the distribution of plant and animal populations all lead to a lack of knowledge about system properties and sometimes, as in the case of marine fisheries, about the distribution of the resource. Uncertainty characterizes decisionmaking whenever information is both scarce and temporary. In an uncertain environment, decision-making takes place through trial and error, through a series of adaptations to changing conditions. The definition of the "best" use of resources or the necessary conditions for ecosystem sustainability may be clouded by a lack of knowledge.

Uncertainty is also manifested in a lack of assurance about the behavior of others. It is difficult to value future potential environmental goods or services when their existence is insecure because of a lack of assurance about the behavior of others (Runge 1984). Without assurance about limits to others' use, people realize that if they don't use environmental goods today they may not be available in the future. For example, even though delaying a fish harvest may result in bigger and more valuable fish which reproduce over a longer period of time, without assurance that they will have those fish in the future people have no incentive to patiently wait for the future returns from foregone current use. Because of the lack of patience, uncertainty creates incentives to value a certain present over an uncertain future ("a bird in the hand is worth two in the bush").

This lack of knowledge, lack of assurance about others, and impatience about future returns all work against long-term sustainability. The uncertainty reflected creates a natural tension between the individual and the group, and between people and ecosystems. For the individual, uncertainty shortens the time horizon and encourages accelerated resource use in order to capture the benefits before others do. But for the group concerned with the collective need to sustain resource productivity, and for the ecosystem, uncertainty calls for a precautionary approach in which rates of immediate use are kept low while more is learned about system structure and processes. These opposing responses are widespread in natural resource management and complicate decisions about appropriate rates of use.

In an uncertain environment, people must adapt to survive. Efforts to create assurance often lead to rules which are coordinated through collective action (Runge 1992; Sandler 1992). Other adaptation strategies are developed by learning and by the formation of expectations. For example, different strategies are used to hunt fish in the ocean. The approach to the hunt will depend on individual and group objectives, learned skills, expectations about the tenure of use rights, attitudes toward risk, and the degree of interdependence with other users (Cody 1974; Hanna and Smith 1993; Smith and Hanna 1993). The effectiveness of the hunt will be influenced by the amount of time invested, type of capital equipment, knowledge, skill, and luck. Among some resource users, the process of hunting may be in itself a source of satisfaction.

Human Organization:
The Individual, Community, and the State

Against the background of uncertainty, resources as capital, and variation in goals and values, we now turn to different types of human organization. People are organized and have identity in several dimensions. They exist as individuals with personal interests, needs, and skills. They live in communities in which relationships to others are developed and maintained. They are citizens of states which set allowable bounds of behavior and define responsibilities. Each level of identity is embedded in a larger social, economic, and political sphere, and interacts with other levels through both cooperation and conflict.

The Individual

The "tragedy of the commons" model depicts an independent system that is unorganized, completely decentralized, and devoid of guidelines for social behavior. This type of system exists as an uncoordinated collection of individuals, in contrast to a "functional system" where a division of labor and behavior is prescribed by social roles, norms, and values (Boudon 1981). It is important to know that misuse of resources may result in either system. In the first instance, it can occur when unrestrained self-centered individuals search for profits. In the second, it can occur as the outcome of external pressures and role conflicts, as when heavy debt forces users to overexploit the resource, or from deviant behavior, as when sanctions are not sufficiently effective to prevent poaching. In the first instance, it is the prospects of profits that lead people to overexploit. In the second, it is an intolerable situation such as extreme poverty and a lack of other sources of income.

These two systems should be considered as extremes. At one extreme, the individual is autonomous ("undersocialized") and thus unfettered by social structure. (cf. Wrong 1961). At the other extreme, the person is a conformist ("over-socialized") with decisions determined by social structure. But individuals are neither free from the social structure nor slaves to it (Etzioni 1988; Granovetter 1992). Rather, while pursuing self-interests, individuals are guided by their rights and duties as social persons, by norms of reciprocity, and redistribution (Polanyi 1957), by cultural values, and by sources of identity. Violations of norms and rules may also occur in communities and groups with strong social ties. But when it happens, when "opportunity makes a thief," violators are met with sanctions.

The Community

Worldwide, resource users form communities that may or may not be linked to a certain locality. Communities may also be of a temporal nature, such as when resource users from different localities group together in a particular resource area for the season. As social entities, these different types of communities are more than the sum of their individual parts (Durkheim 1964). A fishing fleet is more than an aggregate of individual vessels; it is also a system of social relations that under certain circumstances may constitute a corporate group (Jentoft and Wadel 1984). For example, to be a lobster fisherman in Maine, one must first become identified with a particular harbor gang (Acheson 1988). Pastoralist households also form cooperative groups. The Sami of northern Norway create reindeer herding units called "siidas," which change size and composition through the year as the pastoralists divide and regroup their herds (Bjørklund 1990).

Communities may result from deliberate collective action or develop through social interaction over time. Communities often embody a common history and expectations of a common future. Within a community, society is not a constraint; rather, "it is us" (Etzioni 1988). Communities can be thought of not only in structural and geographic terms but also in symbolic terms (Cohen 1985), existing in the minds of people as a repository of meaning, identity, and belonging. Members adhere to norms and values not only because it pays, or from fear of sanctions, but also because they are involved and morally committed. The herdsman playing out the tragedy of the commons is acting rationally, but he is also acting immorally. The solidarity, trust, and altruism that often exists among community members may be limited to a specific group (Portes and Sensenbrenner 1993). Community members are often divided, with inherent conflicts of interest regarding the distribution of the resource. Thus one should be careful not to exaggerate the traits of unity, homogeneity, coherence, and stability within communities. Communities change over time and are often characterized by social fissures (Young 1994).

The State

The state is instrumental in the design, implementation, and enforcement of resource regulations. However well intended, state initiatives frequently have ambiguous impacts. Regulatory schemes often misfire or are directly counterproductive. Side-effects such as social inequity are also produced. Sometimes the impacts of state involvement are even more subtle. From the perspective of the local community, bureaucratic involvement in resource management can disembed management responsibilities from local contexts of interaction (Giddens 1994). Cooperative and symbiotic relations are transformed into competitive and "positional" relationships, in which the social conditions conducive to social action—solidarity, trust, equality—are eroded (Hirsch 1976).

What is assumed about the nature of individual and community behavior influences state actions and therefore also influences resource management outcomes. In fishery management, examples abound of cases where the assumptions of individualistic behavior in the Hardin model set up a situation where the predicted model outcomes are in fact produced. Applying the Hardin model in real management situations may well result in a self-fulfilling prophecy, in which the assumption that communities cannot manage their resources locally leads to the establishment of management regimes which in fact ensure that they cannot (Kasdan 1993). Fishery management based on individual privileges granted by government can remove the identification of the individual fisherman with the collective interest (Davis and Jentoft 1989). Thus, as is currently the case in the small-boat fisheries of Norway and Canada, in the interest of preventing a tragedy of the commons, the tragedy is produced (Maurstad 1992; Davis 1991).

Embedded Systems

Just as individuals are members of communities, communities are situated within states, and states are in turn situated within larger social and economic systems containing different layers and scales. For example, in the grazing lands of Botswana, resource users and their rules are embedded in historical, political, and economic structures which carry cultural meaning and value (Peters 1987). Particular resource rules for the grazing lands can only be understood in the context of these larger systems of which they form a part (Durrenberger and Pálsson 1987). When resource users compete, their interaction is contained within rules of the larger society. Users are guided by the ethical principles, social duties, and responsibilities that prevail within the community or ethnic group to which they belong.

Thus, competition may evolve without causing social disruption and disorder. In fact, competition and cooperation should not be regarded as mutually exclusive activities, because competition cannot take place without cooperation (Taylor 1987). Even among competitive users there must be some agreement as to what the competition is all about, who are allowed to compete, which strategies are permissible, and the rights of winners and losers.

Embeddedness plays an important role in the success of resource management systems. In an international comparative study of user-participation in fisheries management, Jentoft and McCay (1995) conclude that specific patterns of user participation reflect the broader institutional patterns and practices that prevail in each country. The cost of ignoring the importance of embeddedness or of removing its functions is often the disruption of the resource management process (Pálsson 1991; Paine 1994). When resource users find themselves disembedded from the social bonds that connect them to each other and to their community, the dynamic represented in the tragedy of the commons may result. For example, in the Asia–Pacific region, the traditional resource management practices of many local subsistence exchange economies have been weakened or destroyed through interactions with external markets that have undermined the moral authority for resource management (Ruddle 1993). In such cases, the tragedy of the commons is the product of social disruption rather than a natural outcome of individual rational behavior. However, resource overexploitation is not always a sign of disembedding. Spanish or Portuguese trawlers on the Grand Banks outside the Canadian Economic Zone are firmly embedded in their respective national fishery systems and particular cultures, but the solution to overextraction in international waters requires the creation of new embedding structures in the form of supranational institutions.

People are also embedded in social systems which extend beyond geopolitical boundaries, including markets, industries, professions, and national organizations (DiMaggio and Powell 1991). Also, resource users are increasingly exposed to forces that are truly global. Capital knows no national boundaries, trade of natural products meets few barriers, and cultural identities rooted in the local community surrender to the global media (Friedman 1994; Featherstone et al. 1995). The global influence is also easily detected ecologically. Natural degradation, pollution, and overuse pass over national borders. And as ecological crises spread globally, so also do the prescriptive models for solving them. To many managers, problems of Sami reindeer pastoralism are analogous to those facing the Maine lobster fisheries or Botswana cattle ranges, and the solutions they advance are basically the same: enclosure of the commons, preferably through privatization. In all such proposals, planners are inspired by the Hardin model. This, as Boulding (1977) notes, ". . . clearly demonstrates the power that is in metaphor."

Once removed, embeddedness cannot be easily reestablished. For example, reembedding management responsibilities within the local community through the design of comanagement regimes and the inclusion of user-knowledge in resource management is difficult (cf. Inglis 1993; Johannes 1989). For local control to exist, the integration of the community must be restored. The dilemma is that one cannot have comanagement without well-integrated communities, and neither can there be well-integrated communities without comanagement. To work, institutions must have the support of resource users, but this support is often not in place before property-rights regimes are implemented. The restoration of communities and the introduction of comanagement through the delegation of regulatory powers must go hand in hand as part of a coordinated plan. Comanagement institutions must be designed with social integration in mind, and users must be involved in their creation.

Summary and Conclusions

This chapter has used concepts and perspectives drawn from many disciplines to describe some of the fundamental attributes of human–nature interaction. The interaction is importantly shaped by human ideology and beliefs toward the natural environment as well as by the variability inherent to natural systems. The interaction is also the outcome of people acting out various individual and collective goals as they transform nature into resources. In the process of transformation, the productivity of ecosystems is sustainable only when ecosystem resilience, institutional resilience, management efficiency, cultural diversity, and social equity are maintained. Working against sustainability are the twin facts that these goals are difficult to achieve and that people often overlook several values of ecosystems that are left unexpressed in the marketplace, such as the value of biodiversity.

Human behavior is shaped by uncertainty and by the need to adapt. Behavior is also affected by people's identities as individuals, community members, and citizens of states, with each layer of identity embedded in a larger sphere of social, political, and economic influences. The main argument of this chapter is that the complex roles and values held by resource users inform and restrain their actions in relation to nature. It is clear that although there is an individualistic side to human behavior, that side seldom dominates or determines outcomes. People are influenced by the larger spheres within which they are embedded, such as ethnic groups, professions, communities, and states.

The role of the state is particularly important in the design of management institutions to prevent the tragedy of the commons. Property-rights regimes are integral to the role that the state plays in resource use, because they are the way that government intercedes in the relationship between people and nature. Property-rights regimes are a link between the human and natural systems that are granted, codified, and upheld by the state. Sometimes, in its enthusiasm to prevent the tragedy of resource overexploitation, the state implements management regimes that cause the tragedy to occur. This happens because management systems often fail to account for the human complexities that exist in economic and social spheres.

Some of the complexities of the human–nature interaction discussed in this chapter form the basis of the more specific treatments presented in the chapters to follow. Views of nature influence the particular linkage between human and natural systems and are critical to how well ecological productivity endures over time. In addition, people's goals and values, the uncertainty of their environment, and the strategies they form affect the structure of a property-rights regime. They also affect the process by which a property-rights regime is formed and the corresponding costs of forming and sustaining it. And finally, culture threads through different levels of influence, affecting the linkages between regimes of different political entities and nations.

REFERENCES

Acheson, J. M. 1988. *The Lobster Gangs of Maine*. University Press of New England, Hanover, NH.

Axelrod, R. 1984. *The Evolution of Cooperation*. Basic Books, New York.

Berkes, F., ed. 1989a. *Common Property Resources: Ecology and Community-Based Sustainable Development*. Belhaven Press, London.

Berkes, F. 1989b. Co-management and the James Bay agreement. Pages 181–208 in E. Pinkerton, ed. *Co-operative Management of Local Fisheries: New Directions for Improved Management and Community Development*. University of British Columbia Press, Vancouver.

Berkes, F. and C. Folke. 1994. Investing in cultural capital for sustainable use of natural capital. Pages 128–149 in A. M. Jansson, M. Hammer,

C. Folke, and R. Costanza, eds. *Investing in Natural Capital*. Island Press, Washington, D.C.

Berkes, F., D. Feeny, B. J. McCay, and J. M. Acheson. 1989. The benefits of the commons. *Nature* 340:91–93.

Bjørklund, I. 1990. Sami reindeer pastoralism as an indigenous resource management system in northern Norway: A contribution to the common property debate. *Development and Change* 21:75–86.

Boudon, R. 1981. *The Logic of Social Action: An Introduction to Sociological Analysis*. Routledge and Kegan Paul, London.

Boulding, K. 1977. Commons and community: the idea of a public. Pages 280–294 *in* G. Hardin and J. Baden, eds. *Managing the Commons*. W. H. Freeman and Company, San Francisco.

Brody, H. 1987. *Living Arctic: Hunters of the Canadian North*. Faber and Faber Limited, London.

Bromley, D. W. 1989. *Economic Interests and Institutions: The Conceptual Foundations of Public Policy*. Basil Blackwell, Oxford.

Bromley, D. W. 1991. *Environment and Economy: Property Rights and Public Policy*. Basil Blackwell, Oxford.

Bromley, D. W., ed. 1992. *Making the Commons Work: Theory, Practice, and Policy*. Institute for Contemporary Studies Press, San Francisco.

Caldwell, L. K. 1990. *International Environmental Policy: Emergence and Dimensions*, 2nd.ed. Duke University Press, Durham, NC.

Campbell, J. 1988. *The Power of Myth*. Doubleday, New York.

Cartmill, M. 1993. *A View to a Death in the Morning*. Harvard University Press, Cambridge, MA.

Ciriacy-Wantrup, S. V. and R. C. Bishop. 1975. "Common property" as a concept in natural resources policy. *Natural Resources Journal* 15(4): 713–727.

Cody, M. 1974. Optimization in ecology. *Science* 183:1156–1164.

Cohen, A. P. 1985. *The Symbolic Construction of Community*. Tavistock Publications, London.

Costanza, R., H. E. Daly, and J. A. Bartholomew. 1991. Goals, agenda, and policy recommendations for ecological economics. Pages 1–20 *in* R. Costanza, ed. 1991. *Ecological Economics: The Science and Management of Sustainability*. Columbia University Press, New York.

Cronon, W. 1983. *Changes in the Land: Indians, Colonists, and the Ecology of New England*. Hill and Wang, New York.

Dahlman, C. J. 1979. The problem of externality. *Journal of Legal Studies* 22(1):141–162.

Davis, A. 1991. *Dire Straits: The Dilemmas of a Fishery, the Case of Digby Neck and the Islands*. ISER Press, St. Johns, Newfoundland.

Davis, A. and S. Jentoft, 1989. Ambivalent co-operators: Organizational slack and utilitarian rationality in an Eastern Nova Scotian fisheries co-operative. *Maritime Anthropological Studies* 2(2):194–211.

Davis, A. and L. Kasdan. 1984. Bankrupt government policies and belligerent fishermen responses: dependency and conflict in the Southwest

Nova Scotia small boat fisheries. *Journal of Canadian Studies* 19(1):108–124.

DiMaggio, P. J. and W. W. Powell, eds. 1991. *The New Institutionalism in Organizational Analysis*. The University of Chicago Press, Chicago.

Durkheim, E. 1964. *The Division of Labor in Society*. The Free Press, New York.

Durrenberger, E. P. and G. Pálsson. 1987. Ownership at sea: Fishing territories and access to sea resources. *American Ethnologist* 14(3):508–521.

Eggertsson, T. 1990. *Economic Behavior and Institutions*. Cambridge University Press, Cambridge, UK.

Etzioni, A. 1988. *The Moral Dimension: Toward a New Economics*. The Free Press, New York.

Featherstone, M., S. Lash, and R. Robertson, eds. 1995. *Global Modernities*. Sage Publications, London.

Feeny, D. 1992. Where do we go from here? Implications for the research agenda. Pages 267–292 *in* D. W. Bromley, ed. *Making the Commons Work: Theory, Practice, and Policy*. Institute for Contemporary Studies Press, San Francisco.

Friedman, J. 1994. *Cultural Identity and Global Process*. Sage Publications, London.

Gadgil, M. 1991. Conserving India's biodiversity: The societal context. *Evolutionary Trends in Plants* 5:3–8.

Gadgil, M. and R. Guha. 1992. *This Fissured Land: An Ecological History of India*. University of California Press, Berkeley.

Gaski, L. 1993. Snart må man ha stempel under kommagene for å dra på fjellet. Utnyttelse av utmarksressurser; endringer I samhandlingsmønstre og kulturell betydning. M.A. thesis, University of Tromsø, Institute of Social Science, Tromso, Norway.

Giddens, A. 1994. *The Consequences of Modernity*. Polity Press, Stanford, CA.

Granovetter, M. 1992. Economic action and social structure: The problem of embeddedness. Pages 53–84 *in* M. Granovetter and R. Swedberg, eds. *The Sociology of Economic Life*. Westview Press, Boulder, CO.

Hanna, S. S. 1996. The new frontier of American fisheries governance. *Ecological Economics*, in press.

Hanna, S. S. and C. L. Smith. 1993. Attitudes of trawl vessel captains about work, resource use and fishery management. *North American Journal of Fishery Management* 13:367–375.

Hardin, G. 1968. The tragedy of the commons. *Science* 162:1243–1248.

Hardin, G. 1977. An operational analysis of "responsibility." Pages 66–75 *in* G. Hardin and J. Baden, eds. *Managing the Commons*. W. H. Freeman and Company, San Francisco.

Henriksen, G. 1986. Rettigheter, oppgaver og ressurser—tre forutsetninger for likeverd i etnisk sammensatte statssamfunn. Pages 116–128 in R. Erke and A. Høgmo, eds. *Identitet og Livsutfoldelse*. Universitetsforlaget, Oslo.

Hirsch, F. 1976. *Social Limits to Growth*. Harvard University Press, Cambridge, MA.

Holling, C. S. 1973. Resilience and stability of ecological systems. *Annual Review of Ecology and Systematics* 4:1–23.

Hughes, J. D. 1994. *Pan's Travail: Environmental Problems of the Ancient Greeks and Romans*. Johns Hopkins University Press, Baltimore, MD.

Inglis, J. T., ed. 1993. *Traditional Ecological Knowledge: Concepts and Cases*. Canadian Museum of Nature, Ottawa.

Jentoft, S. 1989. Fisheries co-management: Delegating government responsibility to fishermen's organizations. *Marine Policy* 13(2):137–154.

Jentoft, S. and T. Kristoffersen. 1989. Fishermen's co-management: The case of the Lofoten fishery. *Human Organization* 48(4):355–367.

Jentoft, S. and B. J. McCay. 1995. User participation in fisheries management: Lessons drawn from international experiences. *Marine Policy* 19(3):227–246.

Jentoft, S. and C. Wadel, eds. 1984. I samme båt: Sysselsettingssystemer i fiskerinæringen. Oslo: Universitetsforlaget.

Johannes, R. E., ed. 1989. *Traditional Ecological Knowledge: A Collection of Essays*. The World Conservation Union, Gland, Switzerland.

Kasdan, L. 1993. Market rationality, productive efficiency, environment, and community: The relevance of local experience. Paper presented at the International Congress on Ecology, Hermosillo, Mexico, April 15–17, 1993.

Matthews, R. C. O. 1986. The economics of institutions and the sources of growth. *Economic Journal* 96:903–910.

Maurstad, A. 1992. Closing the commons—opening the "tragedy": Regulating North-Norwegian small-scale fishing. Paper presented at the 3rd Conference of the International Association for the Study of Common Property, Sept. 17–20, 1992, Washington, D.C.

McCay, B. J. and J. M. Acheson. 1987. *The Question of the Commons: The Culture and Ecology of Communal Resources*. The University of Arizona Press, Tucson.

Merchant, C. 1980. *The Death of Nature: Women, Ecology and the Scientific Revolution*. Harper and Row, New York.

Morrell, M. 1989. The struggle to integrate traditional Indian systems and state management systems in the salmon fisheries of the Skeena River, British Columbia. Pages 231–248 in E. Pinkerton, ed. *Co-operative Management of Local Fisheries: New Directions for Improved Management and Community Development*. University of British Columbia Press, Vancouver.

North, D. C. 1990. *Institutions, Institutional Change and Economic Performance*. Cambridge University Press, Cambridge, UK.

Norton, B. G. 1987. *Why Preserve Natural Variety?* Princeton University Press, Princeton, NJ.

Ostrom, E. 1990. *Governing the Commons: The Evolution of Institutions for Collective Action*. Cambridge University Press, Cambridge, UK.

Ostrom, E. 1993. The evolution of norms, rules, and rights. Beijer Discussion Paper No. 39, Beijer International Institute of Ecological Economics, The Royal Swedish Academy of Sciences, Stockholm, Sweden.

Paine, R. 1994. *Herds of the Tundra: A Portrait of Saami Reindeer Pastoralism.* Smithsonian Institution Press, Washington, D.C.

Pálsson, G. 1991. *Coastal Economies, Cultural Accounts: Human Ecology and Icelandic Discourse.* Manchester University Press, Manchester, UK.

Pálsson, G. and A. Helgason. 1996. Figuring fish and measuring men: the quota system in the Icelandic cod fishery. *Ocean and Coastal Management* 26.

Pearce, D. W. 1993. *Economic Values and the Natural World.* The MIT Press, Cambridge, MA.

Pearce, D. W. and R. K. Turner. 1990. *Economics of Natural Resources and the Environment.* The Johns Hopkins University Press, Baltimore, MD.

Peters, P. E. 1987. Embedded systems and rooted models: The grazing lands of Botswana and the commons debate. Pages 171–194 *in* B. J. McCay and J. M. Acheson, eds. *The Question of the Commons: The Culture and Ecology of Communal Resources.* The University of Arizona Press, Tucson.

Pinkerton, E., ed. 1989. *Co-operative Management of Local Fisheries: New Directions for Improved Management and Community Development.* University of British Columbia Press, Vancouver.

Polanyi, K. 1957. *The Great Transformation.* Beacon Press, Boston.

Pomeroy, R. S., ed. 1994. *Community Management and Common Property of Coastal Fisheries in Asia and the Pacific: Concepts, Methods, and Experiences.* International Center for Living Aquatic Resources, Manila.

Ponting, C. 1993. *A Green History of the World.* Penguin Books, New York.

Portes, A. and J. Sensenbrenner. 1993. Embeddedness and immigration: Notes on the social determinants of economic action. *American Journal of Sociology* 98(6):1320–1350.

Ruddle, K. 1989. Solving the common-property dilemma: Village fisheries rights in Japanese coastal waters. Pages 168–184 *in* F. Berkes, ed. *Common Property Resources: Ecology and Community-Based Sustainable Development.* Belhaven Press, London.

Ruddle, K. 1993. External forces and change in traditional community-based fishery management systems in the Asia–Pacific region. *Maritime Anthropological Studies* 6(1–2):1–37.

Runge, C. F. 1984. Institutions and the free rider: The assurance problem in collective action. *Journal of Politics* 46(1):154–181.

Runge, C. F. 1992. Common property and collective action in economic development. Pages 17–39 *in* D. W. Bromley, ed. *Making the Commons Work: Theory, Practice, and Policy.* Institute for Contemporary Studies Press, San Francisco.

Sandler, T. 1992. *Collective Action*. University of Michigan Press, Ann Arbor.

Smith, C. L. and S. Hanna. 1993. Occupation and community as determinants of fishing behaviors. *Human Organization* 52(3):299–303.

Taylor, M. 1987. *The Possibility of Cooperation*. Cambridge University Press, Cambridge, UK.

Thomas, K. 1983. *Man and the Natural World*. Penguin Books, London.

Viner, J. 1972. *The Role of Providence in the Social Order*. Princeton University Press, Princeton, NJ.

Weber, P. 1994. *Net Loss: Fish, Jobs and the Marine Environment*. Worldwatch Paper 120, Worldwatch Institute, Washington, D.C.

Wrong, D. 1961. Oversocialized conception of man in sociology. *American Sociological Review* 26(2):183–193.

Young, O. 1994. The problem of scale in human/environment relationships. *Journal of Theoretical Politics* 6:429–447.

CHAPTER 4

Dynamics of (Dis)harmony in Ecological and Social Systems

C . S .   H O L L I N G   A N D   S T E V E N   S A N D E R S O N [1]

Introduction

It has never been more important to understand the conjunction of human and natural systems, and the nature of their interactions. Our world is defined by the management of natural systems by human systems, which represents a radical change from the historical condition of humans being defined by their environments, their grand structuring cycles (plagues, economic epochs), and their slowly changing local ways of living (cultures). Now, perhaps forty percent of the biosphere's net primary productivity is altered directly by human activity (Vitousek et al. 1986). World food demand is expected to double before the year 2025, when the world's population will exceed 8 billion (McCalla 1994). The systemic effects of global environmental change will leave no large landscapes untouched by human hands.

In halting response to this reality, scientists and policymakers have proposed an integrated approach to the human management of natural systems based on "sustainability," which emphasizes economic output more than ecological resilience. In fact, the "sustainable development of the biosphere" (Clark and Munn 1986) has embraced an adaptive management ethic, in which human management and natural systems dynamics interweave. The eventual success of that management, and the degree to which it allows adaptive flexibility, depend on the convergence of human and natural systems cycles.

One of us (Holling 1986) proposed a model to examine dynamics of ecological and social systems from the perspective of ecologists. That model presented new concepts to explain the organization and dynamics of complex adaptive systems. The result involves four phases: exploitation, conservation, creative destruction, and renewal (see Fig. 4.1). This model of adaptive renewal became a vehicle which could be used to compare ecological and social systems. This chapter examines the relevance of adaptive renewal to social systems to illuminate the complexities of human management of natural systems. We ask a central question of the management of the biosphere: to what extent are the design and rhythms of natural and social systems compatible, and under what criteria can we make their purposes coincide? More fundamentally, what do natural systems and social systems have in common? In synchronic terms, the answer is more and more. That is, as the world turns, more of it is dependent on human management. But, in historical, or even evolutionary terms, there are different answers. These are unanswerable questions, but they are critical. In this chapter, we direct our focus to observations about the systemic properties of both (ecological and human) systems.

Key Features of Ecosystems

Ecosystem structure and function conform to the following principles:

- The environment is not constant. Environmental change is not continuous and gradual, but episodic. "Natural capital" (i.e., biomass or nutrients) accumulates slowly, and then is released suddenly, only to reorganize as the result of natural processes or human-imposed catastrophes. Rare events such as hurricanes or the arrival of invading species can also shape structure unpredictably, with longstanding results. Often the previous state can only be reclaimed through management, and even then success is not assured (Walker 1988). These critical processes that structure ecosystems take place at radically different rates covering several orders of magnitude, and these rates cluster around a few dominant frequencies.
- The spatial organization of natural systems is not uniform either. Nor is it the same at different scales. Ecological systems are "patchy" at all scales—from the leaf, to the landscape, to the planet. Each of several different ranges of scale shows different attributes of patchiness and texture (Holling 1992b). Therefore, scaling up from small to large cannot be a process of simple aggregation: nonlinear processes organize the shift from one range of scale to another.
- Ecosystems do not have a single equilibrium. Rather, multiple equilibria define functionally different states, and movement

between these states is a natural part of maintaining structure and diversity. On one hand, destabilizing forces are important in maintaining diversity, resilience, and opportunity. On the other hand, stabilizing forces are important in maintaining productivity and biogeochemical cycles.

These ecological principles fly in the face of modern human management schemes. Human management, which takes place in very short timeframes, masks the discontinuities and irregularities so characteristic of change. Humans manage as if change were continuous and predictable, or they think of the world "in normal times" as the base management state. Likewise, large human systems and their bureaucracies manage as if space and time are not first-order management issues (Hannan and Freeman 1989). Simply put, human managers assume that existing systems constitute "the natural order" of things, and infer that such order is relatively homogeneous from local to global scales. They expect that what exists now will persist. The enervating conviction of "normal times" allows us to ignore the degree to which human intervention itself perverts natural dynamics in ways that may play themselves out beyond the manager's time horizon.

To use the common example of fisheries, humans find it difficult to manage the system at a point below maximum yield (McEvoy 1986; Scott 1955). In fluctuating systems, such as shoaling pelagic fisheries of the Southeastern Pacific, fisheries managers are notoriously incapable of matching human and ecological dynamics. While individual managers may learn a lot, the social system learns little; management operates in a problem-solving mode, and the time horizon assigned to the problem does not necessarily correspond to that of the ecosystem.

Disharmony between natural and social systems results from the "disturbance" of humans modifying landscapes, and the limits of managerial vision. More importantly, policies and management that apply fixed rules to achieve constant yields (e.g., fixed carrying capacity of cattle or wildlife, or fixed sustainable yield of fish or wood) independent of scale, lead to systems that lack resilience and may break down from disturbances that were previously absorbed (Holling 1986). Ecosystems are moving targets, with multiple futures that are uncertain and unpredictable. Therefore human management has to be flexible, adaptive, and experimental at scales compatible with the scales of critical ecosystem functions (Walters 1986).

Yet, modern economics and development require that managers search for optimal, or maximum, output. Sustainable development often means little more than sustained yield over long stretches of time, within a given or possible technology (NRC 1993).

Ecosystem Structure and Function: The Succession Example

Over the last decade, traditional views of succession have been revised. It was earlier thought that a highly ordered sequence of species assemblages moved toward a sustained climax assemblage, whose characteristics were determined by climate and soil conditions (Clements 1916). That theory, based as it is on a single equilibrium, is analogous to theories in neoclassical economics. Both assume relatively steady growth, with regulatory (negative feedback) forces providing the "invisible hand" that guides the system along some trajectory to an optimal state. Goal-directedness is clearly implied.

Recently a revisionist view has emerged from extensive comparative field studies of different ecosystems (e.g., West et al. 1981; Walker 1988) where experimental manipulation of ecosystems establish alternative paths to succession (Schindler 1974, 1988; Bormann and Likens 1981; Vitousek and Matson 1984), from paleoecological reconstructions that demonstrate multiple stable states and much more variable paths to those different states (Delcourt et al. 1983; Davis 1986) and from studies that link systems models and field research (Clark et al. 1979; West et al. 1981; Westoby et al. 1989). In social systems, a similar revision emerges from field research, indicating:

- Human adaptive response to disturbance can be opportunistic, based on a wide range of rational responses to necessity (response to disturbance is not homogeneous) (Richards 1983; Perrings and Walker 1992);
- Both "early" and "late" forms of social organization can coexist in the same conditions over long periods of time (that is, modernization does not leave old patterns of organization behind) (Moore 1986; Brewer 1988; Lansing 1991);
- The cycles of social organization and their modification often are dictated by internal mechanisms (that is, the origins of social change are immanent) (Schumpeter 1954; Elster 1985; Knight 1992);
- Some kinds of social change shift the system to a qualitatively different set of rules and dynamics (that is, quantitative change leads to qualitative change).

Combining these two research traditions, recent work in ecosystems subjected to human management suggests that opportunistic strategies not only discredit the single equilibrium hypothesis, but may offer a path to a kind of optimal flexibility that is sensitive to ecosystem dynamics (Perrings and Walker 1992).

In summary, the notion of a unique optimal path to a sustained optimal climax is static and unrealistic.

The Renewal Cycle

The combination of these advances in ecosystem understanding with studies of population systems has led to one version of a synthesis that emphasizes four primary stages in an ecosystem cycle (Holling 1986). Traditionally, ecosystem succession has been seen as being controlled by two functions: *exploitation*, in which rapid colonization of recently disturbed areas is emphasized, and *conservation*, in which slow accumulation and storage of energy and material is emphasized. In ecology, the species in the exploitive, phase have been characterized as r-strategists (weedy, opportunistic, fast-growing) and in the conservation phase as K-strategists ("climax," slow-growing)—drawing from the traditional designation of parameters of the logistic equation.

Revisions in ecological understanding indicate that two additional functions are needed, as summarized in Figure 4.1. One is *release*, or "creative destruction," a concept borrowed from the economist J.A. Schumpeter (Schumpeter 1950, 1954; Elliott 1980), in which the tightly bound accumulation of biomass and nutrients becomes increasingly fragile (or overconnected) until it is suddenly released by agents such as forest fires, insect pests, or intense pulses of grazing. We designate that the Ω phase.

The second is *reorganization*, in which soil processes minimize nutrient loss and reorganize nutrients so that they become available for the next phase of exploitation. We designate that the α phase.

Biological time flows unevenly throughout the cycle. Progression in the ecosystem cycle proceeds from the exploitation phase (r, Box 1, Fig. 4.1) slowly to conservation (K, Box 2), very rapidly to release (Ω, Box 3), rapidly to reorganization (α, Box 4), and rapidly back to exploitation. During the slow sequence from exploitation to conservation, connectedness and stability increase and a stock of "capital" of nutrients and biomass is slowly accumulated.

As the progression to K (Box 2) proceeds, the nutrient capital becomes more and more tightly bound within existing vegetation, preventing other competitors from utilizing the accumulated capital until the system eventually becomes so overconnected that rapid

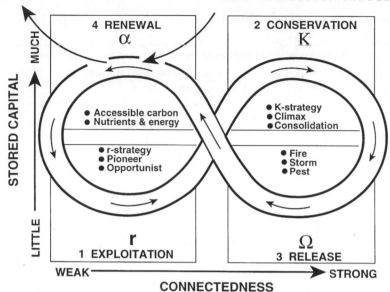

F I G U R E 4.1. The four ecosystem functions (r, K, Ω, α) and the flow of events among them. The arrows show the speed of that flow in the cycle, where arrows close to each other indicate a slowly changing situation and arrows far from each other indicate a rapidly changing situation. The cycle reflects changes in two attributes, (1) y axis: the amount of accumulated capital (nutrients, carbon) stored in variables that are the dominant structuring variables at that moment, and (2) x axis: the degree of connectedness among variables. The arrows entering and leaving a phase suggest where the system is most sensitive to external influence.

change is triggered. The agents of disturbance might be wind, fire, disease, insect outbreak, or a combination of these.

The pattern of change is not smooth but discontinuous, and depends on the existence of changing multistable states that trigger and organize the release and reorganization functions. For example, the release role of the spruce budworm (an insect outbreak species in the eastern North American balsam fir forest) is expressed in the following way. In young forest stands, insectivorous birds control budworm populations. As the forest matures it accumulates a volume of foliage which eventually diminishes the effectiveness of insectivorous birds in their search for food. Essentially, a lower equilibrium density for budworm is set because the birds create a "predator pit" in a stability landscape during the phase of slow regrowth of the forest (Clark et al. 1979; Holling 1988). This stability "pit" eventually collapses as the trees mature, releasing an insect outbreak and revealing the existence of a higher equilibrium density for budworms. A similar argument can be described for release by fire, as a consequence of the slow accumulation of fuel as the forest ages.

To summarize and generalize this example, for long periods in a regrowing forest, the slow variable (trees) controls the fast and intermediate speed ones (budworm and foliage or fire and fuel) until a stability domain shrinks to the point where the fast variables, suddenly and for a brief time, assume control of behavior and trigger release of accumulated capital.

Instabilities trigger the release or Ω phase, which then proceeds to the reorganization or α phase, where the weak connections allow unrestricted chaotic behavior and the unpredictable consequences that can result. Stability begins to be reestablished in the r phase of Box 1. In short, chaos emerges from order, and order emerges from chaos. Resilience and recovery are determined by the fast release and reorganization sequence, whereas stability and productivity are determined by the slow exploitation and conservation sequence.

Moreover, there is a nested set of such cycles, each with its own range of scales. In the typical boreal forest, for example, fresh needles cycle yearly, the crown of foliage cycles with a decadal period and trees, gaps, and stands cycle at close to a century or longer periods. The result is an ecosystem hierarchy, in which each level has its own distinct spatial and temporal attributes (Fig. 4.2). These hierarchies are not static. Levels are transitory structures maintained by processes that change over time and space. The cycles are all operating concurrently, influencing one another. They are rhythms within rhythms, providing not the static structures of a well-oiled machine shop, clanking and vibrating at a myriad of frequencies, but rather those of a jazz band, building rhythms and riffs around each other, coalescing into both short and long rhythmic structures around islands of rhythmic discord. Control in such dynamic hierarchical systems may normally be top-down (Allen and Starr 1982; O'Neill et al. 1986), but the adaptive renewal model indicates periods of fundamental vulnerability to change at the small scale (1) at the transition from growth to collapse (the Ω phase) and (2) at the the transition from reorganization to rapid growth (the α phase).

The accumulating body of evidence indicates key features of discontinuities in processes and structures, and the appearance of multiple stable states. The four-phase cycle of adaptive renewal captures many of these dynamics for ecological systems. But what is the broad value of this analysis for social systems? Do similar dynamics and patterns appear in the management systems established to manage these ecological systems? The remainder of this chapter addresses this

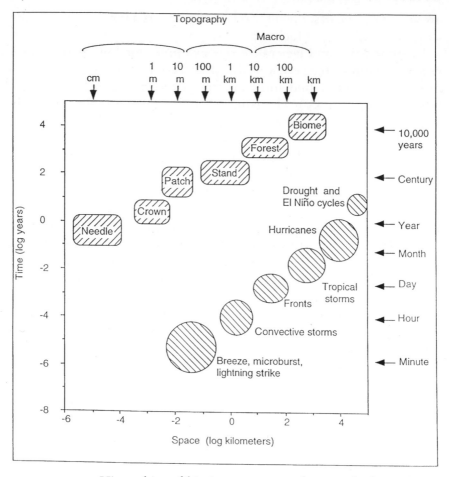

F I G U R E 4.2. Hierarchies of biotic structures and atmospheric processes in the Boreal forest.

question, drawing from lessons learned in a comparison of a series of case studies of regional development and resource management (Gunderson et al. 1995). Of necessity, we restrict the analysis to modern social systems under bureaucratic management. Nonbureaucratic organization in less hierarchically and formally ordered societies presents a separate set of problems beyond the scope of this analysis.

Comparing Ecological and Social Systems
The four-phase cycle of renewal, conservation, creative destruction, and reorganization is an attractive conceptual model for social organization, too. In fact, of course, cyclical theories applied to social sys-

tems have developed more or less independently in international political and economic relations (balance of power and long-cycles theories), agricultural production (livestock cycles, swidden rotation), and even political state formation, war, and revolution (Tilly 1990). So, it is not surprising that to an economist or organization theorist, the properties of the adaptive-renewal cycle mimic the entrepreneurial market or war-making for the exploitation phase and the bureaucratic hierarchy for the conservation phase. The renewal phase is also loosely familiar in human societies in the form of innovation and restructuring—the kinds of social processes that presage social transformation. For a social system—whether economic or cultural—what is termed "natural capital" in Figure 4.1 could be "infrastructure capital," "levels of organizational complexity," or "standard operating techniques" that are incrementally refined and improved over historical time.

One of the puzzles encountered early in a comparison of case studies of ecosystem management (Holling 1986) was the apparently inevitable emergence of a pathology[2] of regional development, at least in its early phases. As a result of initially successful exploitation and human management, the ecosystem and environment became more vulnerable to surprise and crisis. Resilience diminished, management institutions became more rigid and less responsive both to the resource dynamic and to the public, and the citizenry became more dependent on fewer options for self-reliance.

Those case studies were hardly restricted to a narrow type or site; they involved a number of different examples of forest development, fisheries exploitation, semiarid grazing systems, and disease management in crops and people. Since the 1970s, the case studies have grown to include forest management in New Brunswick; water management in the greater Everglades system in Florida; estuarine management in the Chesapeake Bay; salmon and power in the Columbia River; and water quality, fisheries, and development in the Great Lakes and the Baltic Sea.

Two of the initial case studies—forest management in New Brunswick and fisheries issues in the Pacific Northwest—offer insights into the pathology and offer a hypothesis about how to get out of it. In these two examples the pathology up to the mid 1970s has been described as follows:

- Successful short-term management (e.g., suppression of spruce budworm populations in eastern Canada) left the resource (the forest) and hence the economy, more vulnerable to a system-threatening breakdown (more intensive outbreaks of pests persisting over larger areas). This growing vulnerability led to ever-increasing intensity of management, leading to higher vulnerability, and so forth.

- Successful protection and enhancement of resources (salmon spawning through use of fish hatcheries on the west coast of North America) led to more predictable and larger harvests (catches by both sport and commercial fishermen). Success triggered increasing resource pressure and investment, which caused the resource and the resource-based industry to be precariously dependent on artificially enhanced stocks, whose productivity varied according to larger natural system changes.

In both cases, the pathology was broken by a spasmodic readjustment, an adaptive lurch of apparent learning that created new opportunity. That lurch toward innovation gives an evolutionary character to development of a region that might make sustainable development an achievable reality rather than an oxymoron. But under what circumstances, guided by what rules?

Because of the obvious cyclical parallels, the four-phase adaptive cycle emerged as a reasonable way to organize enquiry. But its original form was strictly a representation of an ecosystem cycle as seen in Figure 4.1. That original ecological application has been extensively expanded and its predictions about structure and function of ecosystems tested enough to show its power and relevance, at least in that field of enquiry (Holling 1992b). But, until now, we have avoided the temptation to transfer it from ecological systems to social ones. However, the notion of a complex adaptive system as a general entity in itself has now emerged from a number of different fields and those independent insights have begun successfully to cross-fertilize (Simon 1974; Waldrop 1992; Lansing and Kremer 1993).[3]

More important was the growing suspicion that the model's limitations could be overcome to some degree by linking people, nature, and regional economies. Rather than forcing an ecological model on social systems, therefore, our hope was more to expose its inadequacies and perhaps to expand its generality. At its foundation, the model is essentially a truism of birth, growth, death, and renewal that must apply to any living system and perhaps to nonliving ones as well. But viewed as such, the issue becomes not one of inappropriate transfer from one field to another, but of finding no situation where it does not apply. Explaining everything explains nothing!

The critical feature of the model that can distinguish among different systems lies in the phase of renewal (α phase of Box 4 in Fig. 4.1). Renewal can simply mean the endless repetition of the same initializing condition for the four-phase cycle, as suggested in the initial application of the model to ecosystems. For human systems, however, that would mean humanity was tied to a rack of determinism doomed to repeat the lessons of history with no option for individual will, learning, or history that are the distinguishing features of social science inquiry.[4]

Novelty, and the different futures that novelty creates, however, can unfold as the consequences of unpredictable opportunities provided by the Box 4, α phase where, for a limited time, constraints disappear, and available capital can set the pattern for new and unfamiliar configurations of elements never before connected.

Although Box 4, α phase conditions represent the stage most vulnerable to erosion and loss of accumulated capacity, it also contains the *potential* to jump to unexpectedly different and more productive systems. For example, when fire frequency declined along the prairie–forest border in Minnesota during the Little Ice Age 400 years ago (Grimm 1983), extensive areas changed from oak savanna to maple forest. It was the change in the release function of fire at the Ω phase that opened opportunity for rapid transformation of vegetation at the reorganization, or α phase. Unexpected combinations of previously independent species developed affinities which gave them a key role in future structuring of the ecosystem. At one level, this is similar to the effects of human suppression of fire frequencies on both the structure and dynamics of the ecosystem *and* the propensity for humans to use the system more intensively for their own purposes. This notion can be applied not only to fire management but to the formation of landesque capital (draining swamps, terracing, etc.), or to the elimination of infectious disease (river blindness in Burkina Faso, yellow fever in Panama).

In order to explore further those similarities and differences between ecological and social systems, it is useful now to determine if related concepts and theories, particularly those with an empirical base, have been developed in the social sciences. In doing so, we recognize three fundamental "facts" arising in comparisons of social and natural systems: first, that human actions are guided by intentions, where in natural systems these are of marginal importance; second, that social science's mission is different from that of natural science, in its quest to explain why we are *not* in a state of nature (Elster 1989); and third, that human history and its interpretation has an important role in explaining social systems and, to a greater and greater degree, in explaining the likelihood that the shift from the release phase to the reorganization phase will be a transformative one.

Social Change Theories

We can identify at least three classes of social theories of change that bear on this analysis. The first is the life cycle representation so common to many fields and to the logistic formulation that Marchetti (1987) uses to such good purpose. These life cycle/logistic representations imply growth to some sustained plateau, with senescent elements replaced from some unknown pool. In ecology, that model provided the foundation for Clements' model of ecosystem succession described earlier. In organizational theory, it is the foundation for representing the time course for products (e.g., the product life cycle [Vernon 1966]), processes, and organizations (Kimberly et al. 1980). In economics, however, new theoretical directions expose the abrupt nature of the flip from one mature product to a competing one (Arthur 1990), much as we describe here for the shift from Box 2 to 3, from K to Ω. "Mature" products are seen as capturing a market, and, through increasing returns to scale, may freeze out superior, competing innovations. Patterns of behavior, in the parlance of institutional theory, are "sticky." This aspect could also be applied to the "institutional capture" of political space, in which organized interests dominate a political agenda at the expense of larger publics, or better ideas (McConnell 1966; Olson 1963, 1982).

That addition leads to a second class of social change theory that contrasts gradualist life cycle models with revolutionary change ones. Gersick (1991) has reviewed these using another biological theory as a template for describing change in complex systems: Eldredge and Gould's view (1972) of biological evolution as proceeding by punctuated equilibria, rather than by gradual incremental change. The fossil record suggests that species lineages persist for long periods in essentially the same form or equilibrium, and that new species arise abruptly in sudden adaptive explosions of rapid change. That representation is consistent with the behavior generated by the adaptive–renewal model cycle, but aggregates the four phases into two—one prolonged period of gradual change, and one of rapid transformation. The theory emerged as a description of the fossil record, with explanations for the sudden changes ranging from the consequences of external disturbances (e.g., planetesimal impacts on the earth) to internal senescent/reorganization sequences.

Similar representations have been proposed in the social sciences. For example, in the philosophy of science, Kuhn (1970) distinguished the alternations between long periods of normal science and sudden scientific revolutions leading to a paradigm shift. Abernathy and Utterback (1982) distinguish gradual from radical innovation sequences in industry. Friesen and Miller's (1984) theory of organizational adaptation contrasts periods of momentum with those of revolution. Hannan and Freeman (1989) adopt this dynamic model to a variety of organizations to understand the quick origination of organizational types followed by slower change thereafter. Levinson (1978) sees individual human development as periods of stability alternating with abrupt rapid transitions.

Such theories identify so-called "deep structures" that provide the sustaining rules for the gradual incremental changes that occur throughout the "equilibrium" periods. Those structures can even survive such upheavals as conquest and empire, as has been shown in the case of Balinese water temples, which provided complex water management in an intensively managed agricultural system (Lansing 1991). Revolutions are seen as being brief periods when a system's deep structure collapses to become subsequently reformed around new strategies, power, and alignments. These theories tend to focus on those long-run structuring aspects of history and to dismiss the evanescent fast variables. The "pale lights" of mere "events" glow intermittently, "all without piercing the night with any true illumination. . . .beyond their glow, darkness prevails" (Braudel 1980:10). An ecological parallel was discussed earlier, where long, slow changes in the structure of tree stands control forest dynamics up to the point of collapse, when the budworm "revolution" occurs and the deep structure of the forest is reformed.

But in this case, as with social revolutionary change theories, the model provides more a description of a phenomenon than an explanation of its causes. It leaves important explanatory answers untreated. For example, in historiographical terms, did the European plague represent "an evil made necessary by an ineluctable evolution?" Or was it "a tragic accident at variance with the normal course of events?" (Hawthorn 1991) Does the outbreak of rinderpest in the African Sahel represent a product of natural cycles or a discontinuous system shift caused by the introduction of domesticated animals on an inappropriate scale? (Richards 1983). Recognizing the different variables that control each of the four phases may offer a deeper understanding of the dynamics.

Other, deeper, social theories of change explicitly recognize the four-phase properties of complex evolving systems and the tensions they generate to produce stages of growth and transformation. For example, the Austrian economist Schumpeter (1950) saw socioeconomic transformations proceeding in such a way that market forces controlled the r phase of innovation; institutional hierarchies, monopolism, and social rigidity controlled the K phase of consolidation; forces of "creative destruction" triggered the release or Ω phase; and technological invention determined the source for a phase transformation at α. The essence, and important difference, in such theory is the immanence of the forces of change. That is, the power and potential force of transformation operates from within the system itself, which links Schumpeter with Marx and Marxist interpretations of the evolution of human society (Dobb 1947).

In such theories of revolutionary change, insights focus on the properties of the release or Ω phase. In contrast, the renewal or α phase lies in a fog of mystery by reason of its inherently unpredictable nature. But Schumpeter's designation of capitalism as a "perennial gale of creative destruction" highlights precisely the same paradox in ecosystems at the transition from Box 2 of consolidation, or K, to Box 3 of release, or Ω. There is obviously a destructive element to the collapse of a social formation or to the occurrence of an intensive fire in a mature forest. But there is also a creative element, because previously tightly bound capital is released—organizational energy, political skills, and knowledge in a society; organized carbon and nutrients in a forest.

An even more specific typology comes from cultural anthropology in the works of Douglas (1978) and Thompson (1983). Four explicit types of individuals or institutions are identified and these are organized within two axes very similar to the ones in Figure 4.1. The r-phase is designated as the entrepreneur, the K phase is the caste or bureaucracy, the Ω phase the sects, and the α phase the ineffectual individual (Douglas 1978; Thompson 1983). The insights provided by their descriptions of sects resonates with attributes of the release processes that we describe for ecosystems. The sects are described as being small and tightly organized, often around a charismatic leader with a strong, singular ideological purpose. Their power emerges only occasionally when their tenacious allegiance to internal rules and purpose intersects with the vulnerability of a mature and rigid bureaucracy. This captures their role in triggering release and can illuminate the role of independent environmental activists (or social revolutionaries) in triggering changes in a system.

If we focus more broadly on the organizational scale, there is a tension between those who would characterize organizations as torpid and bureaucratic (see above) versus those who marvel at their imagination and flexibility, as did James March (Hannan and Freeman 1989:69). This scale privileges the manager or charismatic leader much less, especially "in normal times."

This description only partly echoes our previous characterization of the ecological system. Box 4's dissociated, weakly connected state is the very attribute that makes unexpected combinations possible and the influence of the individual most likely. It is the flywheel of the whole system, whose properties determine whether past cycles are simply repeated, or collapse, or emerge in an altogether new system.

The critical difference revolves around whether the weakly connected system state is viewed as one of atomized individuals, or whether it is recognized as a loosely organized social formation with the potential for collective action.[5] A recent example from social responses to crisis helps make the point. After the devastation caused by Hurricane Andrew in South Florida in 1992, the neighborhoods that renewed most rapidly and effectively were ones that drew upon the accumulated experience and contacts of the individuals themselves. The role of elderly people was particularly revealing and critical (Guillette 1993). Their personal contacts, developed over their working lives, allowed them to break through bureaucratic blockages to find aid available from federal, state, and municipal agencies and insurance companies. Contacts and friendships in this example are as much accumulated capital as are money and skills in the α phase of renewal. Other examples from catastrophic cases are readily available in the literature. The opportunities for individuals may only appear, however, in the vacuums created by catastrophe, and we have said nothing explanatory about how individuals optimize versus organizations.

The Box 4, α phase is the one least understood because of its inherently unpredictable nature. The only rigorous theory we have encountered that gives it some specificity is from the body of chaos theory (Stewart 1989). One of the key points of chaos theory is that slight changes in initial conditions can generate a great complexity of behavior and unpredictable outcomes. One of the favorite examples comes from a simple model of the atmosphere developed by Lorenz (Stewart 1989), which showed that slight departures from initial conditions of weather lead to widely divergent futures. The behavior that results looks random, although within a bounded domain, and yet is completely deterministic. There is an inherent unpredictability to outcomes. Lorenz named this the Butterfly Effect, dramatizing the phenomenon with an analogy that a butterfly flapping its wings in Beijing can change storm patterns in New York a month later.

Many examples of chaotic behavior have been identified in physical, biological, and social systems. As in any new theory that gives fresh insight, chaos theory has generated an enthusiastic search for other examples, driven by the desire for universality. Is healthy brain function chaotic and unhealthy function stable? Does heart function have chaotic patterns? Planetary orbits? For ecosystems, at least, the question should be not whether they are chaotic, but when they are chaotic.

To summarize, at times behavior is determined by the r-strategists, by the pioneers and opportunists of Box 1. They set the conditions for control to shift to the K-strategists—to the effective competitors and consolidators of position and power. Resilience is reduced, controls intensified, and the system becomes an accident waiting to happen. As the shift to the Ω phase occurs, the slow, extensive variables lose their control of behavior; fast variables assume control and release the capital that was stored and sequestered in tightly organized form. This capital then becomes dissociated in the α phase where a new set of variables, processes, and random events slow the leakage of capital out of the system, mobilize it in accessible forms, and precipitate possible unexpected associations between previously independent variables.

History and the Slow Variables

This model of human–nature interaction is based on notions of periodicity, contingency, history, learning, adaptation, and reproductive success. The assumptions are that ecosystems and social institutions, to the extent they are to be considered together, operate in complex cycles with opportunities presented at different points in those cycles that may trigger qualitative shifts in the rules and dynamics of the system. Those shifts are contingent upon a concatenation of slow and fast variables, as well as upon chance. In human systems, opportunistic changes are also a function of leadership, social organization, and purposive action.

One of the durable questions of social theory stated in these terms is: If the *intention* of human institutions is to reproduce successfully, then what are the predictors of breakdown? Do they include more than chance? Why must the Holling brittleness hypothesis (human management institutions gravitate to fixed behaviors that make the management system brittle and vulnerable) obtain, or under what conditions does it (not) obtain? A secondary, but still important question is: When are different kinds of management authority relatively important, i.e., When does the maverick appear and why? When is the system most susceptible to individual leadership, or to exogenous forces? Or, when does the success of the system itself predict its "creative destruction"? That is, is it necessary for a social system or a complex human organization to face crisis in order to reform, and if so, is crisis a functional attribute of the system itself? This raises the important analytical question of system boundaries: how much of the four-box dynamic is endogenous, and when are exogenous variables most important?[6]

Both evolutionary biologists and historians might agree that the past is composed (at one level) by contingent particulars (Hawthorn 1991:10), but social scientists would say further that those particulars do not add up to history, either natural or social (no "naked record of facts") (Novick 1988:35). That constitutes the role of theory and historiography in social science, and evolutionary theory and natural history in natural science. Natural and social history are not the same. But just as evolution is path-dependent and irreversible (adaptations do not deconstruct), society does not "repeat its history" except in the most trivialized sense. That is, the four-box cycle in social systems will never accomplish the reorganization phase in the same historical state as it began reorganization in an earlier cycle.[7]

Within this context, theories do make a difference. The organizing principles behind this argument include complexity, hierarchy, cross-scale dynamics, randomness, path dependency, cycles, and non-cyclical courses. The unit of analysis is the system, not the individual or the species. If we take, for the moment, the perspective that human systems are derivative of natural systems rules, we can separate out those elements that are unique to, or principally appropriate to, human systems (intentionality, learning, and history) and those unique to, or principally appropriate to, natural systems (periodicity, adaptation, individual concern with reproductive success).

Simply put (and the raft of literature on this topic precludes anything else), human systems seek to consciously manage their environments based on experience—to learn. Adaptive management has to do with social learning from past experience (Lee 1993). Organizations purportedly "learn" as humans do. This learning model is put in doubt by the depressing hypothesis that "the whole history of humankind reads in some large part as a history of impairment of inquiry"(Lindblom 1990:69). In contrast to a learning model, Lindblom posits a political model in which social groups seek advantage through obfuscation and repression of knowledge. This is not totally inconsistent with learning, where value is measured in terms of the success of future actions, which in turn are based on strategically structuring the field of action. The political model can be restated as part of the accumulated "brittleness" of the K phase, as people's awareness of disinformation culminates in distrust. Moments of political opportunity, combined with this distrust, open the system to strategic restructuring of the field of action—that is, if the polity is organized or mobilized. Politics can be seen as a structuring process that seeks advantage through manipulation of learning.

Among the differences between natural and social systems one fact is critical: that contingency in human systems is addressed by purposive action by institutions organized beyond individual life cycles; that those institutions take on a mission of reproductive success—of pure organizational survival—that may not have much to do with the actual means–end rationality of their original mission; that institutions can pass on learned behaviors that are less adaptive to surprises because they are rigidly adherent to core organizational values (What are the core values of nonhuman animals? What defines their "volitions"? [Lindblom 1990:23]). In human systems, there is a substantive difference between passive adaptation and active learning (Tables 4.1 and 4.2).[8] In natural systems, adaptation is the critical process, and cross-generational social learning (as opposed to adaptation) is unknown.

TABLE 4.1

A Comparison of Passive Adaptation and Active Learning

Adaptation	Learning
Behavior changes as actors add new activities (or drop old ones) without examining the implicit theories underlying their programs. Underlying values are not questioned.	Behavior changes as actors question original implicit theories underlying programs and examine their original values.
The Ultimate Purpose of the organizaztion is not questioned. The emphasis is on altering means of action, not ends. Technical rationality triumphs.	The ultimate purpose is redefined, as means as well as ends are questioned. Substance rationality triumphs.
New ends (purposes) are added without worrying about their coherence with existing ends. Change is incremental without any attempts at nesting purposes logically.	New nested problem sets are constructed because new ends are devised on the basis of consensual knowledge that has become available, as provided by epistemic communities.

Source: Haas 1990.

TABLE 4.2

Attributes of Human Groups That Dominate Activities in Four Phases of the Adaptive Cycle

Attribute	Phase of adaptive cycle[a]					
	$r \to K$	$K \to \Omega$	$\Omega \to \alpha$		$\alpha \to r$	$A \to$ Exit
Group type	Bureaucracy	Activists	Temporary		Adjunct with powers	
Activity focus	Self-serving	Insurgence	Unlearning		New learning; cooperation	Deep transformation; cooperation
Strategy	"Do as before but more"	"Weathering the storm"	"Unlearning yesterday"		"Inventing tommorrow"	
Response to changes	No change	Conflict	Shedding old behaviors		Reframing strategies	Invention
Time horizon	Time of office (linear time)	Present (discontinuous	Time out (multiple scales)		Near future	Distant future (multiple scales)
Space horizon	Building and holding bounds	Destruction of old bounds	Suspension of boundaries		Creating new bounds	
Nature of truth and reality	Constructed	Challenged	Deconstruction		Reconfiguring myths	New myths (visionary)

[a]The listed group dominates during the phase, but is present and functioning in other phases as well. This table represents a centrist view of primarily North American institutions.

Adaptation and Hierarchy
The Adaptive Cycle

In contrast to existing social change theories, the adaptive renewal cycle emphasizes a loop from hierarchical consolidation in Box 2 to two phases of destruction and reorganization where innovation and chance assume a dominant role. As the system cycles through all of its four phases, although control shifts from one set of variables, processes, and events to another set, all variables and processes other than those controlling at the moment are present and functioning in either a maintenance or a "holding" pattern. For example, pioneer species or entrepreneurs are present during the consolidation phases; some trees and bureaucrats (or at least the seeds and saplings of each) persist through the release and reorganization sequence; soil processes or deep social structures function throughout all phases. It is that functional diversity that keeps critical actors in the wings or in a supporting role, while the lead shifts for a period to others. So, the Spanish Communist Party can emerge upon the death of Franco after years of suppression; the Balinese water temples can survive the Green Revolution's attempts to rationalize water allocation through technical expertise. This conclusion reveals our preference for theories that explain systems in terms of immanent change.

Although we see fundamental similarity between adaptive ecological and adaptive human systems, human systems have much greater powers for both rigidity and novelty, for at least three reasons. First, the entire purpose of social institutions is built around the reduction of uncertainty (Ostrom 1990; Sanderson 1994). This means that (a) there is a purpose or purposes within which the periodicity of the four-box heuristic must operate, where none is present in nature; and (b) the purpose tends to lock the system into a smaller loop of conservation and exploitation. J. Elster refers to "binding behavior," which seeks to narrow the domain of possible action (Elster 1984).

Second, the ability of a government bureaucracy—or a firm, for that matter—to control information and resist change seems to show a level of individual and group ingenuity and persistence that reflects conscious control by dedicated and intelligent individuals. This is the modern form of the Weberian observation that organizations are purposive in two senses: they operate within a means–end domain[9] and they are determined to reproduce themselves.

Third, the assumptions with which we began this exercise included the drive of human systems to optimize (in fact, maximize) a given value, not to allow natural system dynamics to run loose. So, if the entire purpose of social systems is to lock the system into the conservation and exploitation loop, they will likely resist both adaptive and learning dynamics that provoke release and reorganization. The overriding temptation of modern human societies is to maximize for a narrow range of values, so that maximum sustainable yield of forest or fishery or rice field forces managers to ignore the importance of long-term successional dynamics, in favor of short-term output. Alternatively, the possibility exists that the locus and speed of the adaptive cycle can be changed by conscious design, so that renewal occurs internally while overall structure is maintained.

Returning to history, we can add a cross-temporal problem to human systems that is not present in natural systems: humans who manage a system for a given set of purposes generally do not consider the system's dynamics beyond the management time horizon. So, in addition to the tendency to manage for a reduced set of values that shortchange the system's natural (unmanaged) dynamics, the very characterization of the system's natural dynamics is short-term. This management myopia explains the difficulty of managing *current* anthropogenic sources of greenhouse gases that will affect *future* climate states and imposing the social costs of mitigation on present-day society (rather than a future society that exists in the abstract).

And, finally, it is difficult in the extreme for human systems to manage natural systems that are unpredictable. Perhaps the most important disjuncture between human and ecological systems involves an inability to manage economically important ecological systems that are inherently unstable or unpredictable. Once again, fisheries offer a classic example of an open, highly variable system managed for short-term yield, often with little regard for chaotic variation in stock/recruitment ratios, biological diversity, total populations, and other system characteristics (Wilson et al. 1990).

Hierarchy

The second feature that distinguishes the scheme presented here concerns the manner in which elements of complex adaptive systems nest one in another. Simon (1974) was one of the first to argue the adaptive significance of such structures. He called them "hierarchies," but not in the sense of top-down sequence of authoritative control. Rather, semiautonomous levels are formed from the interactions among a set of variables that share similar speeds (and, we would add, geometries [Holling 1992a]). Each level communicates a small set of information or quantity of material to the next higher (slower and coarser, in geometric terms) level. This "loose coupling" between levels allows a wide latitude for "experimentation" within levels,

thereby greatly increasing the speed of evolution. A forested landscape example was presented earlier as Figure 4.2.

Ecologists were inspired by this seminal article of Simon's to
transfer the term "hierarchy" to ecological systems (Allen and Starr
1982; O'Neill et al. 1986). But subsequently, the structural, top-
down aspect has tended to dominate, reinforced by the proper, everyday definition of hierarchy as one of vertical authority and control.
The dynamic and adaptive nature of such nested structures has
tended to be lost. It certainly is true that slower and larger levels set
the conditions within which faster and slower ones function. Thus a
forest stand moderates the climate within the stand to narrow the
range of temperature variation that the species experience.

But missing in this representation is the dynamic of each level organized in the four-phase cycle of birth, growth and maturation, death,
and renewal. That cycle is the engine that periodically generates the
variability and novelty upon which experimentation depends. As a
consequence of the periodic but transient phase of destruction and
reorganization, as the cycle progresses from the Ω phase to the α, the
variables can become reshuffled, perhaps to establish different relationships, perhaps to be open to foreign and entirely novel entrants.
This explicitly introduces mutations and rearrangements as a periodic process within each hierarchical level in a way that partially
insulates the resulting experiments from destroying the integrity of
the whole structure. Hence species, physical factors, and biophysical
processes in ecosystems and roles, ideas, and people in institutions
can periodically be reshuffled and invented to explore the consequences of novel associations.

Similarly, it is to be supposed that the very ingenuity that allows
survival of a bureaucracy also provides uniquely human opportunities for change and novelty. Human innovations create new environments independent of, or in concert with, external changes. (The
question of whether hierarchical organization facilitates or impedes
that process is a separate matter.) The development of sedentary agriculture or the industrial revolution might have been conditioned by
climate changes, but it was precipitated by human innovations that
literally created new worlds. At the least, these cultural transformations are in the same domain as the longer term transformations of
biological evolution that created land-dwelling animals or warm-
blooded ones. The organization and functions we now see embracing
both ecological and human systems are, therefore, those that contain
a nested set of the four-box cycles, in which opportunities for periodic reshuffling within levels maintain adaptive opportunity, and the
simple interactions across levels maintains integrity.

The theoretical synthesis indicates that ecological and economic systems exhibit properties of the four-phase adaptive cycle within hierarchical relationships across scales. These properties are characteristic of all complex, adaptive systems.

Summary and Conclusions

We have compared ecologic and social systems by developing concepts to explain dynamics of complex, adaptive systems, of which ecologic and social systems are examples. Two new concepts were presented. In the first, the adaptive renewal model that was developed from ecological theory was applied to management institutions and contrasted with other theories of social change. The reconfiguration phase of the adaptive cycle provides the least recognized, predictable, or understood portion of social dynamics. The second new concept involves the recognition that adaptive cycles are occurring within structures nested and arranged across scales of space and time.

We contend that the essential difference between human and ecological systems is management and purpose. The central question that derives from this has to do with the ability of human-managed systems not only to synchronize with the expected values of natural system dynamics, but to recognize the variability in their flows and functions, and to act accordingly. It is not to be expected that such management will derive from single equilibrium, short-time horizons, and maximization of ecological system outputs, all of which unfortunately describe the modern organization and management of nature. In regard to the design of ecologically adapted property rights, the message is grim: human systems of property rights, built around deterministic (or stipulated) ecosystem models, are not flexible in their application or crafted in light of the temporal or spatial demands of natural systems (Naughton and Sanderson 1995). Until modern human institutions are built on ecological dynamism, and designed to flex with natural variability, their principal impact will be to impede nature, not to sustain it.

NOTES

1. Thanks are due to Arun Agrawal and Rusty Pritchard for their help in improving this chapter.

2. Calling such characteristics pathologies, rather than simply another kind of system characteristic implies a substantive purpose for the organization, or a development design. That itself distinguishes social systems from natural systems, unless the substantive purpose is reduced to reproductive success or survival.

3. Since the late 1980s, the Santa Fe Institute has been providing a prime focus for exploring and deepening these insights and for opening opportunities provided by the identification of adaptive complex systems as a specific object of enquiry, whatever form it takes—economic, social, biological, or ecological.

4. This is not to deny the determinist possibility altogether. How else could Marchetti (1987) so consistently describe the development of various technologies with a simple logistic curve—a Box 1-to-Box 2, an r-to-K conceit? But it is one thing to posit a determinist model, another to suggest that it is THE model of social systems.

5. In fact, of course, this relates to another essential question, unspecified in this description: the power of any theoretical approach to capture the cross-scale changes in social organization. In the methodological individualism of rational choice, this is often relegated to the background, as the approach allows that organizations are sums of individuals to be treated as relatively simple aggregates (Elster 1989:29). Organization theorists tend to concentrate on the aggregated form and to undervalue the role of the individual. A complex systems approach to social organization, on the other hand, focuses on emergent properties of organization that make scaling up more interesting than a simple level of analysis question. None of these approaches *necessarily* focuses on the cross-scale dynamics that are critical to analyzing adaptive management strategies.

6. This would be a convenient formulation, to endogenize crisis and consider episodic and noncyclical drivers of change to be exogenous.

7. Though it sounds trivial, we are simply saying that "history moves on." To the extent that natural systems are influenced by human history (increasingly) over time, one can apply this generalization from human society to natural systems, too.

8. This raises an interesting side argument about whether change in human organizations is "Lamarckian," in its dependency on learned traits, or determined by structural attributes that resist adaptation based on learning. For an entry into the debate, see Hannan and Freeman 1989:22. It is also true that individual species at the ecosystem level produce structure that reinforces their own persistence in the system, which is a kind of active adaptation mimicking volition.

9. This rationality is most often bounded by organizational limits and the triumph of technical rationality over more open-ended optimizing. It is also likely that public and private organizations are constrained by different logics, with the latter more dependent on efficiency and productivity (Haas 1990:55).

REFERENCES

Abernathy, W. and J. Utterback. 1982. Patterns in industrial innovation. Pages 97–108 in M. Tushman and W. Moore, eds. *Readings in the Management of Innovation*. Pitman, Boston.

Allen, T. F. H. and T. B. Starr. 1982. *Hierarchy: Perspectives for Ecological Complexity*. The University of Chicago Press, Chicago.

Arthur, B. 1990. Positive feedback in the economy. *Scientific American* 262: 92–99.

Baskerville, G. L. 1976. Spruce budworm: Super silviculturalist. *Forest Chronicle* 51:138–140.

Baskerville, G. L. 1988. Redevelopment of a degrading forest system. *Ambio* 17:314–322.

Baskerville, G. 1995. The forestry problem: Adaptive lurches of renewal. Pages 37–102 *in* L. H. Gunderson, C. S. Holling, and S. S. Light, eds. *Barriers and Bridges to the Renewal of Regional Ecosystems*. Columbia University Press, New York.

Bormann, F. H. and G. E. Likens. 1981. *Patterns and Process in a Forested Ecosystem*. Springer-Verlag, New York.

Braudel, F. 1980. *On History*. Translated by S. Matthews. University of Chicago Press, Chicago.

Brewer, J. D. 1988. Traditional land use and government policy in Bima, East Sumbawa. Pages 119–135 *in* M. R. Dove, ed. *The Real and Imagined Role of Culture in Development: Case Studies from Indonesia*. University of Hawaii Press, Honolulu.

Clark, S. 1985. The *Annales* Historians. *In* Q. Skinner, ed. *The Return of Grand Theory in the Human Sciences*. Cambridge University Press, Cambridge, UK.

Clark, W. C. and R. E. Munn, eds. 1986. *Sustainable Development of the Biosphere*. Cambridge University Press, Cambridge, UK.

Clark, W. C., D. D. Jones, and C. S. Holling. 1979. Lessons for ecological policy design: A case study of ecosystem management. *Ecological Modelling* 7:1–53.

Clements, F. E. 1916. Plant Succession: An Analysis of the Development of Vegetation. Carnegie Institute of Washington Publication 242:1–512.

Davis, M. B. 1986. Climatic instability, time lags and community disequilibrium. Pages 269–284 *in* J. Diamond and T. Case, ed. *Community Ecology*. Harper and Row, New York.

Delcourt, H. R., P. A. Delcourt, and T. I. Webb. 1983. Dynamic plant ecology: The spectrum of vegetational change in space and time. *Quaternary Science Reviews* 1:153–175.

Diener, M. and T. Poston. 1984. On the perfect delay convention or the revolt of the slaved variables. Pages 249–268 *in* H. Haken, ed. *Chaos and Order in Nature*. Springer-Verlag, Berlin.

Dobb, M. 1947. *Studies in the Development of Capitalism*. International Publishers, New York.

Douglas, M. 1978. *Cultural Bias*. Occasional Paper for the Royal Anthropological Institute No. 35. Royal Anthropological Institute, London.

Eldredge, N. and S. Gould. 1972. Punctuated equilibria: An alternative to phyletic gradualism. Pages 82–115 *in* T. J. Schopf, ed. *Models in Paleobiology*. Freeman, Cooper and Co., San Francisco.

Elliott, J. E. 1980. Marx and Schumpeter on capitalism's creative destruction: A comparative restatement. *Quarterly Journal of Economics* 95: 46–58.

Elster, J. 1984. *Ulysses and the Sirens.* Cambridge University Press, Cambridge, UK.

Elster, J. 1985. *Making Sense of Marx.* Cambridge University Press, Cambridge, UK.

Elster, J. 1989. *Nuts and Bolts for the Social Sciences.* Cambridge University Press, Cambridge, UK.

Friesen, P. and D. Miller. 1984. *Organizations: A Quantum View.* Prentice-Hall, Englewood Cliffs, NJ.

Gersick, C. J. G. 1991. Revolutionary change theories: A multilevel exploration of the punctuated equilibrium paradigm. *Academy of Management Review* 16:10–36.

Grimm, E. C. 1983. Chronology and dynamics of vegetation change in the prairie-woodland region of southern Minnesota. *New Phytologist* 93: 311–335.

Guillette, E. 1993. Role of the aged in community recovery following hurricane Andrew. *Quick Response Report QR56.* Natural Hazards Research and Applications Center, Denver, CO.

Gunderson, L., C. Holling, and S. Light. 1995. *Barriers & Bridges for the Renewal of Ecosystems and Institutions.* Columbia University Press, New York.

Haas, E. B. 1990. *When Knowledge is Power: Three Models of Change in International Organizations.* University of California Press, Berkeley.

Hannan, M. T. and J. Freeman. 1989. *Organizational Ecology.* Harvard University Press, Cambridge, MA.

Hawthorn, G. 1991. *Plausible Worlds: Possibility and Understanding in History and the Social Sciences.* Cambridge University Press, Cambridge, UK.

Holling, C. S. 1986. Resilience of ecosystems; local surprise and global change. Pages 292–317 *in* W. C. Clark and R. E. Munn, eds. *Sustainable Development of the Biosphere.* Cambridge University Press, Cambridge, UK.

Holling, C. S. 1988. Temperate forest insect outbreaks, tropical deforestation and migratory birds. *Mem. Ent. Soc. Can.* 146:21–32.

Holling, C. S. 1992a. The role of forest insects in structuring the boreal landscape. Pages 170–191 *in* H. H. Shugart, R. Leemans, and G. B. Bonan, eds. *A Systems Analysis of the Global Boreal Forest.* Cambridge University Press, Cambridge, UK.

Holling, C. S. 1992b. Cross-scale morphology, geometry and dynamics of ecosystems. *Ecological Monographs* 62(4):447–502.

Holling, C. S., D. D. Jones, and W. C. Clark. 1976. Ecological policy design: A case study of forest and pest management. *IIASA* 1 (1976):139–158.

Kauffman, S. A. 1993. *Origins of Order: Self-Organization and Selection in Evolution.* Oxford University Press, Oxford, UK.

Kimberly, J. R., J. R. Miles, and Associates. 1980. *The Organizational Life Cycle*. Jossey-Bass Inc., San Francisco.

Knight, J. 1992. *Institutions and Social Conflict*. Cambridge University Press, Cambridge, UK.

Kuhn, T. S. 1970. *The Structure of Scientific Revolutions,* 2nd ed.. University of Chicago Press, Chicago.

Lansing, J. S. 1991. *Priests and Programmers: Technologies of Power in the Engineered Landscape of Bali*. Princeton University Press, Princeton, NJ.

Lansing, J. S. and J. N. Kremer. 1993. Emergent properties of Balinese water temple networks: Coadaptation on a rugged fitness landscape. *American Anthropologist* 95:97–114.

Lee, K. N. 1993. *Compass and Gyroscope: Integrating Science and Politics for the Environment*. Island Press, Washington, D.C.

Levinson, D. J. 1978. *The Seasons of a Man's Life*. Knopf, New York.

Libby, C. E. 1962. *Pulp and Paper Science and Technology*. McGraw-Hill, New York.

Lindblom, C. E. 1990. *Inquiry and Change: The Troubled Attempt to Understand and Shape Society*. Yale University Press, New Haven, CT.

Marchetti, C. 1987. Infrastructures for movement. *Technological Forecasting and Social Change* 32:373–393.

Marx, K. 1973. *Grundrisse: Introduction to the Critique of Political Economy*. Edited by Martin Nicolaus. Penguin, London.

McCalla, A. F. 1994. "Agriculture and Food Needs to 2025: Why we should be concerned." Consultative Group on International Agricultural Research. Sir John Crawford Memorial Lecture.

McConnell, G. 1966. *Private Power and American Democracy*. Knopf, New York.

McEvoy, A. F. 1986. *The Fisherman's Problem: Ecology and Law in the California Fisheries, 1850–1980*. Cambridge University Press, Cambridge, UK.

Moore, S. F. 1986. *Social Facts and Fabrications: "Customary" Law on Kilamanjaro, 1880 1980*. Cambridge University Press, Cambridge, UK.

National Research Council. 1993. *Sustainable Agriculture and the Environment in the Humid Tropics*. National Academy Press, Washington, D.C.

Naughton, L. and S. Sanderson. 1995. Property, politics and wildlife conservation. *World Development* 28:1265–1275.

Novick, D. 1988. *That Noble Dream: The "Objectivity Question" and the American Historical Profession*. Cambridge University Press, Cambridge, UK.

Olson, M. 1963. *The Logic of Collective Action*. Harvard University Press, Cambridge, MA.

Olson, M. 1982. *The Rise and Decline of Nations: Economic Growth, Stagflation, and Social Rigidities*. Yale University Press, New Haven, CT.

O'Neill, R. V., D. L. DeAngelis, J. B. Waide, and T. F. H. Allen. 1986. *A Hierarchical Concept of Ecosystems*. Princeton University Press, Princeton, NJ.

Ostrom, E. 1990. *Governing the Commons: The Evolution of Institutions for Collective Action*. Cambridge University Press, Cambridge, UK.

Perrings, C. and B. Walker. 1992. Biodiversity loss and the economics of discontinuous change in semi-arid rangelands. Paper presented at the Second Conference on the Ecology and Economics of Biodiversity Loss. Beier Institute, Stockholm. Manuscript.

Prigogine, I. 1980. *From Being to Becoming: Time and Complexity in the Physical Sciences*. W.H. Freeman, New York.

Regier, H. A. and G. L. Baskerville. 1986. Sustainable redevelopment of regional ecosystems degraded by exploitive development. Pages 292–317 *in* W. C. Clark and R. E. Munn, eds. *Sustainable Development of the Biosphere*. Cambridge University Press, Cambridge, UK.

Richards, P. 1983. Ecological change and the politics of African land use. *African Studies Review* 26:1–72.

Richards, P. 1985. *Indigenous Agricultural Revolution: Ecology and Food Production in West Africa*. Westview Press, Boulder, CO.

Sanderson, S. E. 1994. Human driving forces: Political-economic institutions. Pages 224–252 *in* W. B. Meyer and B.L. Turner II, ed. *Changes in Land Use and Land Cover: A Global Perspective*. Cambridge University Press, Cambridge, UK.

Schindler, D. W. 1974. Eutrophication and recovery in experimental lakes: Implications for lake management. *Science* 184:897–899.

Schindler, D. W. 1988. Experimental studies of chemical stressors on whole lake ecosystems. Baldi Lecture. *Verhandlungen International Limnology* 23:11–41.

Schumpeter, J. A. 1950. *Capitalism, Socialism and Democracy*. Harper and Row, New York.

Schumpeter, J. A. 1954. *History of Economic Analysis*. Oxford University Press, New York.

Scott, A. 1955. The fishery: The objectives of sole ownership. *Journal of Political Economy* 63:116–124.

Simon, H. A. 1974. The organization of complex systems. Pages 3–27 *in* H. H. Pattee, ed. *Hierarchy Theory: the Challenge of Complex Systems*. George Braziller, New York.

Stewart, I. 1989. *Does God Play Dice? The Mathematics of Chaos*. Basil Blackwell, Oxford, UK.

Thompson, M. 1983. A cultural bias for comparison. Pages 232–262 *in* H. C. Kunreuther and J. Linnerooth, eds. *Risk Analysis and Decision Processes: The Siting of Liquified Energy Gas Facilities in Four Countries*. Springer, Berlin.

Tilly, C. 1990. *Coercion, Capital and European States, AD 990–1992*. Blackwell. Cambridge, MA.

Vernon, R. 1966. International investment and international trade in the product cycle. *The Quarterly Journal of Economics* 80:190–207.

Vitousek, P. M. 1994. Beyond global warming: Ecology and global change. *Ecology* 75:1861–1876.

Vitousek, P. M. and P. A. Matson. 1984. Mechanisms of nitrogen retention in forest ecosystems: A field experiment. *Science* 225:51–52.

Vitousek, P. M., P. R. Ehrlich, A. H. Ehrlich, and P. A. Matson. 1986. Human appropriation of the products of photosynthesis. *BioScience* 36:368–373.

Waldrop, M. M. 1992. *Complexity*. Simon and Schuster, New York.

Walker, B. H. 1981. Is succession a viable concept in African savanna ecosystems? Pages 431–447 *in* D. C. West, H. H. Shugart, and D. B. Botkin, eds. *Forest Succession: Concepts and Application*. Springer-Verlag, New York.

Walker, B. H., 1988. Autecology, synecology, climate and livestock as agents of rangelands dynamics. *Australian Rangeland Journal* 10: 69–75.

Walters, C. J. 1986. *Adaptive Management of Renewable Resources*. Macmillan, New York.

West, D. C., H. H. Shugart, and D. B. Botkin. 1981. *Forest Succession: Concepts and Application*. Springer-Verlag, New York.

Westoby, M., B. H. Walker, and I. Noy-Meir. 1989. Opportunistic management for rangelands not at equilibrium. *Journal of Rangeland Management* 42:266–274.

Wilson, J. A., R. Townsend, P. Kelban, S. McKay, and J. French. 1990. Managing unpredictable resources: Traditional policies applied to chaotic populations. *Ocean and Shoreline Management* 13:179–197.

Wynn, G. 1981. *Timber Colony*. University of Toronto, Toronto.

CHAPTER 5

Social Systems, Ecological Systems, and Property Rights

FIKRET BERKES

Introduction

This chapter presents some perspectives on the linkage between social systems and natural systems, and reviews some aspects of the state of knowledge about how natural resource systems and social systems interact under different property-rights regimes, and how that interaction affects the performance of natural resource systems.

The property rights issue of concern here does not include industries, services, most agricultural land and mineral resources, but includes common-property (or common-pool) resources. Further, in the realm of commons, the focus here is not global commons (Dasgupta and Maler 1992; Keohane and Ostrom 1995), or regional commons such as the Baltic Basin or the Caribbean Sea, but mostly local commons managed under different property-rights regimes, which is the major literature base on the interface of natural and social systems. Many of the principles derived from the local commons are applicable to, or have parallels in, the international commons (Keohane and Ostrom 1995).

There are four sections in this chapter. The first presents some background discussion of common-property (common-pool) resources and Hardin's (1968) contention that individuals using resources jointly are helpless to organize and engage in collective action.

The second section discusses some classical and recent views of the interface of natural systems and social systems. The section argues that institutions are the key to analyzing the interface, and that the focus on property rights expands the scope of ecological economics to consider not a two-way linkage (natural systems–economic systems) but a three-way linkage incorporating social/institutional/cultural dimensions also. This three-way linkage may be characterized as natural-capital/cultural-capital/human-made-capital inter-action (Berkes and Folke 1994a), whereby the importance of feed-backs in the linkages is emphasized.

The third and most detailed section includes a review of empirical cases. It shows that there is no clear-cut verdict on the performance of natural resource systems under different property-rights regimes, except that open-access is not viable in the long term.

The fourth and last section addresses the question of criteria of "success." It ends with the conclusion that there are no simple prop-erty-rights solutions. Needed are combinations of property-rights regimes and a diversity of property rights institutions that can be adapted for specific circumstances. The chapter is offered in the spirit of an overview with some key references, and not as an exhaustive analysis of the subject area.

Concepts, Parables, Regimes

Although there is variation in emphasis among scholars (e.g., McCay 1995), most discussions of common property are concerned with resource types which share two key characteristics: (i) exclusion or control of access of potential users is problematic, and (ii) each user is capable of subtracting from the welfare of all other users, that is, there is a jointness problem. On the basis of these two characteristics, some resources are referred to as common-property (or common-pool) resources, and defined as a class of resources for which exclusion is difficult and joint use involves subtractability (Berkes 1989; Feeny et al. 1990). This class of resources usually includes fish, wildlife, forests, grazing lands, irrigation, and groundwater. Most wildlands, parks, and public spaces also show characteristics of common-property, most agricultural land and mineral resources do not.

It has been known that resources that share the above characteris-tics tend to be susceptible to depletion and degradation. This com-mons dilemma has been referred to as "the tragedy of the commons" (Hardin 1968). Costanza (1987) has used the term "social trap" to refer more broadly to any circumstance in which the rational indi-vidual choice is inconsistent with the long-term interests of either the individual or society.

For natural scientists, by far the best known of the various formu-lations of the commons dilemma is the "tragedy of the commons," used by Hardin as a parable to explain overgrazing in a hypothetical medieval English commons. Each herdsman seeking individual gain wants to increase the size of his herd. But the commons is finite, and sooner or later the total number of cattle will exceed the carrying capacity of the land. But it is in the rational self-interest of each herdsman to keep adding animals: his personal gain from adding one more animal (+1) outweighs his personal loss (a fraction of −1) from the damage done to the commons. However, since all herdsmen use the same logic, eventually they all lose. Hence, the overexploitation of the commons is an inevitable result, and a tragedy in the sense of ancient Greek tragedies according to Hardin, in which the characters know that the disaster is coming but are unable to do anything about it.

Hardin's (1968) notion that "freedom in the commons brings ruin to all" was taken quite literally, and accorded by some the status of scientific law. But many scholars knew that the case study would not hold up to historical scrutiny and that the generalization about commons was inappropriate (Feeny et al. 1990). Improving upon Hardin's analysis of the commons required, among others, an organizing framework of property-rights regimes applicable to common-property resources.

Briefly, following Ostrom (1990), Bromley (1992), and Feeny et al. (1990), common-property (common-pool) resources may be held in one of four basic property-rights regimes. *Open-access* is the absence of well-defined property rights. Access is free and open to all. *Private property* refers to the situation in which an individual or corporation has the right to exclude others and to regulate the use of the resource. *State property* or *state governance* means that rights to the resource are vested exclusively in government for controlling access and regulating use. *Communal property* or *common property* means that the resource is held by an identifiable community of users who can exclude others and regulate use. These four regimes are ideal, analytical types. In practice, resources tend to be held in overlapping combinations of them, and there is variation within each.

On the basis of empirical experience, we can hypothesize that three property-rights regimes—private property, state property, and communal property—can under some circumstances, lead to sustainable resource use. By contrast, there is general consensus that open-access is not compatible with sustainability. Hardin's herders, whose access to the resource was free and rulemaking appeared not to exist, were functioning in an open-access regime, not communal property. Hardin's confusion of open-access with common-property has been much discussed as a source of confusion in resource management policies as well (McCay and Acheson 1987; Bromley and Cernea 1989; Berkes 1989; Bromley 1992).

Privatization, advocated as a solution by many economists and others, is often not an option because, by definition, there is an exclusion problem with common-property resources. As Magrath (1989) put it, many of the resources in question are nonexclusive by nature, and not deemed appropriate for private ownership. This has made common-property resources generally difficult to deal with in conventional economic terms. The question of the appropriate property-rights regime is part of the current policy debate for this vast array of resources with exclusion and jointness problems. It is the recognition of these resources as a distinct category that has given rise to a large body of recent literature that cuts across disciplinary boundaries.

Different Views of the Interface

In the history of human ecology, a number of social scientists have attempted to formulate ways of approaching the interface between society and environment. Many of these take into account organization and technology as two key factors in the relationship. Park (1936), the founder of the Chicago school of human ecology, postulated that there was a "cultural superstructure" in human society (as opposed to other species) that imposed itself as an "instrument of direction and control" upon the environment. This cultural superstructure or social complex had three elements: population, artifact (technology), and custom and beliefs (culture). Interaction occurred between the social complex and the environment.

A similar view was expressed by another human ecologist, Duncan (1961), who argued that human societies were characterized by technology and organization. Thus, the link between the human population and environment was not a two-way interaction but rather a four-way interaction of the interdependent variables—population, organization, technology, and environment. The same four variables are also found in Hawley's (1973) view of the ecosystem. His view differs from the others in considering organization and technology as a "lens" that mediates the relationship between a society and its natural environment.

Much of the common-property literature is consistent with classical human ecology in taking into account factors related to organization; there is less emphasis, however, on technology which tends to be treated as an external variable. Much of the common-property literature emphasizes institutions as mediating factors that govern the relationship between a society and the natural resources on which it depends (e.g., Ostrom 1990).

The literature in ecological economics, by contrast, is concerned more with the relationship between "natural capital" and "human-made capital," almost to the exclusion of social factors including institutions (Jansson et al. 1994). Berkes and Folke (1994a) have argued that, in general terms, property-rights institutions are part of the cultural capital by which societies convert natural capital, that is, resources and ecological services, into human-made capital or the produced means of production. The term "cultural capital" refers to factors that provide human societies with the means and adaptations to deal with the natural environment and to actively modify it. Cultural capital includes what others have called "social capital" and "institutional capital." It also includes how people view the natural world, values, and ethics, including religion, and culturally transmitted knowledge of the environment or indigenous knowledge (Gadgil et al. 1993).

Figure 5.1 presents a view of how the three kinds of capital may be interrelated. Natural capital is the basis for cultural capital. For example, property-rights institutions are closely related to the characteristics of the resources used by a society (Geertz 1963). In turn, attitudes and practices of a society regulate the exploitation of its natural capital (Freeman et al. 1991; Posey and Balee 1989). Thus, human-made capital is generated jointly by natural and cultural

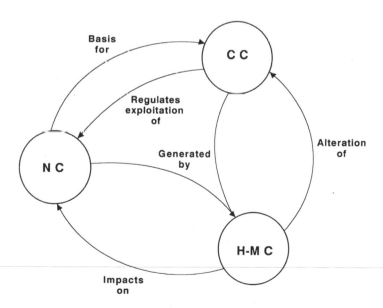

FIGURE 5.1. The main linkages among natural capital (NC), human-made capital (H-MC) and cultural capital (CC). *Source:* Berkes and Folke (1994a).

capital; the use of natural capital under a particular set of institutions, attitudes, and technology produces human-made capital. Human-made capital may, in turn, alter cultural capital; for example, technologies may mask a society's dependence on natural capital and provide a false sense of control over nature. Thus, cultural capital is closely linked to how natural capital will be used; technologies reflect cultural values, worldview, and institutions (Gadgil et al. 1993).

Within a framework of three-way interactions, how would the three capitals interact under different property-rights regimes? The short answer is that we do not know. There is no well developed literature in this area. However, some tentative hypotheses and speculations may be offered:

- New adaptations or a constant elaboration of cultural capital would be necessary to keep up with changes in human-made capital;
- The sustainable use of natural capital will be facilitated by those property-rights regimes capable of responding to feedback from natural capital;
- Ways of enhancing the turnover of information within the larger system will enhance the management of the ecological system; and
- Property-rights institutions must be flexible (rather than "brittle"), diverse, and capable of self-renewal, as Holling (1986) has defined for ecosystem resilience.

The notion of cultural capital, with all the informal and intangible dimensions that it embodies, no doubt complicates the more manageable ecology–economics dichotomy. But it is more consistent with the roots of human ecology and also serves to highlight systems, many of which are informal and thus largely "invisible" to conventional analyses. These informal systems, such as local common-property institutions and traditional knowledge systems, tend to be found more in the Third World than the industrial West, more in rural than in urban areas (e.g., Berkes 1989), and, one may speculate, more in female-dominated than in male-dominated activities. These are not areas in which conventional analyses are known to be strong!

Hardin's seminal "tragedy of the commons," with its group of medieval English herders locked in a downward spiral of resource degradation is a powerful metaphor. But it is not a very good characterization of what really happens in many commons cases; it assumes away institutions and feedbacks. Much of the commons literature suggests instead a "bucket brigade" metaphor. Given a resource management problem, a group of people will often organize themselves in a way that is similar to the formation of a bucket brigade to put out the fire in a rural community.

Figure 5.2 summarizes the two metaphors as simple feedback models of an integrated natural–social system. The major differences between the two models are in the stabilizing feedback loops that connect the social system and the natural system. For common-property resource use to be sustainable, there should be feedback informing the management institution about the state of the resource; there should also be feedback between the regime and the resource user. When these stabilizing feedbacks are absent (or assumed away) then one is left with a runaway positive feedback loop (a vicious circle), and such a system cannot be sustainable in the long term.

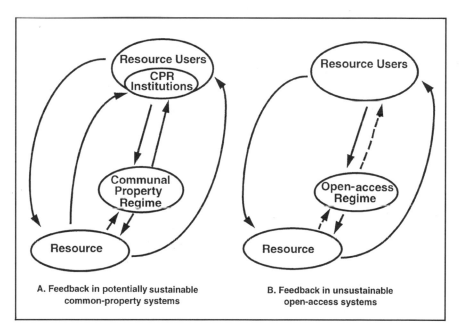

A. Feedback in potentially sustainable common-property systems

B. Feedback in unsustainable open-access systems

FIGURE 5.2. A systems view of the differences between common-property and open-access systems. Common-property systems have two-way feedbacks between the resource, the regime, and the institution. These linkages enable institutions (rules-in-use) to regulate resource use. In the case of open-access systems, however, there are no institutions to respond to signals from the resource and no negative feedback (stabilizing feedback) or rules to regulate resource use. The result is that open-access systems tend to turn into positive feedback loops (vicious circles) whereby resource depletion leads to more intensified use, which leads to more depletion.

Resource Use Under Different Property-Rights Regimes

The importance of these feedbacks may be seen by analyzing empirical cases. Feeny et al. (1990) evaluated the successes and failures of the four pure property-rights regimes, using the criterion of sustainability. Since the definition of common-property emphasizes two characteristics, exclusion and jointness, the evidence for the performance of the four regimes was assessed with respect to how well each met the following two fundamental challenges in the management of common-property resources: (a) the exclusion of other potential users, and (b) the regulation of joint use to ameliorate the problems associated with subtractability. The following sections are based on Feeny et al. (1990), updated to include some of the more recent literature.

Evidence on Exclusion
Open-Access

The evidence is in support of a general "tragedy of the commons" when resources are held as open-access. Examples are many and include the historic case of the depletion of the various whale stocks in the open ocean. Much of the older literature on the commons is replete with examples showing that if there is no exclusion in the use of scarce resources, depletion follows. However, if resources are abundant relative to needs, open-access and lack of exclusion are not necessarily problematic, at least in the short term. Related to this, the literature reveals an important point: in many cases, colonialists dismantled communal property regimes and institutions as a prelude to establishing colonial economies (e.g., Gadgil and Guha 1992). The "tragedy" occurred only after open-access conditions had been created by external factors, after the destruction of existing communal land-tenure and marine-tenure systems.

A number of cases involved the imposition of colonial rule, as in sub-Saharan Africa (Baxter and Hogg 1990), the Pacific Islands (Johannes 1978), India (Gadgil and Guha 1992), the Pacific Coast salmon rivers in the United States and Canada, and elsewhere (Berkes 1985). In a sense, open-access served well when it was deemed desirable that resources be made freely available for converting into economic wealth, and the local people who depended on them for their subsistence were eliminated from the allocation equation. The point is that the creation of wealth in colonial economies is not necessarily (or not usually) consistent with objectives of sustainable resource use.

Private Property

The establishment and enforcement of private property rights have often provided the institutional arrangement for successful exclusion in resources such as agricultural land—so much so that in the contemporary world (i.e., post-USSR, postprivatization China), private property is almost the exclusive way in which farmland is held. Tree-growing on privatized land may be an important mechanism for sustainability. For example, Holmgren et al. (1994) have found increasing tree biomass, mostly on private land, despite population growth in parts of Kenya. With some types of common-property resources, however, private property rights do not provide a sufficiently precise mechanism for solving the exclusion problem.

For example, in fisheries, the system known as individual transferable quotas (ITQs), holds much appeal to some because it enables market forces to direct the allocation of resources, presumably increasing economic efficiency. Under ITQ, each boat owner receives a share of the total allowable catch (a quota) which can be bought, sold, or leased. ITQs have revolutionized fishery management in the last decade or so, but there is also a downside: ITQs may allow a small number of individuals or companies to buy control over the fishery. Also, the quota approach does not work well when allowable catches cannot be forecast well ahead, when there is a mixed fishery and an incidental catch problem, or when the fishing units are small and there is an enforcement problem (Wilson et al. 1994; Weber 1995).

Enforcement problems exist with all types of property-rights regimes, including private property. Common-property resources, by definition, pose exclusion problems, and enforcement of private property may entail high transaction costs (or the cost of doing business). Well-recognized rights of medieval lords to fish and game were routinely violated by poachers. If the local people do not regard private property rights as legitimate, this may drive up the cost of enforcement.

Communal Property

Under communal-property regimes, "exclusion" means the ability to exclude people other than the members of a defined group. Evidence suggests that successful exclusion under communal-property is the rule rather than the exception, but stresses of population growth, technology change, and economic change may contribute to the breakdown of communal-property mechanisms for exclusion (Jodha

1985, 1992). The creation of open-access by external forces, as in colonialism, is particularly damaging. Examples include Amerindian community hunting lands in James Bay, eastern subarctic Canada—where the communal-property regime collapsed as a result of incursions by outsiders, at least twice over two centuries, and recovered with the reestablishment of exclusion by legislation (Berkes 1989).

One of the major conclusions from the literature is that legal recognition of communal resource-use rights, as in Japanese coastal fisheries, is key to the success of exclusion under communal-property regimes. This is true for a variety of resources from wildlife in Africa (IIED 1994) to mangrove forests in the Caribbean (Smith and Berkes 1993). In many parts of the world, however, there is no legal recognition of exclusion under communal property. Nevertheless, in many such cases, the exclusion of outsiders by local users has been informally enforced through such means as threats and surreptitious violence. A remarkable example is the persistence of community-based lobster fishing territories in Maine which are not recognized in government regulation and are technically illegal (Acheson 1988). The Maine lobster example is merely one of many, but it is a significant example because it comes from a country and culture in which the right of individual free-access is a deeply held belief.

State Property

The state-property regime serves an essential purpose in situations in which the general public good is involved, and other property-rights regimes cannot be relied upon to provide sufficient protection for the resource in question. An example is the conservation of watersheds for municipal drinking water supplies. However, for most resources, exclusion problems are not necessarily solved by declaring the resource to be state property, especially if the means of enforcement are lacking. For example, in the Caribbean island nation of St. Lucia, the protection of marine resources through the establishment of a marine park was successful only when the local community supported and helped enforce the boundaries (Smith and Berkes 1991).

Governance of resources by the state has in many cases been sufficient to provide for exclusion, as in national parks in many Western countries. African national parks are heavily guarded, which provides for exclusion for most purposes, but it has not stopped highly organized and motivated groups, such as rhino poachers. As with private property, the legitimacy of state property in the eyes of the local community is important for enforcement. The abrogation of traditional land and resource use rights of local communities in African national parks translates into high transaction costs for exclusion (IIED 1994).

Nationalization of resources, once a popular approach in many postcolonial countries, has resulted in social dislocation and resource degradation (Baxter and Hogg 1990). In a move to curb deforestation, the government of Nepal nationalized forests in 1957, converting what were often communal forests into state property. But the result was the creation of *de facto* open-access. Villagers whose control of nearby forests had been removed, now viewed the state forest as an "ownerless" resource open to anyone's exploitation. Deforestation accelerated; in the face of worsening conditions, the government reversed its policy and began in 1976 to re-create communal-property rights (Messerschmidt 1993). One of the most pressing problems of former Eastern Bloc countries is how to handle the devolution of former state property (Meadows 1995).

Evidence on Regulation of Use and Users
Open-Access

Incentives for sustainable resource use are weak, if not absent, in open-access regimes. Under conditions in which demand exceeds the capacity of the resource to renew itself, and in which technology is available to exploit the resource at a high level, the evidence is that the regulation of use and users generally fails. Examples include the extinction or virtual extinction of the North American passenger pigeon and the bison.

However, in the context of the day, free and unregulated use of resources such as the bison initially made economic sense. To illustrate the individual rationality behind bison depletion, Hardin (1978) invokes the image of the American cowboy-hero Kit Carson shooting bison on the plains, taking only the tongue and leaving the rest. This is not economically irrational, if one considers that the game was then abundant but the hunter's time scarce.

Unregulated resource use, in general, is consistent with objectives of rapid economic growth, as reflected in "frontier economics" (Hardin 1978). If the social problem of traditional use rights is assumed away, the environmental problem only comes up when the resource is depleted. Can regulations be brought in before the resource disappears? Holling (1993) and others have pointed out that scale-dependent time-lags play an important role. In larger scale environmental and resource problems, society does not receive the signals fast enough to act effectively. In the historical case of bison, for example, depletion occurred rapidly, before countervailing institutional arrangements or changing cultural values could prevent it.

Private Property

Privatization usually provides incentives to regulate resource use. If the owner has property rights in the resource and those rights are tradable, both the costs and benefits will accrue to the same owner and will be reflected in the market price of the resource, giving the owner the incentive to regulate resource use in a manner consistent with private objectives. These incentives may be consistent with private economic efficiency, but they are not necessarily consistent with biological conservation. Clark (1973) pointed out that whether incentives created by privatization are consistent with sustainability depends on a combination of the biological characteristics of the resource and the economic characteristics of the market. Suppose a California redwood tree planted for $1 is worth $14,000 at maturity, seemingly a good appreciation in value. But redwood trees may take 2000 years to reach a great size, giving an implied rate of return of less than 0.5 percent per year, well below the rates of return generally available. Thus, planting a redwood tree, or conserving an existing redwood forest, for the wood value does not make economic sense under a private-property regime, no matter how much ecological sense it makes.

Redwoods may be an extreme example, but Clark (1973) has generally shown for slow-growing and late-maturing species such as whales that it may be economically optimal to deplete the resource rather than to use it sustainably. Private-property rights permit the owner to regulate use to maximize the present value of the resource, and not necessarily to regulate use for sustainability.

Communal Property

There is abundant evidence on the ability of social groups to design a variety of mechanisms to regulate use among members. However, a number of conditions have to be satisfied before communal-property regimes can regulate use; Ostrom (1990, 1992) lists eight such design principles and McKean (1992) lists six. Of the various property-rights regimes, communal property provides the most diverse set of regulations and historically the oldest cases.

The medieval English commons, like many other historic commons, were often subject to comprehensive systems of regulation. Scott (1955), one of the earliest commons theorists, pointed out the existence of traditional use-rules such as stinting, which limited the number of heads of animal each owner could graze on the village commons. Many scholars have noted that the commons operated over several hundred years in medieval England, and have questioned if a "tragedy" of the sort described by Hardin (1968) ever occurred widely. Communal-property systems with elaborate regulations are found in virtually every part of the globe and cover virtually all resource types (e.g., McCay and Acheson 1987; Bromley 1992).

Not all examples of successful regulation are historic or are based on long-standing tradition. In a study of several Turkish coastal fisheries, regulations for self-governance were found to have evolved in the order of one decade (Berkes 1992). In Alanya on the Mediterranean coast of Turkey, fishermen developed in the 1970s and the 1980s a system, based on the rotation of fishing sites used, to regulate use and solve the problem of escalating conflicts over prime harvesting areas. These design rules did not solve the problem of increasing numbers of boats but formed the basis for the diversification of fishermen into the developing tourism industry in the late 1980s (Berkes 1992).

State Property

State governance permits the formulation of appropriate regulations for resource use for all citizens, whether it deals with forests, water, or wildlife hunting. It also provides for the expression of public interest and for accountability, but does not necessarily ensure sustainable use. Decisionmakers do not often have the same time horizons and values as resource users, or as seen in the Great Lakes area, officials may adopt the interests of the most powerful user-groups (Regier et al. 1989).

One of the oft-mentioned problems of state-property regimes is the proliferation of regulations. Smith (1988) showed that the combinations of licenses, quotas, allocations, seasons, and trip limitations in the New England fishery added up to more than 100 regulations, leading not to sustainable resource use but widespread noncompliance! In contrast to North America and Europe, state governance of resources in many Third World countries is problematic, not because of the cost of enforcement, but because of the lack of enforcement capability of the state.

Sole reliance on state governance has been declining in recent decades; the failure of central planning in such countries as the former USSR is one reason for this. Public participation in the formulation of regulations in resource management has a long tradition in the West. More recently, resource users have been seeking and obtaining formal powers to participate in the decisionmaking process, referred to as comanagement (e.g. Pinkerton 1989). Such state-level and local-level comanagement is also on the agenda in the Third World. Property rights of local communities are being reasserted within a state governance framework, in a diversity of areas and resource types, from hill forests of India (Gadgil and Guha 1992) to coastal fisheries in Southeast Asia (Pomeroy 1994).

In conclusion, the evidence on exclusion shows that there are enforcement problems with all types of property-rights regimes, including private property. State-property regimes probably fare the worst in this regard. Communal-property regimes do not work well under stress from colonialism, population pressure, technology change, and transformation of subsistence economies to cash economies.

The evidence on the performance of different property-rights regimes in regulating use and users with respect to subtractability is also mixed. Under private property, sustainable use is feasible in many cases but not economically rational for resources which renew themselves very slowly, such as whales. Under communal property, success depends on the ability of users to forge appropriate institutions, which in turn depends on a number of other factors (Ostrom 1990; 1992). Solutions to both exclusion and subtractability problems are feasible under each of private, state, and communal-property regimes. However, no single property-rights regime is sufficient to guarantee the sustainable use of resources (Feeny et al. 1990; Knudsen 1995; McCay 1995).

These findings are generally consistent with Figure 5.2 which postulates the importance of institutions in mediating the relationship between society and environment. In the case of each of the three potentially workable property-rights regimes, success largely depends upon how well institutions are working. Thus, with many former Eastern Bloc and Third World countries, for example, inadequacy of government institutions largely accounts for resource management failure. Under communal-property regimes, success or failure again depends on institutions, in this case, informal constraints, such as norms of behavior, conventions, and codes of conduct. Institutions need not be defined as organizations but rather as systems of working rules (Ostrom 1990; North 1990).

The other point highlighted by Figure 5.2 is the question of feedbacks. Institutions fail to the extent that they are slow to respond to signals from the resource, a characteristic of large, monolithic, old, and "brittle" institutions (Holling 1993). There is accumulating evidence that institutions need to renew themselves and that resource management crises may be useful in that regard (Gunderson et al. 1995). Institutions which are closer to the resource, flexible, diverse, and open to feedbacks from the environment, as is the case with some of communal-property and private-property regimes, stand a better chance of success. Wilson et al. (1994) have made the controversial argument that, in an environment of chaos and uncertainty, local fishery management systems, with their diversity and flexibility, are better adapted for long-term resource management than are government institutions, with their quantitative tools such as quotas.

Performance of Natural Resource Systems: An Outlook

Two major points have been identified for discussion from the ideas and studies reviewed in this chapter. The first pertains to the question of criteria in measuring performance, and the second is about the significance of the observed diversity in apparently successful resource management systems.

The question of the performance of natural resource systems under different property-rights regimes begs the question of criteria. As Knudsen (1995) pointed out, much of the common-property literature deals with supposed cases of "success" in a rather vague way, more by reiteration than by theory-building and hypothesis-testing. How can the "success" of natural resource use cases be assessed? Feeny et al. (1990) used ecological sustainability, wherein the resource in question was used without compromising the ability of future generations to meet their needs (WCED 1987). This is basically a criterion of resource use without depletion, as also used by Ostrom (1990), but it does not necessarily imply that resource use was optimal from either ecological or economic points of view. It does, however, have the advantage of being both human-centric and resource-centric, and not exclusively one or the other (Feeny et al. 1990).

There are, however, other criteria that can be used. In his widely used common-property analysis framework, Oakerson (1986) suggested two criteria—efficiency (defined as Pareto optimality whereby at least one person could be made better off and no one worse off) and equity (distributive justice). These criteria have been applied to a large number of case studies reported in two books by the National Research Council (1986) and by Bromley (1992). Alternative criteria, as proposed by some development specialists (Pomeroy 1994; Titi and Singh 1994), include empowerment (ability of people to control decisions affecting their lives) and livelihood security (ability of people to maintain their means of living).

Other authors have used various economic and institutional criteria to evaluate performance. These include Blomquist (1992) on Southern California groundwater, and Tang (1992) on a number of irrigation case studies. Chopra et al. (1990) and Chopra and Kadekodi (1991) analyzed the performance of participatory institutions in the management of common and private property resources in North-western India village communities. Stevenson (1991) examined the economic performance of private and communal property rights systems in Swiss alpine meadows. He found that in the more productive lower elevations, private property was more efficient. In the less productive higher elevations, remote areas unsuitable for private property because of higher management costs, communal property performed as efficiently as private property.

In contrast to these detailed studies of institutions and economic performance, there seem to be very few studies that focus on the performance of the natural resource itself under different property-rights regimes. Exceptions include Smith and Berkes (1991, 1993).

What is available in abundance, however, is a rich literature on local and traditional management systems. Perhaps the most striking feature of the case studies in the literature is the sheer diversity of property-rights institutions, especially in the older, historically rooted resource management systems, such as in the Swiss Alps (Netting 1981; Stevenson 1991). For example, there is a diverse array of arrangements from island group to island group in the reef and lagoon tenure systems of Oceania (Ruddle and Akimichi 1984; Freeman et al. 1991). Johannes (1978) found that "almost every basic fisheries conservation measure devised in the West was in use in the tropical Pacific centuries ago." The ancient wisdom of traditional management and the populist wisdom of contemporary community-based resource management systems are being rediscovered by the conservation and development community (Pye-Smith and Borrini Feyerabend 1994).

Compared with this diversity of conservation measures and common-property arrangements, resource management prescriptions of the West which have been replacing the traditional systems are rather bland and uniform in nature, such as quota management, as opposed to the diversity of time-tested controls in small-scale fisheries throughout the world (Wilson et al. 1994). Gadgil and Berkes (1991) and McNeely (1991), among others, have pointed out that scientific management has its roots in the utilitarian and exploitive world view that assumes that humans have dominion over nature and is best geared for the efficient utilization of resources as if they were limitless. The replacement of a diversity of local systems by a monolithic scientific management vision has in most cases not led to sustainable outcomes. There are many examples of natural resource depletion or degradation following the replacement of locally adapted, subtle, and complex common-property systems by government management or private property, especially in the Third World (McCay and Acheson 1987; Berkes 1989; Baxter and Hogg 1990; Bromley 1992).

Conventional resource management science, best geared for exploitive development ("business in liquidation") but not for sustainable use, is in need of fundamental rethinking. Based on the empirical evidence from the common-property literature, the range of changes might include those regarding world views and, more pertinent to the present subject, property rights and institutional arrangements. The evidence suggests that the task is to make institutions for resource use more diverse, not less; natural system–social system interactions more responsive to feedbacks; management systems more flexible and more accommodating of environmental perturbations and thus less "brittle." These may be treated as hypotheses and are in fact part of a research agenda (Berkes and Folke 1994b). Some of the more promising lines of inquiry are likely to involve the study of feedbacks, such as those between common property institutions and ecological systems.

ACKNOWLEDGMENTS

I would like to thank many colleagues, most notably Jim Acheson, David Feeny, Carl Folke, C. S. Holling, Bonnie McCay, Meg McKean, and Elinor Ostrom for the development of the ideas in this chapter. Susan Hanna provided expert editorial advice. My research has been supported by the Social Sciences and Humanities Research Council of Canada.

REFERENCES

Acheson, J. M. 1988. *The Lobster Gangs of Maine.* University Press of New England, Hanover, NH, and London.

Baxter, P. T. W. and R. Hogg, eds. *1990. Property, Poverty and People: Creating Rights in Property and Problems of Pastoral Development.* Department of Social Anthropology and International Development Centre, University of Manchester, Manchester, UK.

Berkes, F. 1985. Fishermen and the "tragedy of the commons." *Environmental Conservation* 12:199–206.

Berkes, F., ed. 1989. *Common Property Resources: Ecology and Community-Based Sustainable Development.* Belhaven, London.

Berkes, F. 1992. Success and failure in marine coastal fisheries of Turkey. Pages 161–182 *in* D. Bromley, ed. *Making the Commons Work*. Institute for Contemporary Studies Press, San Francisco.

Berkes, F. and C. Folke. 1994a. Investing in cultural capital for the sustainable use of natural capital. Pages 128–149 *in* A.-M. Jansson, M. Hammer, C. Folke, and R. Costanza, eds. *Investing in Natural Capital*. Island Press, Washington, D.C.

Berkes, F. and C. Folke. 1994b. *Linking Social and Ecological Systems for Resilience and Sustainability*. Beijer International Institute of Ecological Economics, Stockholm.

Blomquist, W. 1992. *Dividing the Waters. Governing Groundwater in Southern California*. Institute for Contemporary Studies Press, San Francisco.

Bromley, D. W., ed. 1992. *Making the Commons Work: Theory, Practice and Policy*. Institute for Contemporary Studies Press, San Francisco.

Bromley, D. W. and M. M. Cernea. 1989. The management of common property natural resources. World Bank Discussion Paper No. 57.

Chopra, K. and G. K. Kadekodi. 1991. Participatory institutions: The context of common and private property resources. *Environmental and Resource Economics* 1:353–372.

Chopra, K., G. K. Kadekodi, and M. N. Murty. 1990. *Participatory Development, People and Common Property Resources*. Sage, New Delhi.

Clark, C. W. 1973. The economics of overexploitation. *Science* 181:630–634.

Costanza, R. 1987. Social traps and environmental policy. *BioScience* 37: 407–412.

Dasgupta, P. and K.-G. Maler. 1992. *The Economics of Transnational Commons*. Clarendon, Oxford, UK.

Duncan, O. D. 1961. From social system to ecosystem. *Sociological Inquiry* 31:140–149.

Feeny, D., F. Berkes, B. J. McCay,. and J. M. Acheson. 1990. The tragedy of the commons: Twenty-two years later. *Human Ecology* 18:1–19.

Freeman, M. M. R., Y. Matsuda, and K. Ruddle, eds. 1991. Adaptive marine resource management systems in the pacific. Special issue of *Resource Management and Optimization*, Vol. 8, No. 3/4.

Gadgil, M. and F. Berkes. 1991. Traditional resource management systems. *Resource Management and Optimization* 8:127–141.

Gadgil, M. and R. Guha. 1992. *This Fissured Land: An Ecological History of India*. Oxford University Press, New Delhi.

Gadgil, M., F. Berkes, and C. Folke. 1993. Indigenous knowledge for biodiversity conservation. *Ambio* 22:151–156.

Geertz, C. 1963. *Agricultural Involution*. University of California Press, Berkeley.

Gunderson, L. H., C. S. Holling, and S. S. Lights, eds. 1995. *Barriers and Bridges to the Renewal of Ecosystems and Institutions*. Columbia University Press, New York.

Hardin, G. 1968. The tragedy of the commons. *Science* 162:1243–1248.

Hardin, G. 1978. Political requirements for preserving our common heritage. Pages 310–317 *in* H.P. Brokaw, ed. *Wildlife and America.* Council on Environmental Quality, Washington, D.C.

Hawley, A. H. 1973. Ecology and population. *Science* 179:1196–1201.

Holling, C. S. 1986. The resilience of terrestrial ecosystems: Local surprise and global change. Pages 292–317 *in* W. C. Clark and R. E. Munn, eds. *Sustainable Development of the Biosphere.* Cambridge University Press, Cambridge, UK.

Holling, C. S. 1993. Investing in research for sustainability. *Ecological Applications* 3:552–555.

Holmgren, P., E. J. Masakha, and H. Sjoholm. 1994. Not all African land is being degraded. *Ambio* 23:390–395.

IIED. 1994. *Whose Eden? An Overview of Community Approaches to Wildlife Management.* International Institute for Environment and Development, London.

Jansson, A.-M., M. Hammer, C. Folke, and R. Costanza, eds. 1994. *Investing in Natural Capital.* Island Press, Washington, D.C.

Jodha, N. S. 1985. Population growth and the decline of common property resources in Rajasthan, India. *Population and Development Review* 11:247–264.

Jodha, N. S. 1992. Common property resources. A missing dimension of development strategies. World Bank Discussion Paper No. 169.

Johannes, R. E. 1978. Traditional marine conservation methods in Oceania and their demise. *Annual Review of Ecology and Systematics* 9:349–364.

Keohane, R. and E. Ostrom, eds. 1995. *Local Commons and Global Interdependence.* Sage, London.

Knudsen, A. J. 1995. *Living with the Commons.* Chr. Michelsen Institute, Bergen.

Magrath, W. 1989. The challenge of the commons. World Bank, Environment Department Working Paper No. 14.

McCay, B. J. 1995. Common and private concerns. *Advances in Human Ecology* 4:89–116.

McCay, B. J. and J. M. Acheson, eds. 1987. *The Question of the Commons. The Culture and Ecology of Communal Resources.* University of Arizona Press, Tucson.

McKean, M. A. 1992. Success on the commons: A comparative examination of institutions for common property resource management. *Journal of Theoretical Politics* 4:247–281.

McNeely, J. A. 1991. Common property resource management or government ownership: Improving the conservation of biological resources. *International Relations* 1991:211–225.

Meadows, D. H. 1995. Privatization of land in the Baltics? *Surviving Together* (Spring 1995), 13–14.

Messerschmidt, D. A. 1993. Common forest resource management. *Annotated Bibliography of Asia, Africa and Latin America*. FAO Community Forestry Note 11.

National Research Council 1986. *Proceedings of the Conference on Common Property Resource Management*. National Academy Press, Washington, D.C.

Netting, R. McC. 1981. *Balancing on an Alp*. Cambridge University Press, Cambridge, UK.

North, D. C. 1990. *Institutions, Institutional Change, and Economic Performance*. Cambridge University Press, New York.

Oakerson, R. J. 1986. A model for the analysis of common property problems. Pages 13–29 in *Proceedings of the Conference on Common Property Resources Management*. National Academy Press, Washington, D.C. (See also in Bromley 1992.)

Ostrom, E. 1990. *Governing the Commons. The Evolution of Institutions for Collective Action*. Cambridge University Press, Cambridge, UK.

Ostrom, E. 1992. *Crafting Institutions for Self-Governing Irrigation Systems*. Institute for Contemporary Studies Press, San Francisco.

Park, R. E. 1936. Human ecology. *American Journal of Sociology* 42:1–15.

Pinkerton, E., ed. 1989. *Cooperative Management of Local Fisheries*. University of British Columbia Press, Vancouver.

Pomeroy, R. S., ed. 1994. *Community Management and Common Property of Coastal Fisheries in Asia and the Pacific*. ICLARM, Manila.

Posey, D. A. and W. Balee, eds. 1989. Resource management in Amazonia: Indigenous and folk strategies. Special issue of *Advances in Economic Botany*, Vol. 7.

Pye-Smith, C. and G. Borrini Feyerabend 1994. *The Wealth of Communities*. Earthscan, London.

Regier, H. A., R. V. Mason, and F. Berkes 1989. Reforming the use of natural resources. Pages 110–126 in F. Berkes, ed. *Common Property Resources*. Belhaven, London.

Ruddle, K. and T. Akimichi, eds. 1984. Maritime institutions in the Western Pacific. *Senri Ethnological Studies*, Vol. 17. National Museum of Ethnology, Osaka.

Scott, A. D. 1955. The fishery: The objectives of sole ownership. *Journal of Political Economy* 63:116–124.

Smith, A. H. and F. Berkes 1991. Solutions to the "tragedy of the commons": Sea-urchin management in St. Lucia, West Indies. *Environmental Conservation* 18:131–136.

Smith, A. H. and F. Berkes 1993. Community-based use of mangrove resources in St. Lucia. *International Journal of Environmental Studies* 43:123–131.

Smith, M. E. 1988. Fisheries risk in modern context. Maritime Anthropological Studies 1:29–48.

Stevenson, G. G. 1991. *Common Property Economics: A General Theory and Land Use Applications.* Cambridge University Press, Cambridge, UK.

Tang, S. Y. 1992. *Institutions and Collective Action: Self-Governance in Irrigation.* Institute for Contemporary Studies Press, San Francisco.

Titi, V. and N. Singh 1994. *Adaptive Strategies of the Poor in Arid and Semi-arid Lands: In Search of Sustainable Livelihoods.* International Institute of Sustainable Development, Winnipeg.

WCED. 1987. *Our Common Future.* World Commission on Environment and Development/Oxford University Press, Oxford, UK.

Weber, P. 1995. Protecting oceanic fisheries and jobs. Pages 21–37 in *State of the World 1995.* Earthscan, London.

Wilson, J. A., J. M. Acheson, M. Metcalfe, and P. Kleban 1994. Chaos, complexity and communal management of fisheries. *Marine Policy* 18: 291–305.

PART II

The Structure and Formation of Property Rights

CHAPTER 6

Common and Private Concerns

BONNIE J. McCAY

Introduction

Formal thinking about the "tragedy of the commons" derives from studies of fisheries. Indeed, the problem of common property resources is also known as "the fisherman's problem" (McEvoy 1986). For fishes and other renewable living resources there are relationships between mortality and production, or effort and yield, that look like a logistic Lotka–Volterra curve. In theory, there is a level of mortality that results in maximum sustained yield (MSY). Those using this model assume that management involves government rules that keep fishing mortality at the MSY level, more or less, and important fisheries today are managed roughly in this way.

Economists added to the biologists' concern with maximum sustained yield their concern with maximum economic yield, or profitability, and showed how open access affects both. The point of marginal returns to capital, where money made from fishing is no greater than the cost of fishing, is the point at which people will stop, but that is far beyond both MSY and the point of maximum sustained profitability. This is the basis for a long-standing argument for limiting access to fisheries that, in the past decade, has become an enthusiastic chorus for creating exclusive rights to fish, the "private concern" of this chapter.

Almost always, the models used to understand the interactive dynamics of fisheries stop at this point, wedded as most of us in America are to two paradigms: conservation and rationalization (Charles 1992:384–385). The first is concerned with taking care of the fish (or birds or forests); the second with the pursuit of economic returns. Conservation in America has long been marked by tension between the two. But there is a third paradigm, "the social/community paradigm," involving questions about distributional equity, community welfare, and other social and cultural benefits.

The "social/community" paradigm is absent in most discussions of tragedies of the commons and natural resource management. It is, however, expressed in the metaphor "comedies of the commons," people as social beings, trying to come to some collective agreement about common problems. In the bioeconomic model, people are asocial beings, responding as individuals to incentives from the natural environment and the market; the limits, if any, on their behavior (such as TACs or limited licenses) implicitly come from the outside, from a wiser government. But we know that even fishers care and try to do something about the resources on which they depend and may play important roles in the creation and enforcement of rules and regulations. This alternative perspective is important in recognizing disproportionality and inequality in both the causes and consequences of environmental problems. And it points toward a focus on collective action and other social responses to environmental problems.

Bad Habits and a New Typology

Common Property ≠ Description of Resources

Scholarly writing, thinking about, and practice concerning problems of the commons have been in a tangle. One reason is the practice of using the phrase "common property" to refer to resources that share certain features (e.g., fluidity, mobility, extensiveness). The error is in the failure to recognize that property derives not from nature but from culture. It does not refer to things but to social agreements about how humans relate to things. A key argument of the revisionist perspective on "commons" issues is therefore that one should distinguish between the features of the resource and those of the ways people choose to relate to the resource and each other. Vincent and Elinor Ostrom (1977) long ago argued for the use of the term *common pool*, rather than *common property*, for that class of resources that are particularly problematic to human institutions because of the difficulties of bounding or dividing them, the likelihood that one person's actions may affect another's enjoyment of the resource, and so forth. Examples of common *pool* resources would then include large bodies of water, rivers, fishes and other wildlife, air and the airwaves, even information and genetic material, all of which have certain natural features in common. Simpler and other definitional schemes abound. The point here is that common pool is not the same as common *property;* there might be cases of common property for non-common pool resources (for example, condominium housing), and of private property for common pool resources (for example, buying tickets for access to camping in public wilderness areas).

Common Property ≠ Open Access

A second reason for an intellectual muddle consists in treating "common property" as synonymous with "open access" or the same as "no property rights." Although *open access* is a distinctive "commons" problem, it is not definitive of common property. The "comedy" perspective insists that there is an important difference. Common property is about property rights. In common property systems, there can be restrictions on who is a proper "commoner" and what people do, or even a social agreement that there will be no restrictions and open access.

To reiterate, common property is a cultural artifact, socially constructed and contested, not a natural or necessary condition. In this way it is distinct from the condition of open access, as this appears in economic models, even though some common property regimes may have been specified, or socially constructed, as open access. In the "thin" (cf. Little 1991) version of this perspective, neoinstitutional economists and others emphasize the contingency of economic behavior on legal–social contexts (Bromley 1989). Property is not created because one or two individuals behave certain ways. Rather property arises from public choice, requiring some degree of community consideration and agreement. Anthropologists are likely to "thicken" the analysis with more detailed specification of content, context, and culture (McCay and Acheson 1987).

Property Rights and Management Regimes: A New Typology

The revisionist view recognizes that the natural environment may be dealt with in many different ways, with many different consequences. Common pool resources may be under a variety of management regimes which are not adequately indicated by the term *common property*. In a recent set of articles, we used regimes loosely identified as open access (or no governance), communal property, state property, and private property (Berkes et al. 1989; Feeny et al. 1990:4, listing many other references to similar distinctions). In traditional analyses, the first three types of management regime are more often lumped as "common property." Splitting the category and examining case studies shows that there is no simple one-to-one relationship between regime and outcome and whether the outcome is sustainable exploitation. This revisionist perspective leads to

doubt that environmental problems are due to the "common property" attribute of some resources plain and simple (Feeny et al.
1990:13).

I propose that we go further to distinguish between property claims
(one class of institutions) and management regimes (another class).
To keep the analysis simple only three general types of property are
listed: private property, common property, and open access. The
management regimes are laissez-faire, market, communal, state, and
international.

Open access is the null condition of no property claims. For some
purposes it may be appropriate to distinguish this case from a socially
constructed agreement that all citizens, inhabitants, or members of
"the public" have rights of use.

Private property is usually defined in terms of exclusivity and transferability (e.g., Regier and Grima 1985). Private property rights are
more exclusive and generally (but not universally) more transferable
than are common property rights. It is essential to recognize the
potential variability of the "bundles of rights," as the lawyers say, for
private as well as common property.

Common property refers to a large class of property rights that can
incorporate much of what is otherwise thought of in these schemes as
"state property" (as in Feeny et al. 1990). One of the anthropological
points to be made is that it is dangerous to generalize, given the specificity of particular property systems and their embeddedness in other
dimensions of social, economic, and political life. However, we can
draw some general outlines of what is often meant in specific cases.
Among the features typically found are a right to use something in
common with others; or, a right not to be excluded from the use of
something (Macpherson 1978); and some expression of equality or
equitability in the allocation of rights. It may also be a situation in
which people have use rights but not exchange rights.

Much more variable are the boundaries of common property. They
may be virtually nonexistent, as for example in the Swedish custom
of *allmennsretten* allowing anyone to harvest wild mushrooms or
berries on private lands. They may be very tightly circumscribed, as
in some village systems, where common rights may be contingent on
citizenship or land ownership. The boundaries of "the commons"
and "the commoners" vary in their permeability. They may be very
permeable in terms of access, such as where a local community, by
community rules, takes care of a resource but allows others to come
in to harvest it. This system is fairly typical of indigenous peoples but
can also be found more widely, as in the case of municipal care of a

coastal beach where the larger public gains access by paying a beach fee or parking fee (e.g., the New Jersey system). But these can be very tightly circumscribed, so that only legitimate members of certain communities have any rights at all.

For purposes of a "thicker" comparative analysis, a first step is to separate property rights from management regimes. Property rights are among the institutional conditions that influence management regimes but are not the same. Following is a crude typology that might emerge from making a distinction between property rights and management regimes.

Laissez-faire or the condition of no management regime, replaces open-access in the scheme of Feeny et al. (1990) (see also Berkes et al. 1989). Systems where people have open-access property rights can also be systems where they must follow rules and are engaged in collective action. It is thus important to be clear that laissez-faire is the big problem, not open-access per se. The combination of laissez-faire with open-access is indeed prone to "tragedies of the commons" if pressure on resources is high enough.

Market regulation should be distinguished from private property. Private property is relevant to management insofar as it allows market mechanisms to work more effectively. On the other hand, governance is required to uphold private property claims and other conditions of the market. This combination may be a source of "tragedies of the commoners" as well as tragedies of misplaced faith in market remedies, particularly where "externalities" and long-term and indirect ecological effects are involved.

Communal governance is distinguished from common or communal property. It highlights the existence and potential of user-governance and local-level systems of common pool resource management, irrespective of whether rights are common or private or a mixture.

State governance is distinguished from state property, recognizing the central role of the state to most common pool systems whether property is state-owned or not. "State property" can be the property owned outright and used exclusively by agents of the state, on the one hand, or it can be property deemed public, over which the state exercises governance—the latter is most important, and the concept of state governance reflects that fact.

A very important addition is *international governance*. It has features and challenges to common pool management that differ from state governance, if not communal governance, such as the absolute lack of centralized enforcement.

In sum, property rights are not the same as management systems, although they are logically connected. Open access is not the same as laissez-faire: although most laissez-faire systems are open-access, there are many open-access systems where rules and regulations abound. Private property is not the same as market regulation, even though the "tragedy of the commons" theory is that the problem with the commons is that market regulation does not work. Market forces certainly apply across the board, wherever the activity is linked to markets, but the regulatory incentives of markets do work best where there is something like private property. On the other hand, private property rights are no guarantee that their owners will care about resource conservation. Moreover, a "tragedy of the non-commons" (May 1990) can occur when privatization benefits the few but further marginalizes the many, who are forced to increase their uses and weaken their management of common pool resources. Common property is not the same as communal regulation, either. It is possible for communal regulation to exist where access is open. It is also very possible that a community can regulate how private property owners use their properties (e.g., zoning), because of concern about externalities and shared community values. But communal regulation probably works best where members of a community have special rights—property rights. For example, after independence from colonial domination, many new nations did away with communal or common property rights because these were linked with clans and other groups that were seen as problematic to the emerging nation-state, and this weakened and destroyed customary systems of resource management.

State and international management regimes—as are usually meant by "governance"—cross-cut all forms of property. "The state"—meaning the centralized government that holds a virtual monopoly on the use of force and is the final arbiter of law—is critical to the existence of both private and common property. It legitimizes and protects (or can be used to challenge) such property claims. The international level of governance is particularly challenging for the solution of regional and global environmental problems, because the so-called "free rider" problem inherent to all commons dilemmas is writ large and there is no real centralized system of enforcement.

Problems with the Typology

The virtue of this typology is that it underscores the diversity of management regimes that can and do exist, beyond the laissez-faire commons, and can be used to ask questions about the ecology, economics,

and sustainability of natural resource systems. However, it too is misleading in suggesting that there is something universal about each of
its categories, that there is something homogeneously known as private property or common property (as opposed to recognition of
complex, varying "bundles of rights" as lawyers say), or that "the
market" and "the state" are homogeneous and virtually the same in
form and effect everywhere.

Moreover, this model and its predecessor beg for additions and
subtypes, and one is quickly led to the point that they are all potentially interrelated. For example, there can be no market regulation
without private property, and no private property without some level
of governance. Communal regulation is often dependent on authority
granted from central government powers. Examining relationships
between communal and state governance leads to further questions.
For example, what is "the community"? Some may be defined in
terms of the geography of people's residences and working places;
others in terms of occupations or occupational specialization; others
in terms of interest groups. Some common pool governing communities may in fact be comprised of members of a local elite rather than
the larger populace, raising questions about how social, economic,
and political hierarchy and heterogeneity affect the nature and success of common property governance.

How do we conceptualize and understand overlapping, changing,
and contentious property and governance claims? There are also
trickier questions about what "community" means in experiential,
moral, and social-organizational terms and how it affects various
forms of common property governance (Taylor 1987; Singleton and
Taylor 1992; Ostrom 1992).

Comedies of the Commons

The "tragedy of the commons" approach leads to arguments for
strong, centralized governance or for privatization, letting the market
do the job. From the revisionist point of view, a broader, more complex range of alternatives comes into view. These include a stronger
emphasis on the potentials of people as social actors to manage their
affairs and on more decentralized and cooperative management,
what is here meant by "comedy of the commons" (cf. Smith 1984;
Rose 1986). Tragedy in the classic Greek sense is the drama of an
individual, with a tragic flaw or relationship with the gods who is
inevitably propelled to some tragic destiny. In a comedy, people recognize that something is wrong and try, for better or worse (often
"comically"), to do something about it.

Communal Management

Margaret McKean recently compared what she has learned about common property land management on the north slope of Mount Fuji, Japan, over two centuries, with what others have learned from studying landed commons in medieval England, Nepal, Switzerland, Morocco, India, and the Andean highlands, as well as some irrigation and fisheries management cases (McKean 1992:258–261; see also Ostrom 1987, 1990). In her analysis, successful communal management involves:

(1) Clear understanding of who is and is not eligible to use the commons

(2) Some way that the eligible users or their representatives regularly meet to air grievances, adjudicate problems, and make decisions and rules

(3) Jurisdiction mostly independent of larger government powers

(4) Limited transferability of property rights

(5) Ability of the system to handle social and economic differences

(6) Close attention to monitoring and enforcement

A good example can be found in New Jersey in the late 1970s and early 1980s (McCay 1980). The Fishermen's Dock Cooperative of Point Pleasant had developed a complex system of catch limits for two species that were critical to the fishery during the winter months and were subject to sharp price declines when the market was glutted. The system met all of the criteria emphasized by McKean: only members of the cooperative were eligible; they met regularly to make decisions and air grievances; rights to sell through the cooperative were not transferable; complex ways of administering the catch rules were created to handle differences in capital and skill while rewarding both and yet maintaining a sense of fairness; and both monitoring and enforcement were relatively easy. The boats had to land their catches and follow the rules to stay in the co-op. In addition—speaking to a question not handled very well by most scholars of common property management—the Point Pleasant fishermen were capable of expanding the boundaries of their "self-regulation" to others within the larger region when it seemed important and necessary.

Some might say the system was too specific and limited to be applicable elsewhere and therefore to be of interest to fisheries managers in government agencies. However, "this very same factor may also be used to suggest that a reasonable alternative or adjunct to centralized, large-scale systems of fisheries management does exist. Some management systems may persist and work best where they remain on a scale small and flexible enough to be adjusted to the particular problems and circumstances of the people inherent in them, and yet capable at times of being extended to a regional level [as I had shown in the description]" (McCay 1980:36).

There are many other systems of communal management, including some that are relatively new. A general notion arising from the case studies is that if a group of people has some sort of territorial or jurisdictional claim to a valuable resource, they will be motivated and empowered to manage it better. This is critical where government resources and the political will required for enforcement of regulations are scarce. Some systems are experiments introduced by outsiders. Others have developed locally.

Major obstacles exist to the self-governance way of managing the commons. It may be impractical where resources are migratory or overlap jurisdictions, as in the fisheries of the temperate and northern regions. In addition, self-governance may be unacceptable where it excludes people with claims to common use-rights based on historical use or other notions of right. For example, it is possible to interpret New Jersey's system of giving municipalities the power to regulate access to coastal beaches as being a good example of self-governance. People who go to the beach must pay for beach badges and/or parking, and that money is used by the towns to maintain the beaches. Very little of the coast is a state or federal park. However, courts have accepted that the intent and consequence is often exclusionary, favoring local residents, and they have delimited the power of the towns because under public trust law all citizens have common rights of access to the tidewaters and oceans.

Comanagement and User Participation

The revisionist perspective emphasizes communal management and self-governance, but clearly there are limits and drawbacks to self-governance, including the migratory or fugitive nature of some resources, overlapping jurisdiction, and competing claims (such as the special rights of local people who depend on a particular resource, versus the rights of citizens or the public to the use of the resources). Put another way, the question is often about the ways that common pool resource users interact with the state in developing, implementing, and changing systems of governance. The term "comanagement" has come to be used to introduce the topic, but comanagement is but one of a variety of forms of interaction between a government and its public. Accordingly, another dimension of the study of "comedies of the commons" is the study of the political arrangements that affect relations between governing agencies and groups of resource users (Jentoft and McCay 1995).

Comanagement, where power is actually shared, promises an institutional response to the "commons" problem, which is essentially the question of how private interests can better intermesh with collective interests. In theory (Jentoft 1989; Pinkerton 1989), comanagement will improve both the effectiveness and the equitability of fisheries management. Comanagement may also improve compliance with agreed upon rules. Effectiveness is partly a question of accurate appraisal of the situation and the effects of changing the rules. Resource assessment is critical. It seems logical that under a comanagement system, resource users would be more likely to share accurate information than they would under other systems. This would reflect more fundamental changes in behavior and attitudes as fishers or others become and are treated as responsible comanagers. Comanagement is one of the ways that "indigenous" and nonexpert knowledge and interests can be meaningfully brought into management.

There are other arguments for comanagement systems, such as the likelihood that they will be more equitable, based on the premise that resource users are more familiar with the intricacies of local social and economic situations and therefore are more able to respond to the special needs and interests of different groups or individuals than are governments, which usually try to treat everyone alike. In addition, a comanaged regulatory process may be more responsive to changing conditions. The organizations of resource users involved may be able to change rules more quickly, and are in general more flexible and responsive than government.

Private Concerns

Few would disagree with the proposition that open access can generate resource abuse and economic losses. This is really what Hardin (1968) was modeling in his sketch of "the tragedy of the commons" and what H. Scott Gordon meant by common property fishing in his seminal article on the dynamics of overfishing (1954). Nor is there much to argue about concerning the value of delineating and enforcing property rights when conservation is a problem. *Some* specification of property rights is a necessary foundation to the development of regulation. What is of concern is the rapid jump over Gordon's prescription of limiting access to the prescription of creating private property in rights to resources.

In fisheries privatization involves the creation of exclusive use-rights in fish stocks (typically as percentages of a quota), with more or less freedom to transfer these rights, the hallmarks of a marketable commodity. The idea rests on work by economists on problems of environmental pollution, including the idea of tradeable emissions permits, later extended to fisheries. These "ITQs," or individual transferable quotas, are widely praised as solving the problems of "the commons," combining a quota for conservation purposes with a way of restoring the ability of the market to generate efficiencies in the use of a resource.

There is nothing inherently right or wrong, bad or good, about market-based solutions to environmental and resource management problems (Young and McCay 1995). They enable the use of market regulation for common property, but they change the property rights in the direction of exclusion. Whether right or wrong, good or bad, depends on the specifics of a particular situation including the goals of management—framed within the goals and expectations of a society. Studies are now underway in a variety of regions to look at the implications of ITQs and related measures in fisheries (McCay et al. 1996; Pálsson and Helgason 1996).

Whether private ownership creates conditions for stewardship and resource conservation that compensate for the social costs entailed in the concentration of power and alienation of many from the means of production involved is an important question. It is difficult to discern the mechanisms by which privatized fishing rights translate into conservation; ITQ systems are still dependent on government-imposed or comanaged regulations of catches and technology (Mace 1993). Moreover, private property owners are quite willing and able to over-exploit and push to extinction "their" resources, if the price is right and the future holds other options, as Colin Clark long ago demonstrated for whaling (Clark 1973). Moreover, privatization can create new pressures on the remaining commons, as shown throughout the world, where the privatizing accumulation of property by the few pushes the majority to more marginal lands or to overexploit their customary, communal lands.

A Different Metaphor?

The "tragedy of the commons" discourse is profoundly modernist, based on the asocial individual who is naturalized and individualized in the model. The self-seeking behavior of the herdsman is only natural, given his identity as both Economic man and Everyman, and there is, in the model, only one possible alternative to atomistic, mutually destructive social relations: government intervention. A particular view of the nature of human nature leads to a view of the process of environmental abuse as inevitable and inexorable. And natural greed must be harnessed if natural greed is the cause.

One alternative, I have suggested, is comedy. It may be appropriate to use the concept of comedy for the focus and narrative style of the revisionist approach to the question of the commons, where game theory, public choice approaches, and other economistic approaches are used to show conditions under which cooperation to prevent or resolve problems of the commons occur. Comedy in literature is, as Donald Donham has pointed out, a common plot or persistent theme of neoclassical economic analyses, "so-called Pareto optimality typically providing the healthy resolution to apparent contradiction" (Donham 1990:192).

This revisionist approach risks being interpreted as being prescriptive ("thou shalt be small-scale and self-governed") and overly optimistic ("when left to their own devices, people will reach viable solutions to their collective dilemmas"). In addition, it is still squarely modernist, with but a shift in assumption about human nature and the degree of social interaction. A more satisfying approach would add concerns about the interplays of conflicting interests, contested and agreed-upon meanings and definitions. It would look at the "thick" specification of property rights and other "institutional arrangements," in particular intersections of history, politics, culture, time, and space (McCay and Acheson 1987).

For an example of the cultural and historical specificity and embeddedness of "the commons," note that the misuse of the term "common property" as the same thing as no property rights at all is arguably a distinctive part of the American experience. In language and culture, Americans have generally lost a sense of "common property" as property. With the rise of radical individualism, capitalist practice, and liberal economic theory, property came to be seen *only* as an individual right to exclude others from the use or benefit of something—that is, private property—when logically and historically it pertains to a broader class of individual rights, including the individual right not to be excluded from something (Macpherson 1978:202). It is telling that the Library of Congress cataloging system does not have a subject heading for common property except for the very recent use of "commons," and "natural resources, communal," for the "revisionist" literature I have cited. This is at the core of one of the major political problems affecting environmentalist goals in the United States today: the rise of a "private property rights" movement in reaction to attempts to use the common property dimensions of the legal doctrine of "public trust" for environmentalist objectives. Common property has lost its status as anything other than the general power of the state, under the rubric of legal doctrines and the general sentiment of "public trust," reducing the issue to one of compensable "taking" versus private property rights.

When I first ventured to use the metaphor "comedy," what I had in mind was what M. Estellie Smith (1984) had defined as comedy in an encyclopedia's version of classic Greek comedy: the drama of humans "as social rather than private beings, a drama of social actions having a frankly corrective purpose" (Smith 1984). It might be better then, to try the metaphor of "the romance" of the commons. In romance, conflict drives the narrative and is not overcome in the manner of neoclassical analyses (Donham 1990). Romance implies a far more complex development of character, situation, and plot and hinges upon the tension of not knowing what the outcome will be, but hoping for the best. As a literary metaphor, it comes closer to the anthropological endeavor.

The culture of the commons is a strong and unifying perspective from which one can approach the problem of property rights and natural resources. It includes both the "high" culture of academics, politics, and law and the "low" culture of people who claim, contest, and exercise property rights in the course of their lives. A number of research questions and topics follow. For example, how do these two cultures interact? What about the contested terrain of privatizing common property rights? What about the nature of community?

Culture includes the realm of people's expectations about nature, themselves, and each other—whether people are seen as far too greedy and selfish to ever get together on anything "common," whether they see themselves as significantly affecting the natural world and its resources, and how these things affect how people behave, including their ability to come to terms with the management of common property. We could and should also include expectations about the relationships between citizens and their governments, with respect to the management of natural resources—expectations which, when not met, may lead to unexpected responses. Culture also includes the values and beliefs people hold about social and ecological relationships, how they are prioritized and linked to each other, and how these affect how people behave. Can we even imagine a world in which people actually cooperate with each other and sacrifice their immediate self-interests to achieve a better balance with the rest of the natural world? These and other dimensions of culture are both various and changing, and should be incorporated into any theory about human ecology and the commons.

ACKNOWLEDGMENTS

Parts of this chapter were included in a talk given at the Plenary Session, 123rd Annual Meeting, American Fisheries Society, Portland, Oregon, August 30, 1993. Other parts are from a document called "Management Regimes" prepared for the Meeting on Property Rights and the Performance of Natural Resource Systems, September 2–4, 1993, The Beijer Institute, Royal Academy of Sciences, Stockholm, Sweden, and from a paper prepared for a Seminar in the Program in Agrarian Studies, Yale University, October 8, 1993, as well as from a paper given at a symposium "Antropologien og naturen" at Tórshavn, Faroe Islands, Denmark.

This chapter was published in *Advances in Human Ecology,* edited by Lee Freese, Volume 4 (1995): 89–116; it is reprinted here in a much abridged and revised form with permission of the publisher, JAI Press, Greenwich, CT. I am indebted to those who listened and criticized the various presentations of these papers, in particular David Nugent, James Scott, Carol Rose, and Angelique Haugerud at a Yale Seminar and to Gísli Pálsson, Torben Vestergaard, and Poul Pedersen at a Faroe Islands symposium. Research was supported in part by the National Sea Grant College Program and the New Jersey Agricultural Experiment Station. It was also sponsored by the Beijer International Institute of Ecological Economics, the Royal Swedish Academy of Sciences, Stockholm, Sweden, with support from the World Environment and Resources Program of the John D. and Catherine T. MacArthur Foundation and the World Bank. The research was conducted as part of the research program Property Rights and the Performance of Natural Resource Systems.

REFERENCES

Berkes, F., D. Feeny, B. J. McCay, and J. M. Acheson. 1989. The benefit of the commons. *Nature* 340:91–93.

Bromley, D. W. 1989. *Economic Interests and Institutions: The Conceptual Foundations of Public Policy.* Basil Blackwell, New York.

Charles, A. T. 1992. Fishery conflicts; a unified framework. *Marine Policy* (Sept.):379–393.

Clark, C. W. 1973. The economics of over-exploitation. *Science* 181: 630–634.

Donham, D. 1990. *History, Power, Ideology.* Cambridge University Press, Cambridge, UK.

Feeny, D., F. Berkes, B. J. McCay, and J. M. Acheson. 1990. The tragedy of the commons: Twenty-two years later. *Human Ecology* 18(1):1–19.

Gordon, H. S. 1954. The economic theory of a common property resource: The fishery. *Journal of Political Economy* 62:124–142.

Hardin, G. 1968. The tragedy of the commons. *Science* 162:1243–1248.

Jentoft, S. 1989. Fisheries co-management: Delegating government responsibility to fishermen's organizations. *Marine Policy* April:137–154.

Jentoft, S. and B. J. McCay. 1995. User participation in fisheries management: Lessons drawn from international experiences. *Marine Policy* 19(3):227–246.

Little, D. 1991. *Varieties of Social Explanation: An Introduction to the Philosophy of Social Science.* Westview Press, Boulder, CO.

Mace, P. M. 1993. Will private owners practice resource management? *Fisheries* 18(9):29–31.

Macpherson, C. B., ed. 1978. *Property: Mainstream and Critical Positions.* University of Toronto Press, Toronto.

May, P. H. 1990. A tragedy of the non-commons: Recent developments in the babaçu palm based industries in Maranhao, Brazil. *Forests, Trees and People Newsletter* 11:23–27.

McCay, B. J. 1980. A fishermen's cooperative, limited: Indigenous resource management in a complex society. *Anthropological Quarterly* 53: 29–38.

McCay, B. J. and J. M. Acheson. 1987. *The Question of the Commons: The Culture and Ecology of Communal Resources.* University of Arizona Press, Tucson.

McCay, B. J., C. F. Creed, A. C. Finlayson, R. Apostle, and K. Mikalsen. 1996. Individual transferable quotas (ITQs) in Canadian and U.S. fisheries. *Ocean and Coastal Management* 26.

McEvoy, A. F. 1986. *The Fisherman's Problem: Ecology and Law in the California Fisheries, 1850–1980.* Cambridge University Press, Cambridge, UK.

McKean, M. A. 1992. Success on the commons: A comparative examination of institutions for common property resource management. *Journal of Theoretical Politics* 4(3):247–281.

Ostrom, E. 1987. Institutional arrangements for resolving the commons dilemma: Some contending approaches. Pages 250–265 *in* B. J. McCay and J. M. Acheson, eds. *Capturing the Commons.* University of Arizona Press, Tucson.

Ostrom, E. 1990. *Governing the Commons: The Evolution of Institutions for Collective Action.* Cambridge University Press, New York.

Ostrom, E. 1992. Community as the endogenous solution of commons problems. *Journal of Theoretical Politics* 4(3):343–351.

Ostrom, V. and E. Ostrom. 1977. A theory for institutional analysis of common pool problems. Pages 157–172 *in* G. Hardin and J. Baden, eds. *Managing the Commons.* W.H. Freeman, San Francisco.

Pálsson, G. and A. Helgason. 1996. Figuring fish and measuring men: The quota system in the icelandic cod fishery. *Ocean and Coastal Management* 26.

Pinkerton, E., ed. 1989. *Cooperative Management of Local Fisheries: New Directions for Improved Management and Community Development.* University of British Columbia Press, Vancouver.

Regier, H. A. and A. P. Grima. 1985. Fishery reserve allocation: An explanatory essay. *Canadian Journal of Fisheries and Aquatic Sciences* 42:
845–859.

Rose, C. 1986. The comedy of the commons: Custom, commerce, and inherently public property. *The University of Chicago Law Review* 53(3):
711–781.

Singleton, S. and M. Taylor. 1992. Common property, collective action and
community. *Journal of Theoretical Politics* 4(3):309–324.

Smith, M. E. 1984. The triage of the commons. Paper presented to annual
meeting of the Society for Applied Anthropology, March, 14–18,
Toronto, Canada.

Taylor, M. 1987. *The Possibility of Cooperation.* Cambridge University
Press, New York.

Young, M. and B. J. McCay. 1995. Building equity, stewardship, and
resilience into market-based property right systems. Pages 87–102 *in* S.
Hanna and M. Munasinghe, eds. *Property Rights in Social and Ecological Context: Concepts and Case Studies.* The World Bank, Washington, D.C.

CHAPTER 7

The Formation of Property Rights

ELINOR OSTROM AND EDELLA SCHLAGER

Introduction

The twenty-first century looms ahead. Will the natural resources upon which all life depends be adequately protected in the decades to come? Will the local, self-organized resource communities that have governed and managed so many natural resource systems continue into the next century? Or, will they slowly disappear as the last relics of a dying past? So many have disintegrated during the past century that some scholars worry that they will all be destroyed and taken over by either markets or states.[1] Are self-organized resource governance and management regimes really something that can cope with the problems of a modern age? Are locally developed institutions, which rely on knowledge acquired over time, effective when modern science provides better ways of managing local resources than those of individuals who are illiterate and lack knowledge of modern scientific techniques?

The research on this topic has developed rapidly during the past decade.[2] The establishment of the Panel on Common Property Resources at the National Academy of Sciences during the mid-1980s was an important turning point in this area of research. The initial publication of the summary volume of the National Academy of Sciences Panel (National Research Council 1986), the many important books recently published (McCay and Acheson 1987; Fortmann and Bruce 1988; Wade 1988; Berkes 1989; Pinkerton 1989; Ostrom 1990; Sengupta 1991, 1993; Blomquist 1992; Tang 1992; Martin 1989/1992; Thomson 1992; Dasgupta and Mäler 1992; Ostrom et al. 1993; Netting 1993; Ostrom et al. 1994a; Keohane and Ostrom 1995), the revision of the National Academy of Sciences volume (Bromley et al. 1992), the influential article by Feeny et al. (1990), and recent important work on property rights (Libecap 1989; Eggertsson

1990; Bromley 1991; North 1990) all have contributed to this progress.

The most important findings from this extensive research regarding the emergence and consequences of property-rights systems in field settings can be summarized as follows:

(1) Overuse, conflict, and potential destruction of natural resources producing highly valued products is likely to occur where those involved act independently due to lack of communication or incapacity to make credible commitments.

(2) If those who directly benefit can communicate, agree on norms, monitor each other, and sanction noncompliance with agreements, individuals can establish rules to control overuse, conflict, and the destruction of natural resources.

(3) The variety of locally selected norms, rules, and property-rights systems used in field settings is immense, but can be characterized by general design principles.

(4) Locally selected systems of norms, rules, and property rights that are not recognized by external authorities may collapse if their legitimacy is challenged, or if large exogenous economic or physical shocks occur.

(5) Control of natural resources by state authorities is effective in some settings but is frequently less effective and efficient than control by those directly affected especially related to smaller-scale, natural resource systems.

(6) Efforts to establish marketable property rights to natural resource systems have substantially increased efficiency in some cases and encountered difficulties of implementation in others.

At a very general level, these findings can be summarized with two statements. Open-access resources—those characterized by no property rights—will be overused, will generate conflict, and may be destroyed. All types of property-rights regimes—including private property, common property, and state property, whether locally selected or externally imposed—may reduce the costs of open-access regimes, but perform differentially depending on the attributes of the resource, the local community, and the specific rules used. Thus, evolved or self-consciously designed property-rights regimes are essential to regulate the use of natural resource systems.

The complexity of natural settings is immense. The likelihood is small that any set of uniform rules for all natural resource systems within a large territory will produce optimal results. Instead of attempting to derive or identify the single best set of rules for governing natural resources, theoretical and empirical research is better used to help inform those who are close to particular natural resource systems, as well as those in larger, overarching agencies, about principles they can use to improve performance.

In our effort to do just that, we focus on the following questions:

- What are the attributes of common-pool resources?
- What are property rights?
- How do property rights get established, and what are the effects of diverse property-rights regimes?
- What social and physical factors affect the formation of property rights?
- Why are local, self-organized property-rights regimes important, but not sufficient, in achieving sustainable natural resource systems?
- Why are property-rights regimes organized at many diverse scales necessary to achieving sustainable natural resource systems?

Common-Pool Resources

Most natural resources can be classified as common-pool resources — one of four very general ways of classifying the goods and services that enter into transactions. Common-pool resources are natural or human-made facilities or stocks that generate flows of usable resource units over time. Common-pool resources share two characteristics: (1) it is costly to develop institutions to exclude potential beneficiaries from them, and (2) at least one of the valued resource units obtained from a common-pool resource that are harvested by one individual are not available to others (Ostrom et al. 1994a; Gardner et al. 1990). The first characteristic is shared with those goods and services referred to in the economics literature as public goods, and the second characteristic is shared with those goods and services referred to as private goods. Because designing institutions that successfully exclude potential beneficiaries from access to common-pool resources is nontrivial and costly, many common-pool resources are *de facto* open-access resources: anyone who wishes can gain access and appropriate resource units. Given that at least one of the resource units appropriated by one user is not available to others, overuse or even destruction of the resource is a frequent consequence of allowing common-pool resources to be left as open-access resources.[3]

Common-pool resources may be "renewable" or "nonrenewable." Those common-pool resources that are renewable have the capability, if use patterns are kept within limits, of sustaining a flow of resource units over a long period of time. Nonrenewable common-pool resources, such as oil pools, are an extremely interesting type of natural resource, but one where the crucial questions relate to the timing of the withdrawal of flow units and not to the sustainability of the system itself. This chapter will focus on renewable common-pool resources.

All common-pool resources have both stock and flow aspects. An irrigation system, a grazing area, a mainframe computer, or a bridge are examples of natural or human-made renewable resource systems. Water, fodder, CPUs, and bridge-crossing units are examples of resource flow units from such systems. In order to sustain a common-pool resource, both its stock and flow must be governed. For an irrigation system to continue to produce irrigation water, the system must be maintained. For irrigators to receive adequate amounts of water in a timely fashion, use must be coordinated. Thus, governance arrangements that have successfully coped with the provision, production, appropriation, and use of common-pool resources are frequently complex property-rights systems that do not fit easily into neat and fashionable dichotomies.

Property Rights

The terms "property rights" and "rules" are frequently used interchangeably in referring to uses made of natural resources.[4] The way that we use these terms is to recognize that "rights" are the product of "rules" and thus not equivalent to rules. A property right is enforceable authority to undertake particular actions related to a specific domain (Commons 1968). For every right an individual holds, rules exist that authorize or require particular actions in exercising that property right. Because rights define actions that individuals can take in relation to other individuals as regards some "thing," if one individual has a right, someone else has a commensurate duty to observe that right. The duty that an individual owes another defines the actions the individual may, must, or must not take in relation to another and that other's property.

In regard to the use of common-pool resources, the most relevant operational-level property rights are "access" and "withdrawal" rights. These are defined as:

Access: The right to enter a defined physical area and enjoy
               nonsubtractive benefits (e.g., hike, canoe, sit in the
               sun).
Withdrawal: The right to obtain the resource units or "products" of
               a resource (e.g., catch fish, appropriate water, etc.).[5]

If someone pays the entry fee into a park, they have purchased the
temporary right to enter that park so long as they observe the rules
defining what the entry fee allows them to do or not to do. In turn,
other park users face a duty not to interfere with the right of another
to enjoy the park. If a group of fishers hold rights of access, they also
have the authority to enter a fishing ground. Rules specify the requirements the fishers must meet in order to exercise the right of access. For
instance, fishers may be required to reside in a specified jurisdiction
and to purchase a license before entering a fishing ground.

In addition to simple access, users may be authorized to harvest
resource units at a particular location, during a specified time, or
using particular technologies.[6] Fishers, for example, may be assigned
particular fishing spots through a lottery (Faris 1972; Martin 1973).
Being assigned a set of fishing spots is an operational-level withdrawal right authorizing harvesting from a particular area.[7] Withdrawal rights may also be related to what will be done with the
resource units after they are harvested. In some settings, individuals
have rights to withdraw only enough resource units to meet their subsistence needs and are not authorized to sell resource units so harvested. Or, some areas of a forest may be allocated for the harvesting
of thatch for constructing roofs while another area may be allocated
for harvest of grasses for the making of baskets.

Individuals who have access and withdrawal rights may or may not
have more extensive rights authorizing participation in collective-
choice decisions. The distinction between rights at an operational
level and rights at a collective-choice level is important. It is the difference between exercising a right and participating in the definition
of future rights to be exercised. The authority to devise future operational-level rights is what makes collective-choice rights so powerful.
In regard to common-pool resources, collective-choice property
rights include management, exclusion, and alienation. They are
defined as follows:

Management: The right to regulate internal use patterns and trans-
               form the resource by making improvements.

Exclusion: The right to determine who will have an access right,
                  and how that right may be transferred.
Alienation: The right to sell or lease either or both of the above
                  collective-choice rights.

The right of management is a collective-choice right authorizing its holders to devise operational-level withdrawal rights governing the use of a resource. Individuals who hold rights of management have the authority to determine how, when, and where harvesting from a resource may occur, and whether and how the structure of a resource may be changed. For instance, a group of fishers who devise a zoning plan that limits various types of harvesting activities to distinct areas of a fishing ground are exercising rights of management for their resource (see, for example, Davis 1984; Cordell 1972).

The right of exclusion is a collective-choice right authorizing its holders to devise operational-level rights of access. Individuals who hold rights of exclusion have the authority to define the qualifications that individuals must meet in order to access a resource. For instance, fishers who limit access to their fishing grounds to males above a certain age who live in a particular community and who utilize particular types of gear are exercising a right of exclusion.[8]

The right of alienation is a collective-choice right permitting its holder to transfer part or all of the collective-choice rights to another individual or group. Exercising a right of alienation means that an individual sells or leases the rights of management, exclusion, or both.[9] Having alienated those rights, the former rights-holder can no longer exercise these authorities in relation to a resource or a part thereof.

Arranging these rights as shown in Table 7.1 enables us to make meaningful distinctions among five classes of property-rights holders. The five property rights are independent of one another, but are frequently held in the cumulative manner arranged as shown in Table 7.1. It is possible to have entry rights without withdrawal rights, to have withdrawal rights without management rights, to have management rights without exclusion rights, and to have exclusion rights without the rights of alienation.[10] In other words, individuals or collectivities may, and frequently do, hold well-defined property rights that do not include the full set of rights defined above. On the other hand, to hold some of these rights implies the possession of others. The exercise of withdrawal rights is not meaningful without the right of access; alienation rights depend upon having rights to be transferred.

TABLE 7.1
Bundles of Rights Associated with Positions

	Owner	Proprietor	Claimant	Authorized user	Authorized entrant
Access	X	X	X	X	X
Withdrawal	X	X	X	X	
Management	X	X	X		
Exclusion	X	X			
Alienation	X				

Source: Adapted from Schlager and Ostrom (1992:252).

We call individuals who hold operational-level rights of access, "authorized entrants."[11] Most recreational uses of such common-pool resources as national parks involve rights to enter and enjoy the park but not to harvest timber or other forest products. We call those who have both entry and withdrawal rights, "authorized users." If specified in operational rules, access and withdrawal rights can be transferred to others either temporarily, as in a lease arrangement, or permanently when these rights are assigned or sold to others. Transfer of these rights, however, is not equivalent to alienation of management and exclusion rights as we discuss later.

The rights of authorized users are defined by others who hold collective-choice rights of management and exclusion. Authorized users lack the authority to devise their own harvesting rules or to exclude others from gaining access to fishing grounds. Even though authorized users may be able to sell their harvesting rights, they nevertheless lack the authority to participate in collective action to change operational rules.

An example of authorized users are the salmon and herring fishers of Alaska. In 1972, the Governor's Study Group on Limited Entry was created to research and develop limited entry legislation, which the Alaskan legislature adopted in 1973 (Adasiak 1979). The Alaskan limited entry system divides Alaskan salmon and herring fisheries into a number of different fisheries. An entry commission determines the number of permits available for each fishery. The commission can make adjustments in the numbers as circumstances change, either by issuing additional permits or by buying back existing permits. Fishers cannot hold more than one permit per fishery. The permits are freely transferable, but cannot be used as collateral. The Alaskan fishers who hold permits are authorized users. The Alaskan legislature in conjunction with a study group devised the fishers' rights of access and withdrawal, which fishers can transfer. The fishers do not directly participate in making collective choices, and thus cannot devise their own operational-level rules concerning the use of the fisheries.

We define as "claimants" individuals who possess the same rights as authorized users plus the collective-choice right of management.[12] With the right of management, claimants have the collective-choice authority to devise operational-level rights of withdrawal. They cannot, however, specify who may or may not have access to resources, nor can they alienate their right of management. For instance, the net fishers of Jambudwip, India, are claimants (Raychaudhuri 1980). Jambudwip is an island in the Bay of Bengal that is only occupied during fishing seasons when fishers establish camps and fish off its southwestern shore. The Jambudwip fishers, exercising management rights, have devised a set of withdrawal rules that permit them to coordinate their use of the fishing grounds. At the beginning of a fishing season, each crew chooses a spot on which to set its net. A large bag net is suspended between two posts that are then driven into the ocean floor. Rules, as well as environmental conditions, govern the placing of nets. As Raychaudhuri (1980) explains:

> According to the convention of the fisherfolk, one is not allowed to set his net in a line, either in front or behind another's net. But there is no bar to set on any side of it. . . . If one net is set in front of another, both lose the catch, either of the tide or of the ebb.

In addition, a spot once claimed by a fishing crew belongs to that crew for the remainder of the fishing season. Even if the crew removes its net from the spot and moves to another spot, no other crew can fish the abandoned spot unless first gaining permission from the original crew (Raychaudhuri 1980). While the Jambudwip fishers have exercised management rights by devising rules that define withdrawal rights, they do not exercise the authority to decide who can and who cannot enter the fishing grounds that they utilize. Consequently, the Jambudwip fishers are claimants and not "proprietors."

John Bruce (1995), in his analysis of common-property regimes, refers to the wide diversity of management and use rights found in relation to land-based natural resources as "tenure niches." Examining the territory that a group uses, one frequently finds the surface (even when it is water) divided into regions allocated to different types of uses. Each of these agreed-upon uses, Bruce calls a tenure niche. As he stresses, tenure niches are rarely simple or static.

They may vary seasonally, as when household fields become after harvest a commons where all community livestock can graze crop residues. In swidden-fallow systems, tenure niches move and rights to resources change in a locality as cultivation is undertaken and then moves on to other areas. Tenure niches may overlap when there are distinct tenure regimes for two resources which physically overlap, as when tenure in trees is defined independently from that in land (Bruce 1995).

Thus, one may find multiple claimants using the same terrain or multiple areas over time in systems where access and withdrawal are quite well defined. Rights are precisely defined regarding temporal-area-technology-use attributes (Bruce et al. 1993).

"Proprietors" are defined as individuals who possess collective-choice rights to participate in management and exclusion. Proprietors authorize who may access resources and how resources may be utilized; however, they do not have the right to alienate either of these collective-choice rights. Scholars who have recently undertaken theoretical and empirical research on "common-property regimes" focus primarily on those regimes organized by proprietors (Berkes 1989; Bromley et al. 1992; McCay and Acheson 1987; Ostrom et al. 1993; Ostrom 1990).

The fishers who participate in the cod trap fisheries of Newfoundland are proprietors. Cod trap berths are allocated by lottery. To gain access to a berth, a fisher must participate in a lottery. Only fishermen from the local community are allowed to participate in the lottery or to sit on the local cod trap berth committee that operates the lottery (Martin 1979). The lottery system is significant in that the organization of cod trap committees since 1919 has legally codified the boundaries of the fishing space over which a community has political jurisdiction (Martin 1973).

Turkish fishers who harvest from coastal lagoons are also proprietors. The Turkish government leases lagoons to fishers' cooperatives. For instance, it leases the Ayvalik–Haylazli lagoon to a fishers' co-op of the same name. To access and harvest fish from the lagoon, a fisher must belong to the co-op. In order to belong to the co-op, a fisher must reside in one of the three adjacent villages for at least six months and not have wage employment income (Berkes 1986).

The fishers of Ayvalik–Haylazli lagoon have exclusive and legal rights to the fish of the lagoon and the lagoon's adjacent waters. All fishermen are cooperative members, and all cooperative members are active fishermen. They protect their rights by patrolling the boundary of their fishing area and chasing off or apprehending intruders. (Three outside fishing boats were apprehended in 1983.) (Berkes 1986).

Neither the fishers of Ayvalik–Haylazli lagoon nor the cod fishers of Newfoundland, however, can sell or lease their rights of management and exclusion.

If in addition to collective-choice rights of management and exclusion, individuals also hold the right of alienation, that is, they can sell or lease their collective-choice rights, then they are defined as "owners."[13] For instance, fishers of Ascension Bay, located in Quintana Roo State, Mexico, are members of the Vigia Chico cooperative. Co-op members have divided Ascension Bay into "individually held capture areas (*'parcelas'* or *'campos'*) ranging from 0.5 to more than 3 km²" from which they harvest lobster (Miller 1989). Each co-op member holds complete sets of rights over specific areas. The fishers may transfer their rights of management and exclusion over their particular spot to other fishers of Ascension Bay. Several *campos* are sold or bartered each season and such transactions are common knowledge. On occasion, sales are registered with the co-op (Miller 1989). Once having sold their *campos,* however, fishers no longer can exercise rights of exclusion or management in relation to Ascension Bay lobstergrounds.

Another example of full ownership is the Thulo Kulo irrigation system in Nepal. When this system was first constructed in 1928, some 27 households contributed to a fund to construct the canal and received shares to the resulting system proportionate to the amount they invested. Since then, the system has been expanded several times by selling additional shares. Measurement and diversion weirs or gates are installed at key locations so that water is automatically allocated to each farmer according to the proportion of shares owned. Shares also define duties. Routine monitoring and maintenance is allocated to work teams composed of the owners of about an equal number of shares. Thus, everyone participates in routine maintenance proportionally to the benefits obtained.[14] Voting on general policies, including the extension of the system and the sale of new shares, is also based on the number of shares held by a participant (see Martin and Yoder 1983; Martin 1986).

A still different type of "ownership" was developed by local irrigators in Valençia, Spain, in the fifteenth century. In 1435, some 84 irrigators served by two interrelated canals in Valençia gathered at the monastery of St. Francis to draw up and approve formal regulations to specify who had rights to water from these canals, how the water would be shared in good and bad years, and how responsibilities for maintenance would be shared. The modern *Huerta* of Valençia, composed of these plus six additional canals, now serves about 16,000 hectares and 15,000 farmers. The right to water inheres in the land itself and cannot be bought and sold independently of the land. Rights to water are approximately proportionate to the amount of land owned, as are obligations to contribute to the cost of monitoring and maintenance activities (see Maass and Anderson 1986). Thus, in this instance, the ownership of what is considered common property—an irrigation system—is tied specifically to the ownership of what is considered private property—land. By transferring the rights to one good, the extensive rights and duties involved in a second good are also transferred.

Well-Defined Property Rights

As discussed earlier, without enforceable property rights, those who value the benefits that can be derived from common-pool resources have every incentive to harvest any volume of resource units they can obtain so long as the expected benefits are equal to or greater than the expected costs. No incentives to conserve exist without assurance that resource units saved today will be available for use at a later time by the one who conserves. Further, there are no incentives to invest in activities that enhance the performance and value of a common-pool resource if those benefits cannot be captured by those who produced them.

The significance of a well-established property-rights system is the security that enforced property rights gives to individuals and groups of individuals that their access, withdrawal, management, exclusion, and/or alienation will be recognized in the future by potential competitors for these rights. With such assurance, individuals can make credible commitments to one another to develop long-term plans for investing in and harvesting from a common-pool resource in a sustainable manner.

The concept of a well-established property-rights system has been interpreted, however, by some analysts to refer only to systems that include alienability.[15] In this view, proprietors, who have the rights of exclusion, management, withdrawal, and access, do not have well-defined property rights to a resource system and will not make efficient long-term decisions about investment and harvesting from a resource. Unless individuals can personally withdraw their share of the accumulated assets resulting from their prior investments in conservation or enhancement activities, individuals will not make such investments. The right of alienation is viewed as the essential right allowing individuals to obtain the residuals (benefits minus costs) of past investment. Some empirical research supports this view. A major World Bank study examined the impact of increasing the assurance that *de facto* owners of farm land could sell their land by providing them with formal titles to their land. In a careful econometric study, Feder et al. (1988) found that land in Thailand without a formal title was one-half to two-thirds of the value of land with a formal title. The value of crops obtained per unit of land on lands that had a secure title were between one-tenth and one-fourth higher than those without secure title. Further, the more secure titling provided better access to credit and led to greater investments in improved land productivity (see also Feder and Feeny 1991).

Undoubtedly, the right of alienation promotes the efficient use of property. However, other empirical studies suggest that while it is an important incentive, it is not a necessary condition for promoting efficient use.[16] Proprietors—those who hold rights of exclusion but not of alienation—also make decisions that promote long-term investment and harvesting from a resource. Place and Hazell (1993) collected survey data from Ghana, Kenya, and Rwanda to ascertain if indigenous land-rights systems, which are "proprietorship" systems, were a constraint on agricultural productivity. Many of the African land tenure systems enable "all eligible members of a local lineage or kinship groups to have assured access to at least some land. But at the same time, full ownership rights over land traditionally reside with the community, and individuals have a more restricted set of use, exclusion, and transfer rights over the land they farm" (Place and Hazell 1993). Having the rights of a "proprietor" as contrasted to an "owner" did not affect investment decisions and productivity. Other studies conducted in Africa (Migot-Adholla et al. 1991; Bruce and Migot-Adholla 1994) also found little difference in productivity, investment levels, or access to credit. There is also considerable evidence that traditional tenure systems are dynamic and change as local population densities, activities, and needs change over time (Berry 1993). Seabright (1993) also notes that dividing previously shared property can cause considerable conflict and reduce the level of trust among former coproprietors needed for other forms of collective action.

In our own studies of common-property systems, we have found that groups of individuals who jointly hold proprietorship rights exercise considerable governance and management initiative to regulate the long-term use of common-pool resources. In a series of studies of inshore fisheries, self-organized irrigation systems, forest user groups, and groundwater institutions, Schlager (1994), Tang (1994), Agrawal (1994), and Blomquist (1994) all found that when resource users who had withdrawal rights also had access to collective-choice arenas in which they could make management and exclusion decisions, that they:

- developed boundary rules to exclude noncontributors;
- crafted authority rules to allocate withdrawal authorizations; and
- devised forms of active monitoring and graduated sanctions.[17]

Many of the negative externalities that unregulated use of these systems would produce were controlled as a result of the rules crafted by users in either their own collective-choice arenas or in such arenas provided by larger governmental entities.

Closely related to the assumption that only those property rights that include alienation among the bundle of rights held are "well defined" is a second assumption that property rights are established and monitored by "the state." There is no question that national governments play an important role in the establishment and the monitoring of property rights of all types. This is especially true in countries that are based on Roman-law traditions. In countries based on a common-law tradition, the national government is, however, rarely the *major* actor in establishing and monitoring property rights related to natural resource systems, except for national lands that it actively establishes, manages, monitors, and enforces. The various types of property rights described (in the section entitled "Property Rights," for example) were not established by external governments. They were established by those individuals involved who also have taken the major responsibility for enforcing these rights. It is only when there is a major conflict over rights that those who themselves feel deprived take this dispute to arenas outside the immediate circle of users. Even then, seeking intervention by national government officials is a relatively rare method of establishing local rights.

General agreements about the rules to be used are achieved in what we have called "collective-choice arenas." Collective-choice arenas can involve settings that are not thought of as official legislative or judicial settings. The rotation of fishing spots in Alanya, Turkey, that Berkes (1986) has described so well, was worked out in a local coffeehouse over a long period of time during which several initial maps were subjected to trial and error by the fishers involved. The very well-defined ownership rights of the shareholders of Thulo Kulo were worked out over several decades in meetings of local farmers held under the shade of a pipal tree.

When conflict arises over locally self-established systems, the conflict may be articulated in any of a wide diversity of conflict-resolution arenas. The first line of resolution is typically the local community itself, either through informal mechanisms of threats or peer pressure, or formal judicial settings. On occasion, national governments do become involved. National governments that provide fair and low-cost judicial arenas for the resolution of those conflicts that are not resolved in other arenas do provide essential fora in which competing claims to property rights can be articulated and, hopefully, settled in a manner perceived by those involved to be legitimate.

In many tragic cases, on the other hand, national governments have either failed to take actions that help increase the security of diverse forms of property or have actively undermined efforts to achieve common agreement about entry, use, management, exclusion, and alienation rights to natural resources. Much of the uncertainty related to property rights of some natural resources—such as tropical forests—is a direct result of the action of national governments rather than the direct action of local users. Until very recently, the property-rights systems that regulated the use of tropical forests were communal or traditional systems where owners shared the rights of proprietors as defined above. During the past century and a half, however, national governments have asserted formal claims to the ownership of the vast bulk of these lands. Panayotou and Ashton (1992) identify six reasons why national governments have been powerless to enforce their claims to ownership and thus achieve an enforceable set of rights. These include:

(1) the vastness of the areas transferred to state ownership (in most countries over 50 percent of total land area);
(2) the speed and manner in which the transfer of ownership has been made;
(3) the failure to recognize and accommodate the customary rights of individuals and communities to the forest, which has created resentment among local populations;
(4) the limited budget and administrative, technical, and enforcement capacities of the newly established estates;
(5) growing pressures from expanding rural populations; and
(6) the failure of rural development to provide alternative employment and income opportunities.

The establishment of property rights, as contrasted to the assertion of a claim to a property right, requires substantial commitment of resources to back up the claims. For a "right" to be established, those who hold the right must assert that they hold the right to take specific types of actions within a well-defined domain, and all others who might have an interest in that domain must acknowledge that right and perceive that they have a duty to refrain from interfering in the exercise of that right. They must have the ability and wherewithal to monitor compliance with their asserted rights and to sanction non-compliance. Monitoring and enforcement must occur in relation to those who owe a duty to observe these rights, and in relation to the agents assigned to exercise those rights on behalf of the state.

With the assertion of rights but the failure to adequately monitor and enforce those rights, numerous unsavory things may occur. In many instances, forest lands have reverted to open-access conditions as traditional use rights have been challenged as a result of the state asserting a property right claim. As a consequence, "pervasive encroachment, squatting, log poaching, slash-and-burn (shifting cultivation), and illegal forest conversion to other uses," has occurred (Panayotou and Ashton 1992). In addition, individual government officials (i.e., agents of the state) have obtained substantial personal returns when they have granted short-term concession agreements to logging companies. Thus, instead of presuming that national governments are the essential factor affecting the definition of property rights, empirical evidence indicates that there are many factors associated with the set of users and how these users are embedded in a larger governance system that explain when property rights will tend to be well-defined.

Factors Affecting the Formation of Property Rights

The variety of specific rules used in field settings for regulating use is immense. Not only is there a substantial variety of rules used to reduce the cost of externalities from unregulated use of natural resources, but neighboring systems that appear to face similar situations frequently adopt different solutions. Within a few miles of Valençia is Alicante, where irrigators long ago adopted rules separating water from the land and participate in an active weekly market for water. Adjacent to Thulo Kulo is Raj Kulo, where the allocation of water (and labor responsibilities) is according to the amount of land owned and not the number of shares owned in the irrigation system.

The variety of rules selected by local users who appear to face similar circumstances raises the question whether institutional change is an evolutionary process involving a selection process that picks the most efficient institutions over time. In an important article, Alchian (1950) demonstrated how the pressure of competitive markets would select surviving firms that used profit-maximizing strategies whether they had chosen these strategies self-consciously or not. Some advocates of spontaneous orders (von Hayek 1967; Schotter 1981; Sugden 1986) have argued that individuals will slowly establish new and more efficient institutions through a series of spontaneous individual decisions. The improved group outcome is conceptualized as an unintended result of individual learning and adjusting behavior over time. It is not quite clear, however, what selection principle is at work outside of competitive markets.

Others, including Knight (1992) and Ostrom (1990, 1994), point out that changes in rules usually occur within a meta set of rules at a collective-choice or constitutional level and within settings that vary in terms of pressure for survival or excellence. The meta rules may assign differential advantages to participants in the rule-changing process. Those with the most voice in collective-choice processes may not benefit from rule changes even though the aggregate benefit is greater than costs. Thus, to explain a change in rules, one needs to analyze not only the status quo distribution of costs and benefits but also the distributional effects of proposed rules (Libecap 1989, 1994) and how these relate to the meta rules used for making and changing rules. Institutional change need not represent an efficiency-enhancing outcome (North 1990).

Many of the efforts of national governments to claim vast tracks of land as government-owned land, for example, cannot be explained as socially efficient changes in land tenure. To explain institutional change, one needs to analyze the relationships among variables characterizing the resource, the community of individuals involved, and the meta rules for making and changing rules. Sufficient theoretical and empirical research has been conducted on this and the closely related theory of collective action to enable one to specify important variables and the direction of their impact. The following variables appear to be conducive to the selection of property rights that reduces externalities related to the use of natural resources:

(1) Accurate information about the condition of the resource and expected flow of benefits and costs are available at low cost.
(2) Participants are relatively homogeneous in regard to information and preferences about the use of the resource.
(3) Participants share a common understanding about the poten-

tial benefits and risks associated with the continuance of the status quo as contrasted with changes in norms and rules that they could feasibly adopt.

(4) Participants share generalized norms of reciprocity and trust that can be used as initial social capital.

(5) The group using the resource is relatively small and stable.

(6) Participants do not discount the future at a high rate.

(7) Participants have the autonomy to make many of their own operational rules which if made legitimately, will not be interfered with, and even potentially supported and enforced by, external (local, regional, and national) authorities.

(8) Participants use collective-choice rules that fall between the extremes of unanimity or control by a few (or even bare majority) and thus avoid high transaction or high deprivation costs.

(9) Participants can develop relatively accurate and low-cost monitoring and sanctioning arrangements.[18]

Cumulatively, individuals must perceive that the long-term costs of controlling externalities will be less than long-term benefits — both for the group and for those individuals who undertake collective action.

Many of these variables are in turn affected by the type of larger governance regime in which users are embedded. If the larger regime facilitates local self-organization by providing accurate information about natural resource systems, providing arenas in which participants can engage in discovery and conflict resolution processes, and providing mechanisms to backup local monitoring and sanctioning efforts, the probability of participants adapting more effective and efficient rules over time is higher than in regimes that ignore resource problems or presume that all decisions about governance and management need to be made by the national government. However, where the case that when the users of very large resource systems are themselves a large and heterogeneous group that has not established arenas in which collective-choice rules can be designed, agreed upon, challenged, and altered over time, that national governments (and international regimes) have a very substantial role to play — not only in the provision of information and arenas for local decisionmaking but in the actual design and enforcement of rules specifying property rights for large resource systems. When national governments attempt to do more than these crucial activities, they reduce their credibility and capability to play the role in property-rights formation that is desperately needed.

Besides the factors listed above that affect whether the users of natural resource systems will themselves devise rules, it is also important to understand how various physical attributes of the resource itself affect the bundles of rights that can be crafted and enforced over time. Schlager et al. (1994) identify two important variables—the presence of storage and the mobility of resource units—as strongly affecting the type of property rights that can be used. In resources where there is no storage and resource units flow from one resource system to another—most fisheries, for example—devising withdrawal rights to a specified quantity of resource units over time has repeatedly proved to be extraordinarily difficult. While individual transferable quantity rights (ITQs) have been a favorite prescription in the fisheries literature for several decades, proportional ITQs have become the norm to avoid this problem (Maloney and Pearse 1979; Scott 1989). It is simply too costly to gather sufficient information about an unpredictably fluctuating resource flow to establish workable fixed quotas, and it is also too costly to adequately monitor and enforce them. A resource system with stationary resource units and with storage, on the other hand, may develop relatively fixed rights to flow units over time. A groundwater basin, for example, where sufficient information is known about the long-term safe yield, may be one type of common-pool resource where alienable rights to water can relatively easily be designed (Blomquist 1992). Such rights, however, are only to the flow from the resource, and questions of who owns, governs, and manages the groundwater basin itself are always of crucial importance in the design of property-rights systems.

Closely related to storage and flow characteristics are: whether the resource system generates a high yield and whether the yield occurs uniformly across space or in unpredictable "patches." These can also affect the kinds of property rights that users design (Netting 1972, 1976). If the yield is relatively low per unit of space, the costs of coming to an agreement about how to parcel it out among users, as well as of fencing, and of enforcing individual claims may be higher than the benefits. Creating a common grazing land or communal forest may cost substantially less than trying to devise individual parcels. Similarly, keeping resources that yield patchy outcomes in a larger unit may be a less expensive risk-sharing institution than developing a form of "crop" insurance. Other factors that increase the difficulty of achieving local property-rights systems that control externalities relate to events that occur over very long time dimensions and/or over very large space.

Importance of Local Property-Rights Systems

Systems of property rights and rules defined, implemented, monitored, and enforced by resource users themselves are likely to perform better than systems of property rights and rules defined, implemented, and enforced by an external authority. Locally devised property-rights systems require less information about the nature and structure of the resource and about the norms and social mores of the resource users. Rules devised by resource users are based on years, decades, and sometimes centuries of experience in using a common-pool resource. Such information is gleaned while engaging in everyday harvesting activities. Fishers learn which spots in a fishing ground are most productive and which areas of the grounds are most compatible with various types of gear, by fishing day after day. Consequently, the rules that resource users devise are well matched to the physical environment in which they will be used. For instance, the fishers of an estuary near Valença, Brazil, divided their fishing grounds into dozens of spots, depending upon the tides, the fish harvested, and the types of technologies used (Cordell 1972). Access to the fishing spots was gained through a variety of rules, such as drawing lots, or through prior announcement. These rules reduced intense conflict among the fishers caused by gear interference and competition over the most productive spots (Cordell 1972).

Not only are the rules well matched to the physical environment, but they are also well matched to the social and cultural environment of the resource users. Oftentimes, rules governing the use of a resource are simply incorporated into existing cultural and political structures. For instance, Berkes (1987) argues that the rules governing the harvesting of fish by the Cree Indians of Canada are grounded in the Cree's views and beliefs about nature and maintaining a right relationship with nature. Lansing and Kremer (1993) and Lansing (1991) describe the decisionmaking, monitoring, and enforcement roles of water priests in Bali irrigation systems.

Locally devised property-rights systems also economize on monitoring and enforcement costs. Most of these costs are borne by the resource users themselves; that is, rules are devised in ways that provide powerful incentives for resource users to monitor one another and that make it easy for monitoring to occur. For instance, in the case of coastal fisheries, rule compliance is relatively easy to monitor. Gear used on a boat can be determined by looking at the boat or examining its harvesting activities. Whether a boat is using gear in the appropriate zone can be determined by viewing its harvesting activities, and the gear it is using. Whether a boat is harvesting from its assigned spot can easily be determined by looking at the boat's location. Also, it is difficult for fishers to hide or cloak rule infractions. Either a boat is on its assigned spot or not. Thus, monitoring can be engaged in as fishers go about their business. Where the costs of monitoring are high, however, it may be difficult to design any effective institutions at all.

Enforcement is also likely to be effective. Fishers face relatively powerful incentives to report and/or sanction rule breakers. To avoid being foreclosed from harvesting fish, fishers face strong incentives to ensure that their assigned spots are not utilized by others. Or, if a fisher notices another boat using gear in an area forbidden to that gear, the fisher, in confronting the transgressor, acts to protect his own gear. The victims of rule breakers face strong incentives to take action to enforce the rules.

The Necessity of Diverse Scales

Locally devised systems of property rights and rules are anchored in detailed time and place information, cultural norms, and the self-interest of the resource users. External authorities would be hard-pressed to devise such institutions because they lack the information and the understanding to devise such institutions, and because they lack the commitment to ensuring their viability and longevity. While the livelihoods of resource users depend upon such institutions, the livelihoods of external bureaucrats depend on numerous other considerations. Empirical evidence is beginning to mount that locally devised governance systems perform better in regulating small- to moderate-sized resources than systems devised by an external authority. In a recent study of more than 100 irrigation systems in Nepal, Lam (1994) found that farmer-organized irrigation systems tended to generate higher agricultural yields and more equitable outcomes than government-organized systems serving similar terrain (see also Ostrom et al. 1994b). Lansing and Kremer (1993) and Lansing (1991) reach much the same conclusion concerning Bali irrigation systems.

Just as individuals can find themselves in commons dilemmas if they fail to coordinate their use of shared resources, so too can local-level organizations, such as fishing villages whose citizens harvest from shared fish stocks, or irrigation organizations whose members use a common irrigation system. While a given community of resource users may have devised property rights and rules that reduce negative externalities among its members, the collective actions that they take, or fail to take, may have adverse consequences for adjoining communities of resource users. For instance, even though fishing villages may carefully govern the access and harvesting activities of their own grounds, all the villages together may be taking too many fish, thereby depleting the fish stock. Or, an irrigation organization situated at the head end of a canal may take as much water as its members want, leaving the irrigation organizations situated lower on the canal facing severe water shortages. Or, a common method of discouraging damaging insects is to provide adequate amounts of fallow times and areas to deprive them of food sources. If farmers in adjoining irrigation systems fail to coordinate their fallow times, they may unleash a critical pest population.[19] In other words, local-level institutions are limited in their ability to address spillover effects individually.

Problems that extend beyond the boundaries of a local-level organization are extremely difficult to address by that organization. A response in the policy literature to the limits of local-level organizations and to the externalities they may create is to devise a single, comprehensive organization that can integrate and rationalize diverse, competing uses of an entire resource, particularly if the resource is located within the boundaries of a single nation. (See Dycus 1984; Dzurik 1990; Gottlieb and FitzSimmons 1991; Mallery 1983; and National Groundwater Policy Forum 1986, for managing watersheds and groundwater basins.) As discussed above, however, such a centralized management regime is likely to disrupt and destroy locally designed governance structures and is unlikely to produce the integration or rationalization so desired (Nakamura and Born 1993; Deyle 1995; Schlager 1995). An alternative approach that holds the promise of supporting local-level institutions, retaining the benefits of such institutions, and addressing their limits is to nest these organizations in a larger institutional environment that facilitates coordination among them, and that can address large-scale problems that local-level organizations share in common (Ostrom 1991).

The form that such coordination takes depends upon the nature of the problem and the magnitude of the interdependencies among local organizations. For small-scale problems that can be easily addressed, perhaps coordination simply amounts to two organizations agreeing to a one-time exchange of goods and services to address the problem. As problems become more persistent, and complex, involving larger numbers of local organizations, a more formal, umbrella organization may be created to better coordinate the actions of its members and to address shared problems that no individual member can address alone. To protect the integrity of local-level organizations, such nesting is best accomplished through a federal, not a hierarchical, approach. Each local-level organization retains exclusive jurisdiction over its own local issues and affairs, and the larger organization serves as a mechanism to support and enhance the viability of local-level organizations, to provide collective benefits to its various member organizations, and to exercise authority in areas that its member organizations have ceded to it. Just as individuals collaborate to devise local-level, self-governing organizations, so too do local-level, self-governing organizations devise regional-level organizations.

Conclusion

Will local, self-organized resource communities that have governed and managed so many natural resource systems continue into the next century? The answer depends upon revising the approach scholars and policymakers take toward such communities and the resources they govern. First, no single, uniform set of rules can possibly address the myriad problems faced by most resource users. For local-level governance structures to work well, they must first take into account the nuances of the physical and cultural environment in which they operate. Second, no one knows those nuances better than the resource users themselves. Resource users are capable of cooperating and defining governance structures that address their shared dilemmas and that maintain and enhance the resources on which their livelihoods rest. Third, local-level organizations are not panaceas. There are difficult and complex resource problems that local-level organizations are incapable of addressing on their own. These types of problems require that local-level organizations define rules to coordinate their actions in order to address the shared problems. Coordination can be as simple as two organizations addressing a common problem or multiple organizations forming a well-defined, more permanent institution to support the activities of the local-level organizations.

Local-level governance structures are not anachronisms. They are not relics clung to by culture-bound, illiterate, or isolated groups of resource users. They have been consciously designed and adopted to resolve pressing resource use issues. They will continue to be adopted, adapted, and redesigned into the twenty-first century to the degree that local-level resource users exercise the authority to govern themselves and to make fundamental decisions about their livelihoods.

NOTES

1. See the very interesting articles by Scott Atran (1986, 1993) on common-property institutions that are not likely to survive into the twenty-first century.

2. Of course, the progress of this decade draws on the immense scholarly work that already had existed in diverse sources. The theoretical break-throughs would not have been likely if many scholars in different disciplines had not undertaken the in-depth and detailed studies of particular natural resource systems. See Martin (1989/1992) for a bibliographic overview of this immense literature.

3. In a resource that generates multiple resource units—such as forests—some of the uses made of these benefits may not be subtractive. One person's use of a forest for recreation or religious purposes does not normally reduce the availability of the system for other nonsubtractive uses unless the particular use involves loud noises or other externalities.

4. This section draws heavily on Schlager and Ostrom (1992).

5. Rules defining the rights of access and withdrawal may or may not permit those rights to be transferred.

6. Lueck (1994) provides a formal analysis of the difference between sharing access, which is frequently an inefficient rule, and allocating the yield by a formula, which is frequently an efficient rule.

7. See Copes (1986) for an analysis of quota systems in relation to fisheries. See Wilson (1982) for an effective critique of standard economic theory's limited view of institutional alternatives in relation to fisheries, and Wilson (1995) for a discussion of when common-property institutions are efficient.

8. If these same fishers revise the conditions that constitute the right of access by expanding the number of fishers who can enter their fishery, they have not exercised a right of alienation. They have not transferred rights to additional individuals. Rather, they have exercised their right of exclusion to redefine who may or may not enter. The right of alienation refers only to the authority to alienate collective-choice rights, that is, to sell or lease such rights. The Turkish government, which leases inshore lagoons to coopera-tives, exercises the right to alienation (Berkes 1986).

9. By alienation, we specifically mean the authority to sell or lease collec-tive-choice rights. We do not include the ability to bequeath. In most common-property regimes, users have the ability to bequeath their rights in a resource. Rights rarely die with an individual. In many situations, how-ever, resource users do not have the right to sell or lease their rights to others. Limiting alienation to sale or lease also brings it closer to its eco-nomic usage. The importance of a right of alienation for many economists is that it provides the possibility that resources will be transferred to their highest valued use. While being able to sell or lease collective-choice rights provides that potential, the right to bequeath these rights is usually pre-sumed by economists to be an insufficient property right to achieve full

efficiency. Larson and Bromley (1990) effectively challenge this commonly held view and argue that much more needs to be known about the specific values of a large number of parameters in a particular setting before analysts can make careful judgments about whether the right of alienation leads to higher levels of efficiency than the right to bequeath. See also Anderson and Hill (1990) for an analysis of three different alienation rules that the U.S. government used in transferring public lands to individuals.

10. While theoretically it is possible to hold entry rights without withdrawal rights, in practice this rarely occurs. The distinction between access and withdrawal becomes crucial at a collective-choice level. Oftentimes, individuals who hold rights of management and thereby define withdrawal rights are not the same individuals who hold rights of exclusion and thereby define access rights. We provide a number of examples throughout the remainder of the chapter.

11. One could also define a position called "squatter" to consist of individuals who possess no rights at any level in relation to a common-pool resource. Squatters use natural resources, such as fisheries, but they do so at their own risk. If challenged by a person who holds collective-choice or operational rights, squatters lack authority to enforce their claims. Squatters stand entirely exposed to the actions of others where the use of a resource is concerned.

12. Alchian and Demsetz (1973) refer to the possession of the right of management, but not exclusion or alienation, as "communal rights."

13. The rights of alienation can be exercised in total or as a limited set of rights for a limited duration. Given the latter capability, "hybrid" legal arrangements related to the same resource are possible and occur frequently. Alchian and Demsetz (1973) point out that some of the "ambiguity in the notion of state or private ownership of a resource" occurs "because the bundle of property rights associated with a resource is divisible." In fact, all coastal fisheries in the United States are apt to be hybrid legal arrangements of one or another variety since the ownership rights to the coastal waters are vested in states. Each state decides whether to assign claimant status to all residents, to all residents who obtain licenses, or to allow various forms of proprietorship to come about through self-organization or through formal leasehold arrangements.

14. Participation in emergency repairs, however, requires labor input from all shareholders regardless of the size of their share. If the irrigation system is destroyed because of a landslide, all shareholders would lose their property rights.

15. This interpretation has been made both by social scientists and by courts of law. In the latter case, the consequence for indigenous peoples who have held clear group rights to land for centuries has been the loss of their claim. In the Philippines and elsewhere, national governments have not recognized group ownership where individuals have no claim to alienability and have declared such lands to be owned by the state. Courts in many countries have upheld these claims (see Fegan 1995).

16. A recent study by Binswanger et al. (1993) strongly suggests that both the emergence and continuance of large, privately held farms were due more to government intervention through land grants or differential taxation rather than greater efficiency.

17. See also Tang (1992), Schlager (1990), and Blomquist (1992).

18. See Ostrom (1990: ch. 6) for a discussion of these factors.

19. Conversely, providing public benefits across multiple local-level organizations is also problematic. For instance, a fishing village is unlikely to invest in a hatchery to supplement a fish stock if those fish will be harvested by fishers from other communities. Just as with negative externalities, incentives to free-ride on other communities must be overcome if public benefits are to be provided.

ACKNOWLEDGMENTS

This chapter draws in part on a paper by Elinor Ostrom, "The Evolution of Norms, Rules, and Rights," presented at a workshop of the Social and Ecological System Linkages Project of the Property Rights and Performance of Natural Resource Systems Group at the Beijer International Institute of Ecological Economics, The Royal Swedish Academy of Sciences in September 1993. It also updates a section of an earlier paper by the authors (Schlager and Ostrom 1992).

REFERENCES

Adasiak, A. 1979. Alaska's experience with limited entry. *Journal of the Fisheries Research Board of Canada* 36(7):770–782.

Agrawal, A. 1994. Rules, rule making, and rule breaking: Examining the fit between rule systems and resource use. Pages 267–282 *in* E. Ostrom, R. Gardner, and J. M. Walker, eds. *Rules, Games, and Common-Pool Resources.* University of Michigan Press, Ann Arbor.

Alchian, A. 1950. Uncertainty, evolution, and economic theory. *Journal of Political Economy* 58(3):211–221.

Alchian, A. and H. Demsetz. 1973. The property rights paradigm. *Journal of Economic History* 33(1) (March):16–27.

Anderson, T. L. and P. J. Hill. 1990. The race for property rights. *Journal of Law and Economics* 33:117–197.

Atran, S. 1986. *Hamula* organization and *Masha'a* tenure in Palestine. *Man* 21:271–295.

Atran, S. 1993. Itza Maya tropical agro-forestry. *Current Anthropology* 34(5) (Dec.):633–700.

Berkes, F. 1986. Local level management and the commons problem: A comparative study of Turkish coastal fisheries. *Marine Policy* 10 (July): 215–229.

Berkes, F. 1987. Common property resource management and Cree Indian fisheries in Subarctic Canada. Pages 66–91 *in* B. J. McCay and J. M. Acheson, eds. *The Question of the Commons: The Culture and Ecology of Communal Resources.* University of Arizona Press, Tucson.

Berkes, F., ed. 1989. *Common Property Resources. Ecology and Community-based Sustainable Development.* Belhaven Press, London.

Berry, S. 1993. *No Condition is Permanent: The Social Dynamics of Agrarian Change in Sub-Saharan Africa.* University of Wisconsin Press, Madison.

Binswanger, H. P., K. Deininger, and G. Feder. 1993. Power, distortions, revolt, and reform in agricultural land relations. Working paper. Agriculture and Rural Development Department, The World Bank, Washington, D.C.

Blomquist, W. 1992. *Dividing the Waters: Governing Groundwater in Southern California.* ICS Press, San Francisco.

Blomquist, W. 1994. Changing rules, changing games: Evidence from groundwater systems in Southern California. Pages 283–300 *in* E. Ostrom, R. Gardner, and J. Walker, eds. *Rules, Games, and Common-Pool Resources.* University of Michigan Press, Ann Arbor.

Bromley, D. W. 1991. *Environment and Economy: Property Rights and Public Policy.* Basil Blackwell, Oxford.

Bromley, D. W., D. Feeny, M. McKean, T. Peters, J. Gilles, R. Oakerson, C. F. Runge, and J. Thomson, eds. 1992. *Making the Commons Work: Theory, Practice, and Policy.* ICS Press, San Francisco.

Bruce, J. 1995. *Securing Common Property: Confronting Issues in Law and Policy.* Food and Agriculture Organization of the United Nations, Forests, Trees and People Programme, Rome.

Bruce, J. and S. E. Migot-Adholla, eds. 1994. *Searching for Security of Land Tenure in Africa. Kendall/Hunt Publishing Co.,* Dubuque, IA.

Bruce, J., L. Fortmann, and C. Nhira. 1993. Tenures in transition, tenures in conflict: Examples from the Zimbabwe social forest. *Rural Sociology* 58(4):626–642.

Commons, J. R. 1968. *Legal Foundations of Capitalism.* University of Wisconsin Press, Madison.

Copes, P. 1986. A critical review of the individual quota as a device in fisheries management. *Land Economics* 62(3) (Aug.):278–291.

Cordell, J. C. 1972. "The Developmental Ecology of an Estuarine Canoe Fishing System in Northeast Brazil." Ph.D. Dissertation. Stanford University.

Dasgupta, P. and K.-G. Mäler. 1992. *The Economics of Transnational Commons.* Clarendon Press, Oxford, UK.

Davis, A. 1984. Property rights and access management in the small boat fishery: A case study from Southwest Nova Scotia. Pages 133–164 *in* C. Lamson and A. J. Hanson, eds. *Atlantic Fisheries and Coastal Communities: Fisheries Decision-Making Case Studies.* Dalhousie Ocean Studies Programme, Halifax.

Deyle, R. 1995. Integrated water management: Contending with garbage-can decisionmaking in organized anarchies. *Water Resources Bulletin* 31(3):387–398.

Dycus, J. S. 1984. Development of a national groundwater protection strategy. *Boston College Environmental Affairs Law Review* 11(2): 211–271.

Dzurik, A. 1990. *Water Resources Planning.* Rowman and Littlefield, Savage, MD.

Eggertsson, T. 1990. *Economic Behavior and Institutions.* Cambridge University Press, Cambridge, UK.

Faris, J. C. 1972. *Cat Harbour: A Newfoundland Fishing Settlement.* Newfoundland Social and Economic Studies No. 3. University of Toronto Press, Toronto.

Feder, G. and D. Feeny. 1991. Land tenure and property rights theory and implications for development policy. *World Bank Economic Review* 5:135–153.

Feder, G., T. Onchan, Y. Chalamwong, and C. Hangladoran. 1988. *Land Policies and Form Productivity in Thailand.* Johns Hopkins University Press, Baltimore, MD.

Feeny, D., F. Berkes, B. J. McCay, and J. M. Acheson. 1990. The tragedy of the commons: Twenty-two years later. *Human Ecology* 18(1):1–19.

Fegan, B. 1995. Layers of land claims: State law, indigenous group territories, majority settler, landlord, tenant, trees in the Philippines. *Common Property Resource Digest* 34(June):2–6.

Fortmann, L. and J. W. Bruce, eds. 1988. *Whose Trees? Proprietary Dimensions of Forestry.* Westview Press, Boulder, CO.

Gardner, R., E. Ostrom, and J. M. Walker. 1990. The nature of common-pool resource problems. *Rationality and Society* 2(3) (July):335–358.

Gottlieb, R. and M. FitzSimmons. 1991. *Thirst for Growth: Water Agencies as Hidden Government in California.* University of Arizona Press, Tucson.

Keohane, R. O. and E. Ostrom, eds. 1995. *Local Commons and Global Interdependence: Heterogeneity and Cooperation in Two Domains.* Sage, London.

Knight, J. 1992. *Institutions and Social Conflict.* Cambridge University Press, Cambridge, UK.

Lam, W. F. 1994. "Institutions, engineering infrastructure, and performance in the governance and management of irrigation systems: The case of Nepal." Ph.D. Dissertation. Indiana University, Bloomington.

Lansing, J. S. 1991. *Priests and Programmers: Technologies of Power in the Engineered Landscape of Bali.* Princeton University Press, Princeton, NJ.

Lansing, J. S. and J. Kremer. 1993. Emergent properties of landscape. *American Anthropologist* 95(1):97–115.

Larson, B. A. and D. W. Bromley. 1990. Property rights, externalities, and resource degradation: Locating the tragedy. *Journal of Development Economics* 33(2) (Oct.):235–262.

Libecap, G. D. 1989. *Contracting for Property Rights.* Cambridge University Press, Cambridge, UK.

Libecap, G. D. 1994. The conditions for successful collective action. *Journal of Theoretical Politics* 6(4) (Oct.):563–592.

Lueck, D. 1994. Common property as an egalitarian share contract. *Journal of Economic Behavior and Organization* 25:93–108.

Maass, A. and R. L. Anderson. 1986. . . . *and the Desert Shall Rejoice: Conflict, Growth and Justice in Arid Environments*. R. E. Krieger, Malabar, FL.

Mallery, M. 1983. Groundwater: A call for a comprehensive management program. *Pacific Law Journal* 14(4):1279–1307.

Maloney, D. G. and P. Pearse. 1979. Quantitative rights as an instrument for regulating commercial fisheries. *Journal of the Fisheries Research Board of Canada* 36(7):859–866.

Martin, E. G. 1986. "Resource Mobilization, Water Allocation, and Farmer Organization in Hill Irrigation Systems in Nepal." Ph.D. Dissertation. Cornell University.

Martin, E. G. and R. Yoder. 1983. The Chherlung Thulo Kulo: A case study of a farmer-managed irrigation system. Pages 203–217 in *Water Management in Nepal: Proceedings of the Seminar on Water Management Issues,* July 31–August 2, Appendix I. Ministry of Agriculture, Agricultural Projects Services Centre, and the Agricultural Development Council, Kathmandu, Nepal.

Martin, F. 1989/1992. *Common-Pool Resources and Collective Action: A Bibliography,* Vols. 1 and 2. Workshop in Political Theory and Policy Analysis, Indiana University, Bloomington.

Martin, K. O. 1973. "The law in St. John's says . . . : Space Division and Resource Allocation in the Newfoundland Fishing Community of Fermeuse." Master's Thesis, Department of Anthropology, Memorial University of Newfoundland.

Martin, K. O. 1979. Play by the rules or don't play at all: Space division and resource allocation in a rural Newfoundland fishing community. Pages 276–298 in R. Anderson, ed. *North Atlantic Maritime Cultures: Anthropological Essays on Changing Adaptations*. Mouton, The Hague.

McCay, B. J. and J. M. Acheson. 1987. *The Question of the Commons: The Culture and Ecology of Communal Resources*. University of Arizona Press, Tucson.

Migot-Adholla, S. E., P. Hazell, B. Blarel, and F. Place. 1991. Indigenous land rights systems in sub-Saharan Africa: A constraint on productivity? *The World Bank Economic Review* 5(1):155–175.

Miller, D. 1989. The evolution of Mexico's spiny lobster fishery. Pages 185–198 in F. Berkes, ed. *Common Property Resources: Ecology and Community-Based Sustainable Development*. Belhaven Press, London.

Nakamura, L. and S. Born. 1993. Substate institutional innovation for managing lakes and watersheds: A Wisconsin case study. *Water Resources Bulletin* 31(3):807–821.

National Groundwater Policy Forum. 1986. *Groundwater: Saving the*

Unseen Resource. The Conservation Foundation, Washington, D.C.

National Research Council. 1986. *Proceedings of the Conference on Common Property Resource Management.* National Academy Press, Washington, D.C.

Netting, R. McC. 1972. Of men and meadows: Strategies of Alpine land use. *Anthropological Quarterly* 45:132–144.

Netting, R. McC. 1976. What Alpine peasants have in common: Observations on communal tenure in a Swiss village. *Human Ecology* 4:135–146.

Netting, R. McC. 1993. *Smallholders, Householders: Farm Families and the Ecology of Intensive, Sustainable Agriculture.* Stanford University Press, Stanford, CA.

North, D. C. 1990. *Institutions, Institutional Change and Economic Performance.* Cambridge University Press, New York.

Ostrom, E. 1990. *Governing the Commons: The Evolution of Institutions for Collective Action.* Cambridge University Press, New York.

Ostrom, E. 1994. Constituting social capital and collective action. *Journal of Theoretical Politics* 6(4) (Oct.):527–562.

Ostrom, E., R. Gardner, and J. M. Walker. 1994a. *Rules, Games, and Common-Pool Resources.* University of Michigan Press, Ann Arbor.

Ostrom, E., W. F. Lam, and M. Lee. 1994b. The performance of self-governing irrigation systems in Nepal. *Human Systems Management* 13(3):197–207.

Ostrom, V. 1991. *The Meaning of American Federalism: Constituting a Self-Governing Society.* ICS Press, San Francisco.

Ostrom, V., D. Feeny, and H. Picht, eds. 1993. *Rethinking Institutional Analysis and Development: Issues, Alternatives, and Choices,* 2nd ed. ICS Press, San Francisco.

Panayotou, T. and P. S. Ashton. 1992. *Not by Timber Alone: Economics and Ecology for Sustaining Tropical Forests.* Island Press, Washington, D.C.

Pinkerton, E. 1989. *Co-operative Management of Local Fisheries. New Directions for Improved Management and Community Development.* University of British Columbia Press, Vancouver.

Place, F. and P. Hazell. 1993. Productivity effects of indigenous land tenure systems in sub-Saharan Africa. *American Journal of Agricultural Economics* 75 (Feb.):10–19.

Raychaudhuri, B. 1980. *The Moon and the Net: Study of a Transient Community of Fishermen at Jambudwip.* Government of India Press, Anthropological Survey of India, Calcutta.

Schlager, E. 1990. "Model Specification and Policy Analysis: The Governance of Coastal Fisheries." Ph.D. Dissertation. Indiana University, Bloomington.

Schlager, E. 1994. Fishers' institutional responses to common-pool resource dilemmas. Pages 247–265 *in* E. Ostrom, R. Gardner, and J. Walker, eds. *Rules, Games, and Common-Pool Resources.* University of Michigan Press, Ann Arbor.

Schlager, E. 1995. Drawbacks of centralized and local level management of groundwater basins: An Arizona case study. Working paper. University of Arizona, Tucson.

Schlager, E. and E. Ostrom. 1992. Property-rights regimes and natural resources: A conceptual analysis. *Land Economics* 68(3) (Aug.): 249–262.

Schlager, E., W. Blomquist, and S. Y. Tang. 1994. Mobile flows, storage, and self-organized institutions for governing common-pool resources. *Land Economics* 70(3) (Aug.):294–317.

Schotter, A. 1981. *The Economic Theory of Social Institutions.* Cambridge University Press, Cambridge, UK.

Scott, A. 1989. Conceptual origins of rights based fishing. Pages 11–38 *in* P. Neher, R. Arnason, and N. Mollett, eds. *Rights Based Fishing.* Kluwer Academic Publishers, Dordrecht, Netherlands.

Seabright, P. 1993. Managing local commons: Theoretical issues in incentive design. *Journal of Economic Perspectives* 7(4) (Nov.):113–134.

Sengupta, N. 1991. *Managing Common Property: Irrigation in India and the Philippines.* Sage, London.

Sengupta, N. 1993. *User-Friendly Irrigation Designs.* Sage, New Delhi, India.

Sugden, R. 1986. *The Economics of Rights, Cooperation and Welfare.* Basil Blackwell, London.

Tang, S. Y. 1992. *Institutions and Collective Action: Self-Governance in Irrigation.* ICS Press, San Francisco.

Tang, S. Y. 1994. Institutions and performance in irrigation systems. Pages 225–245 *in* E. Ostrom, R. Gardner, and J. M. Walker, eds. *Rules, Games, and Common-Pool Resources.* University of Michigan Press, Ann Arbor.

Thomson, J. T. 1992. *A Framework for Analyzing Institutional Incentives in Community Forestry.* Food and Agriculture Organization of the United Nations, Rome.

von Hayek, F. A. 1967. Notes on the evolution of systems of rules of conduct. Pages 66–81 *in* F. A. von Hayek, ed. *Studies in Philosophy, Politics and Economics.* University of Chicago Press, Chicago.

Wade, R. 1988. *Village Republics: Economic Conditions for Collective Action in South India.* Cambridge University Press, Cambridge, UK.

Wilson, J. A. 1982. The economical management of multispecies fisheries. *Land Economics* 58(4) (Nov.):417–434.

Wilson, J. A. 1995. When are common property institutions efficient? Working paper. Department of Agriculture and Resource Economics, University of Maine, Orono.

CHAPTER 8

The Economics of Control
and the Cost of Property Rights

THRÁINN EGGERTSSON

Introduction

All theories of social phenomena abstract from the real world by styl-
izing select characteristics of human behavior, organization, and
physical environments. The economic perspective on property rights
is no exception to this feature of social science. The economics of
property rights (1) models people as rational purposive persons; (2)
characterizes the institutional environment as formal and informal
rules that constrain and direct individual action; and (3) emphasizes
features of the physical environment that affect the cost of control,
particularly the costs of measurement and enforcement (Barzel 1989).

The first of these assumptions is known as the rational choice
model. The rational choice model assumes that people know their
goals or *preferences* and also their alternatives or *choice sets* and
make choices with logical consistency. The rational choice approach
shares with representative democracy the status of being roundly criticized but lacking a superior alternative (Cook and Levi 1990; Bell et
al. 1988). Critics have argued that the approach portrays people as
asocial lighting-fast calculators, but this criticism is not entirely true.
The economics of property rights does not ignore the social environment: the theory recognizes both formal rules, such as laws or regulations, and informal rules that reflect norms, customs, and other
social values, and it has introduced the notion of costly information
to make the choice process more realistic.[1]

Until we have a better model of choice, the rational choice model is
needed for building theories that derive economic and social outcomes from individual responses to particular structures of property
rights.[2] By deriving results from individual behavior, it is possible to
show how certain property rights structures create a conflict between

individual and group rationality. The conflict arises when people, acting consistently with their individual preferences, produce overall outcomes that no one prefers (Olson 1965; Gordon 1954).

The chief weakness of the rational choice model is that it takes the goals and preferences of people as given and does not analyze how they are formed and why they change. Values that people hold influence the cost of maintaining systems of property rights. For instance, strong public commitment to a clean environment lowers the cost of enforcing environmental legislation. Values also influence legislators and others who make rules, and new values often spawn institutional change. Economics has little to say about changes in preferences and the emergence of shared social values, but recently many economists have become deeply interested in these issues (Denzau and North 1994).

This chapter focuses on the costs of establishing and maintaining property rights. The following section introduces some of the main concepts in the economics of property rights. The chapter's third section examines why incomplete rights are found to a varying degree in all systems of property rights. The section also discusses how incomplete property rights motivate people to waste or dissipate scarce resources and outlines how the same people often use private contractual arrangements to limit the waste. The fourth section is concerned with the complexity of social systems and with theoretical approaches for understanding and mastering this complexity. I argue that our theories can explain with considerable success various features of alternative systems, but their capacity to successfully design new arrangements that produce desired results is much more limited. The final section offers some conclusions.

The Economics of Control

When resources are scarce, they are always rationed by some means, which may include prices, standing in line, or even wars. Property rights specify the system of rationing in a community: the rights to use a valuable resource, to earn income from it, and to transfer these rights. The utilization of resources depends on how the control of their many dimensions is divided among various people, including those who represent the state, and how securely they control their assets (Alchian 1965). Economics is not concerned with rights that only exist in name but with actual control.

Control is a manifestation of power. Traditional economics of the market place (neoclassical economics) did not focus on questions of power and control, but studied the consequences of an ideal control structure: a market with fully defined and fully enforced exclusive property rights. The emergence of the economics of property rights and the new economics of institutions reflects attempts to bring the issue of control directly into economic analysis. The new institutionalism has a twofold purpose: (1) to explain how a particular structure of control emerges, survives, and decays; and (2) to examine the implications of various systems of control for the organization of economic activity and for economic results, such as growth, the distribution of wealth, and environmental quality.

Control has many dimensions, and the detailed nature of control matters for people in economic and other activities and influences their behavior: short-term control shortens the planning horizon; uncertain control discourages investment in potentially profitable ventures; lack of control may incite costly races for possession; restricted control may allocate assets to inferior uses. As the nature of control over resources in a community derives from the social and political environment, the study of control calls for an interdisciplinary approach. The scholar must roam across the borders of several disciplines, such as economics and the other social sciences, psychology, history, and law. Below I suggest a framework for analyzing control.[3]

A person's control of resources has an *internal* and an *external* element. The external element is the person's institutional environment: social rules that define rights and duties in the use of resources. The institutional environment of people varies with their standing in the community and is outside their sphere of influence at any point in time. The internal element of control is determined by the people themselves and can be seen as an investment. People are ready to invest in better control (with locks, fences, burglar alarms, monitoring) provided that the additional benefits outweigh the extra costs.

The costs of establishing control and preventing loss of control are called *transaction costs*. People can lose their control of valuable attributes of a resource, or of the resource as a whole, in two ways: (1) through forceful expropriation or theft (involuntary exchange) or (2) when their trading partners in voluntary exchange cheat. People are able to cheat in voluntary exchange when their behavior and their character is not fully known to their partners.

Transaction costs, which emerge because information is costly and therefore incomplete, profoundly influence systems of property rights and the logic of economic organization. The personal cost of enforcing control over resources is inversely related to the support provided by the institutional environment. For instance, transaction costs are likely to be high in a new settlement prior to the establishment of some form of government, or during a civil war when there is no single authority with police power and courts to help people protect their property and enforce contacts. In all institutional environments, transaction costs depend on the measurability of resources and on the ease of monitoring their use, which in turn depend on physical characteristics of the resources and the technology of measurement and monitoring.

In exchange relationships, transaction costs also are related to the nature of the exchange, such as the social links between the traders, and duration, frequency, and synchronization of the exchanges (for instance whether both parties deliver simultaneously). Legislators who trade votes for the projects of each other frequently face high transaction costs because of the many opportunities for cheating. The projects need not come up for a vote at the same time, or one project may require only a single authorization (the location of a highway) and another continued annual support (a welfare program). The transaction costs of maintaining control in exchanges are particularly high, when resources are specific to, or dependent on, transactions between specific parties and have relatively little value in other uses. Dependence on a partner puts a trader at risk and increases the possibility of a hold up. With dependence, a partner may unilaterally reduce the price she pays all the way to the value of the resources in their second best uses. In the case of investment goods designed for a specific user, their second best value may be the scrap value. The threat of hold ups will diminish the supply of specific resources (Williamson 1971, 1985; Klein et al. 1978).

In any environment, people will attempt to cooperate and seek mutually advantageous ways of lowering their transaction costs, put their resources to valuable uses, and gain from trade. Mistrust often prevents successful cooperation, but frequently people succeed in designing a private governance system for regulating the exchange of property rights. Private arrangements are embodied in *contracts*.[4] The structure of a contract usually is influenced both by the external institutional environment and by private (internal) considerations. In the extreme case, a detailed institutional framework leaves no choice to private persons: it prescribes all the details of an exchange relationship and makes specific contracting by the traders redundant. In practice, the structure of contracts usually is prescribed in part externally and is in part designed by the traders.

Long-term exchange relationships must cope with the impossibility of designing institutions or private contracts that anticipate all future events in our uncertain world. In response, the designers of institutions and contracts often create specific procedures for conflict resolution (rather than explicit solutions) for coping with uncertain future events (Goldberg 1976a).

There is considerable confusion in the literature about the distinction between institutions and organizations. I prefer the following definitions: Institutions are rules that assign control of resources—through rights and duties—to individual persons or associations of persons. Organizations are social groups, people who work together. A network of contracts, nested in the institutional environment, defines the structure and boundaries of organizations. In this view, organizations are the key action component of social systems (North 1990). Institutions influence the structure and goals of organizations, but over time the actions of social, political, and economic organizations affect the system of property rights and bring about institutional change.

Incomplete Control and the Waste of Resources

In the real world, people and their organizations confront institutions of bewildering complexity. To identify aspects of institutions that are critical for economic behavior, without being overwhelmed by detail, scholars have defined certain ideal-type institutional environments or systems of property rights. In the literature, a fourfold classification of control regimes is most common: (1) open access, (2) communal (common) property, (3) private property, (4) state property.

Open access exists when no rights to a resource have emerged and the resource is in the public domain. Communal property refers to arrangements where a community of individuals controls a resource. Communal property (usually) cannot permanently be transferred to people outside a particular social group. I prefer the term *communal property* to the more popular *common property* because the latter often is confused with open access. The confusion partly is due to the fact that communal property arrangements sometimes break down and degenerate into *de facto* open access, but retain their formal structure. Private property refers to exclusive ownership by one or more individuals who freely can transfer their rights to other people. In practice, the term *state property* is a misleading category because of the variation in the nature of the state. What is called state or public property may resemble open access, communal property, or even private property (for instance when agents of the state are out of control or when dictators treat state resources as their personal property).

In short, researchers have found that these categories are unsatisfactory for dealing with many empirical cases. The nature of property rights must be specified in more detail to capture how rights influence behavior. Resources usually have several valuable dimensions and uses and, similarly, control structures typically have various dimensions that must be considered. Schlager and Ostrom (1993), in an empirical study of control structures in 44 coastal fisheries around the world, identified for their purposes four dimensions of control: (1) access and withdrawal, (2) management, (3) exclusion, and (4) alienation. Schlager and Ostrom established for each group of fishers how many of these dimensions they controlled and found that the number varied from only one to all four dimensions. Further they found that differences in control structures affected behavior systematically and predictably. The Schlager–Ostrom study was concerned only with the use of coastal waters as fisheries, but coastal waters have other, often conflicting, uses—for instance, the waters can be used for pleasure boating, to receive sewage, or as a harbor.

The division of controls between people, both within each category of uses and between use categories, has implications for behavior and economic results. People often share the control of their resources or have restricted control over them, although officially they are the single owner. There are various reasons for these restrictions on full control. First, it is costly or even impractical for owners to personally attend to all their affairs, which often makes it advantageous to hire agents and transfer certain dimensions of control to them. Organizations act as agents and manage bundles of resources through contractual arrangements: owners of labor resources, financial resources, and various physical assets often transfer certain rights to those who manage firms. Second, the state frequently restricts individual control of resources in various ways—and not only through taxation. The state may determine that a building only can be used as a home or that a building cannot be demolished or altered substantially (because it is a historical landmark). The debate over the (de)regulation of industry, extending back to the Industrial Revolution, is another reminder of how the state gives and takes various dimensions of control. Finally, informal rules limit the control that people have over their resources. Informal local standards and sanctions may compel people to paint their houses in other colors than they desire, or wear other clothes than they wish, or charge less for food during a famine than the market can bear.

The most important insight that the economics of property rights offers is that incomplete control wastes resources—income that is not exclusive to a particular individual or organization is dissipated. The analytics of dissipation were worked out initially for open access to natural resources, such as a fishery (Warming 1911; Gordon 1954). The core of the argument is relatively simple: Consider the discovery of a productive fishery, which could add substantially to the wealth of a community. The fishery will draw people from other activities, if the prospective value of their output (and pay) in the fishery is greater than in their current employment. New entrants will continue to flow into the fishery until the value of their output (and pay) is the same in the fishery as elsewhere in the economy. When the inflow finally stops, the community's potential additional income from the fishery has been wasted. All that has changed is that a portion of the labor force has moved from one type of employment to another, but the total income and output of the economy has not increased.

The problem of dissipation arises because too many fishers enter the grounds—somewhat like drivers who crowd a highway and bring the traffic to a crawl. In both cases, new entrants ignore the costs they impose on present users by crowding the field. Fewer would enter if new entrants to a highway or a fishery had to compensate those present for slowing them down or reducing their catch. If these costs were somehow included when people contemplate the costs and benefits of entry, the potential income or value added from the resource would not be wasted. The utilization of the resource would be at a level where its value to the community is maximized.

A resource that no one controls is referred to as a *nonexclusive resource*. The waste associated with nonexclusive resources involves more than excessive utilization of the resource: the very method of utilization is likely to be wasteful. In an open-access fishery, fishers may race to the grounds in boats with inefficiently large engines and engage in other activities that raise production costs. Races to appropriate nonexclusive income usually are motivated by the rule of capture, which states that nonexclusive oil in an underground reservoir, fish in the ocean, or other resources become exclusive property once they are captured by individuals. Another wasteful feature of open access is that people have little incentive to improve the quality of the resources they use, for instance by applying fertilizers to land, because they cannot control the yield—it is nonexclusive income. Nonexclusivity even affects the choice of outputs. Farmers are more likely to use nonexclusive land for grazing cattle than for cultivating orchards, even when orchards are preferred on comparable exclusive plots.

Those, who ignore the impact of their actions on the productivity of other people are said to cause *external effects*. When people allow for these effects, they are said to *internalize* the external effects. It is obvious that external effects are internalized, when one person or one organization controls a contiguous natural resource. A single firm managing all the fishing boats in a fishery would consider the effects of crowding on output and costs for the whole fleet. In the case of several firms, the problem would disappear—resources would not be wasted—if the various individuals at little or no cost could negotiate with each other and make binding agreements (Coase 1960). However, such agreements usually are impractical when the rights to control are not socially recognized and enforced. Fishers who agree to limit their use of a fishery may expect several waves of new entrants who ignore all agreements among the insiders. In reality, contracting always involves costs—transaction costs—and high transaction costs can prevent any agreement among the insiders, even when there is no threat of new entry.

Nonexclusive income and waste are not limited to open-access resources (Barzel 1989). The problem also is found in all systems of exclusive property rights because transaction costs make control incomplete. The practice of not pricing salt and pepper in restaurants or of charging the same price for good and bad seats in a theater are everyday examples of incomplete control.

Incomplete control implies that some dimensions of a resource are nonexclusive, which invites wasteful behavior that lowers the value of the resource. In agriculture under exclusive private ownership, tenants with fixed rent contracts may find it in their interest to maximize the short-run output from the fields that they rent and deplete the soil of nutrients. As for the landlords, high transaction costs can make it impractical for them to monitor how their tenants treat the soil. When these conditions hold, soil nutrients become a nonexclusive dimension of the resource, the tenants ignore the external effects of intensive utilization, and part of the potential long-run income (and output) from the land is wasted.

The prevalence of nonexclusivity due to transaction costs has major implications for focusing research in the economics of institutions. The prospect of nonexclusivity creates an incentive for people to design institutions and contractual arrangements that reduce transaction costs and limit waste (Milgrom and Roberts 1992). In addition to measures such as legal and regulatory restraints and monitoring systems, these responses include contracts that reconcile conflicting interests of individuals. At first glance such contracts may appear irrational, but in the context of incomplete information and transaction costs they can make good economic sense. In the landlord–tenant case above, the landlords might offer incentive contracts to their tenants under which the landlords provide the tenants with fertilizers at a subsidized (or even zero) price to give them incentives to maintain the quality of the land (Barzel 1989).

In a community, the institutional structure constitutes a stock, just as the community's collection of physical assets (its capital) is a stock. At any point in time, the stock of institutions reflects a cumulative process rooted in history. New rules governing particular resources are only a marginal addition to the existing stock of institutions, and the effectiveness of new rules depends in part on the nature of existing rules and values.

From a purely economic viewpoint, the decision to establish exclusive control over a resource is an investment decision: Are the benefits of registering, fencing, and monitoring land greater or less than the costs? In a well-known paper, Demsetz (1967) argues that communities introduce exclusive rights when the benefits exceed the costs for the people involved. The straightforward benefit–cost approach to exclusive rights does not consider bargaining problems and struggles for the division of wealth, which frequently prevent the emergence of efficient property rights. Therefore, the benefit-cost approach has been called the *naive theory of property rights* (Eggertsson 1990).

The naive theory of property rights is not a general theory but a special case that has received empirical support, particularly in certain stable homogeneous local communities that are relatively independent of central authorities (Ostrom 1990). In such communities, wasteful arrangements are rather obvious and their costs impinge directly on people who are in a position to remedy the situation. Distant bureaucrats are more likely to be poorly informed and have weak personal incentives to repair inefficient property rights.

A sophisticated version of the naive theory of property rights is a valuable benchmark, a good tool for illustrating various issues regarding the establishment of exclusive rights, particularly how the struggle for control raises transaction costs and often leads to distorted systems of property rights that waste resources. Below, I outline a model derived by Field (1986, 1989; Eggertsson 1992). The model suggests what factors must be considered, when people who harvest the yield of a contiguous resource such as a pasture, attempt to create a system of control that maximizes their joint wealth.

To simplify, assume that exclusive rights only involve one issue: how the land should be divided among the cultivators. Should they all share the land? Should each person have a private plot? Or should the land be divided into a number of large plots with several people sharing each of the intermediate commons? If two or more persons share the use of an exclusive plot, the arrangement contains the seeds of an open-access problem because people may compete destructively to use the resource, unless they are regulated. Let us refer to such regulations as *governance* and assume that on each plot the (transaction) costs of governance increase steadily as the number of people increases. Governance costs, then, reach a maximum when all the members of the community share the same plot. In each case, the nature of the measurement and enforcement problems determines the best contractual arrangements for dealing with the governance problem (Lueck 1993).

In addition to internal governance on each plot, the community must defend its resource against intrusion by outsiders and against incursion by its own members onto each others plots. Let us refer to the act of protecting borders as *exclusion* and assume that the (transaction) costs of exclusion are related directly to the length of the borders. The borders reach maximum length when each person has a private plot and they are shortest when everyone works the same plot. Therefore exclusion costs peak under individual private property. This simple model now can be used to draw several lessons.

First, the cost–benefit calculations required for finding an ideal (wealth maximizing) system of property rights have become rather complicated once we allow for exclusion and governance. In traditional economics, producers maximize their profits by minimizing the cost of production for each level of output. In our case, the community must simultaneously economize on three fronts—in production, in exclusion, and in governance—in order to minimize total costs.

The second point is that there is no general solution to the problem of maximizing the net yield of the resource. No system of property rights is universally ideal. Depending on circumstances, the optimal solution may involve open access, communal property, intermediate plots, or exclusive individual plots. In each case, the answer depends on the characteristics of costs in production, exclusion, and governance. Prohibitive exclusion costs render any form of exclusive ownership impractical and make open access the optimal solution; relatively low internal governance costs and high exclusion costs can make communal property the ideal arrangement; and factors that sharply reduce exclusion costs make individual private property more attractive.

The third lesson is that a host of factors influences governance and exclusion costs. These factors include the physical characteristics of the resource, production methods, the technology of measurement and enforcement, the relative prices of inputs used to enforce exclusion, existing institutions, and political and social organizations, and natural barriers to entry by outsiders (such as distance or high mountains).

The fourth point is that cultural factors or social values (norms and customs) appear to have an independent impact on the costs of governance and exclusion, but their role is not well understood. Social values can encourage self-control, obedience to authorities, and a communal spirit. Most scholars agree that cultural factors evolve slowly and often spontaneously, rather than as the product of a purposive action by organizations. Therefore, it is unlikely that governments will be able to use social values as instruments of public policy and manipulate norms and customs—like monetary authorities manipulate nominal interest rates. Yet, good knowledge of informal institutions will help policymakers design effective formal rules that do not clash with prevailing social values. Recent work by game theorists suggests that the growth of trust and cooperation is a delicate and time-consuming process, but the end of cooperation—defection—can come swiftly (Milgrom and Roberts 1992). Cooperation in games characterized by the prisoners' dilemma requires more stringent assumptions (such as repeated play) than does defection.[5] In the long run, people who initially cooperate for selfish reasons may acquire a taste for cooperation, and policymakers may enhance this process by creating formal institutions that reinforce cooperation.

Our fifth lesson concerns the (tacit) assumption of the naive theory of property rights that communities always will agree on arrangements that maximize the joint wealth of their members. The assumption is arbitrary and neglects the role of redistribution. To illustrate the point, consider a situation where external changes make it economical to shift from communal property all the way to individual plots. Even though the change would increase the joint wealth of the community, some people may decide to block the reforms because they fear that the powerful among them will take the opportunity to increase their share of the resource. The possibility also exists that a subgroup within a community, primarily motivated by redistribution, may force an uneconomical change in property rights in order to increase their shares of a shrinking pie.

The sixth and final point is that our model takes for granted that communities of users are in full control of their resources. In practice, the rules of the game often are set, not by the local users of a resource, but by a high and distant authority such as a central government. The goals of distant politicians and administrators often conflict with the goals of the users, and pure information problems multiply, the further authority is removed from the operational level. Inappropriate division of authority can waste resources (Ostrom 1990).

Levels of Analysis

A theory of social systems has three components: (1) the institutional environment of the people and their organizations, which shapes their behavior; (2) the responses of individuals and organizations to their environment; and (3) the collective outcome of the individual responses.[6] A scholarly study can focus on any or all of these components. The different research approaches are distinguished by what phenomena they try to explain and what factors they take as given. Another important distinction is drawn between theories for explaining or predicting phenomena and prescriptive theories of institutional design. In general, theories for describing social systems or predicting their response to outside stimuli can be more abstract and stylized than prescriptive theories of institutional design without losing their relevance (Eggertsson, in press). In other words, it is simpler to describe how an established social system functions than to analyze what happens when the authorities intervene and try to change the nature of the system. People may respond to new institutional arrangements in various ways, which depend on circumstances and are hard to predict.

The different levels of analysis are best described with examples from the literature. First consider Cheung's (1974, 1975, 1979) excellent studies of rent control in twentieth century Hong Kong. For his purposes, Cheung takes the institutional environment as given and concentrates both on individual responses to new regulations and on the collective outcome of individual responses (the micro-to-macro transition). Cheung relies on applied price theory, detailed specification of the legal constraints, and on the notion of transaction costs. The analysis provides a powerful and convincing explanation of the market response, but it also makes clear that the outcomes depend on particular institutional arrangements in Hong Kong that a scholar could not have anticipated. The Cheung studies illustrate how people often respond to institutional change with adjustments on several margins. Successful design of new regulations for achieving specific results, while avoiding undesirable side-effects (such as premature demolition and restructuring of tenements in order to escape rent control), frequently requires extensive information that can be obtained only through an extended trial-and-error process of learning. These difficulties suggest that, in institutional design, small-scale experiments often are needed to avoid the cost of large-scale errors.

Next, consider studies of the logic of economic organization within a given institutional framework. These studies focus on how people set up internal governance systems and contract with each other to increase the value of their assets and limit the waste of resources. This work includes Williamson's (1985, 1993) investigations of capitalistic organization, Barzel's (1982) analysis of market practices, Goldberg's (1976a, 1976b) work on relational contracting, McCloskey's (1989) examination of the English open-field system, and Ostrom's (1990) study of the utilization of common-pool resources.[7] In these studies the use of standard microeconomics and game theory, augmented by transaction costs and attention to institutional constraints, gives reasonably good results.

Another set of studies attempts to explain how people and their social and political organizations bring about marginal changes in the institutional framework. Scholars working in this area have used the rational choice model and the information and transaction costs perspective to study collective decisions, the structure of political organizations, and the interaction between political and economic organizations. A sample of this work is found in Alt and Shepsle (1990). Also, Weingast's (1984) use of agency theory to study the U.S. congressional bureaucratic system and work by Weingast and Marshall (1988) on the industrial organization of Congress belong to this category, as do various studies in the economics of regulation and in public choice. This line of work has taught us that the pure market analogy usually is not appropriate for analyzing political processes and decisions, whereas tools such as agency theory, the theory of contracts, and other elements of the new theory of institutions are more helpful (Bates 1991).[8]

The final example are studies that seek to explain large-scale changes in the institutional framework (North 1981, 1990; Ensminger 1992). The evolution of social and political foundations of secure markets is a critical research topic in this area, but secure markets are important for the development of modern decentralized economies. When markets are insecure, people are reluctant to make long-term specialized investments or engage in exchange with anonymous or unrelated partners. Secure markets emerge when the state can make credible commitment to honor its contracts and avoid predatory behavior, and when private individuals are able to make such commitments to each other (North and Weingast 1989; Weingast 1993). Although these studies have identified political developments that support secure markets—such as emerging balance of power between the crown and parliament or a federal system which combines local autonomy in economic affairs with the free flow of resources between members of the federation—these studies also suggest that credible commitments require the support of appropriate social norms and cultural traits (Weingast 1993; North 1993). Arrow (1990) uses the term "commercial morality" in this context. A theory of commercial morality is critical for a better understanding of long-term institutional change, such as the transition to secure markets in the Third World or in the former Soviet Union and Eastern Europe, but a sound theory of the formation of culture still evades us (Eggertsson 1993b).

Conclusion

I have argued that secure control of resources is a critical component of a sound economic system, but cost considerations often make control insecure or nonexistent. A critic may argue that secure control is not enough; it is also essential how control of the various dimensions of resources is divided among various categories of people. The critic is both right and wrong. With full control of their resources, rational people will negotiate partitions of control and exchange rights of control, if the rearrangement increases their joint wealth. However full control is an ideal concept, a nonexisting state of affairs, and the costs of transacting may restrict and distort the transfer of control. In reality, the people who generate systems of property rights are constrained by history, ignorance, and transaction costs, and they primarily pursue their self-interest. The resulting division of control also reflects outcomes of processes for collective action, such as the workings of legislatures. The notion that people generally can agree on arrangements that maximize the joint wealth of their community is a theoretical myth.

Some critics seem to believe that the economics of institutions maintains the hypothesis that all institutions are efficient and that all institutional change is designed to increase wealth. The critics seem to attribute to practitioners of our approach the absurd belief that the institutions of Tropical Africa, Eastern Europe, Iceland, the United States, and Cuba all rate at the top of some general scale for economic efficiency. Our story is different. Although the theory discussed above has all people rationally pursuing their goals, their actions are constrained by various factors, including political processes that sometimes wash out individual attempts to seek optimum solutions. Only in special cases do we find support for Becker's (1992 p. 67–68) formulation of the *weak efficiency hypothesis* that "institutions evolve for various reasons, but whatever their intent including 'exploitation' of weak groups, they accomplish their goal efficiently; that is to minimize 'transaction costs.'"

In the discussion above, I frequently substituted the word "control" for the term "property rights" in order to avoid confusion caused by multiple definitions of property rights in the literature. Property rights have a specific meaning in law that is narrower than in the economics of property rights. Similarly, the concepts of rights and duties have various normative connotations in social science and political philosophy that differ from the use of the concept in the economics of property rights.

My final words relate to the limits of the rational choice model and the need to experiment with alternative models of behavior. In economics and the other social sciences, the new concern with information—how people collect information and how they behave with incomplete information—signifies a revolution, but the *information revolution* is still young. So far research has focused on measurement and enforcement problems and to some extent on the limited capacity of the human brain to process large batches of data. Limited information also implies that people lack complete or correct models of their worlds, which compels them to use a variety of incomplete models of reality to process data (North 1993, Denzau and North 1994). To understand the nature of learning and the paths of the human mind, we must move to a new level of scholarship and study man (rather than society) as a system. The topic is an important frontier of research. In the future it is likely that scholars will use not one but several models of man of varying sophistication, depending on the nature of their work.

NOTES

1. In social science there is considerable confusion over vocabulary in the new subfields that use the rational choice model to study institutions. In this chapter, I use the term *property rights economics* interchangeably with terms such as the *economics of institutions,* the *new institutionalism,* or *neoinstitutional economics.* Although there are differences among them, I choose to emphasize their commonality.

2. I use the terms, *systems* or *structure of property rights,* interchangeably with the terms, *institutional environment* or *framework.*

3. The discussion is based on my 1990 survey of the economics of institutions (Eggertsson 1990), but the framework has been extended and clarified (Eggertsson 1993a).

4. In the economics of institutions, contracts can be formal or informal, written or unwritten. The view of exchange relationships as being embodied in a network of contracts, and the recognition that the structure of contracts involves informal rules (Landa 1994), opens a bridge to the economic sociology of Granovetter (1992) and others.

5. In game theory, the *prisoners' dilemma* refers to strategic situations where cooperation among all the players is the best alternative, but for each individual player the best expected outcome (payoff) comes from not cooperating with the other players. As a result, all the players defect and receive a smaller payoff than they would have received under cooperation. The problem or dilemma arises because of lack of trust. Cooperation by one person, when the others defect, brings her heavy losses, and she cannot trust that other people will cooperate—they cannot credibly commit themselves to cooperation. Ostrom et al. (1993, 1994) have studied cooperation in the use of common pool resources, employing the tools of theoretical, applied, and experimental game theory.

6. In his important study of the foundations of social theory, Coleman (1990, pp. 1–23) argues that a complete theory of social systems should have a macro-to-micro component, an individual action component, and a micro-to-macro component. In other words, the theory should show how the physical and social environment defines the opportunities that people have, then analyze how typical individuals respond to their environments, and finally explain how individual actions interact and sum up to become final outcomes.

7. Milgrom and Roberts (1992) provide a user-friendly survey of analytical methods and results. Also see Werin and Wijkander (1992) for a collection of papers on contract economics by leading scholars.

8. Agency theory examines the relationship between an agent and a principal who has transferred control over her resources to the agent. Both the principal and the agent may cheat because usually they don't share the same goals and have incomplete information about the motives and actions of each other. The theory studies the outcome of such relationships and also how various contractual arrangements limit agency problems.

REFERENCES

Alchian, A. A. 1965. Some economics of property rights. *Il Politico* 30:816–829. Originally published in 1961 by the Rand Corporation; reprinted in A. A. Alchian, 1977. *Economic Forces at Work*. Liberty Press, Indianapolis.

Alt, J. E. and K. A. Shepsle, eds. 1990. *Perspectives on Positive Political Economy*. Cambridge University Press, Cambridge, UK.

Arrow, K. J. 1990. Pages 133–151 *in* R. Swedberg, ed. *Economics and Sociology. Redefining their Boundaries: Conversations with Economists and Sociologists*. Princeton University Press, Princeton, NJ.

Barzel, Y. 1982. Measurement costs and the organization of markets. *Journal of Law and Economics* 25:27–48.

Barzel, Y. 1989. *Economic Analysis of Property Rights*. Cambridge University Press, Cambridge, UK.

Bates, R. H. 1991. Perspectives on the new political economy. A critique. Pages 261–272 *in* G. M. Meier, ed. *Politics and Policy Making in Developing Countries*. ICS Press, San Francisco.

Becker, G. S. 1992. Comments. Pages 66–71 *in* L. Werin and H. Wijkander, eds. *Contract Economics*. Basil Blackwell, Oxford, UK.

Bell, D. E., H. Raiffa, and A. Tversky 1988. *Decision Making. Descriptive, Normative and Prescriptive Interactions*. Cambridge University Press, Cambridge, UK.

Cheung, S. N. S. 1969. Transaction costs, risk aversion, and the choice of contractual arrangements. *Journal of Law and Economics* 12:23–42.

Cheung, S. N. S. 1970. The structure of a contract and the theory of nonexclusive resources. *Journal of Law and Economics* 13:49–70.

Cheung, S. N. S. 1974. A theory of price control. *Journal of Law and Economics* 17:53–71.

Cheung, S. N. S. 1975. Roofs or stars: The stated intents and actual effects of a rent ordinance. *Economic Inquiry* 13:1–21.

Cheung, S. N. S. 1979. Rent control and housing reconstruction: The postwar experience of prewar premises in Hong Kong. *Journal of Law and Economics* 22:27–53.

Coase, R. H. 1937. The nature of the firm. *Economica* 4:386–405.

Coase, R. H. 1960. The problem of social cost. *Journal of Law and Economics* 3:1–44.

Coleman, J. S. 1990. *Foundations of Social Theory*. Belknap, Harvard University Press, Cambridge, MA.

Cook, K. S. and M. Levi 1990. *The Limits of Rationality*. University of Chicago Press, Chicago.

Cooter, R. D. and T. Ulen 1988. *Law and Economics*. HarperCollins, New York.

Demsetz, H. 1967. Toward a theory of property rights. *American Economic Review* 57:347–359.

Demsetz, H. 1988. *The Organization of Economic Activity* (2 vols.). Basil Blackwell, Oxford, UK.

Denzau, A. T. and D. C. North 1994. Shared mental models: Ideologies and institutions. *Kyklos* 47:3–31.

Eggertsson, T. 1990. *Economic Behavior and Institutions*. Cambridge University Press, Cambridge, UK.

Eggertsson, T. 1992. Analyzing institutional successes and failures: A millennium of common mountain pastures in Iceland. *International Review of Law and Economics* 12:423–437.

Eggertsson, T. 1993a. The economics of institutions: Avoiding the open-field syndrome and the perils of path dependence. *Acta Sociologica* 36:223–237.

Eggertsson, T. 1993b. Mental models and social values: North's institutions and credible commitment. *Journal of Institutional and Theoretical Economics* 149:24–28.

Eggertsson, T. 1994. The economics of institutions in transition economies. Pages 19–50 *in* S. Schiavo-Campo, ed. *Institutional Change and the Public Sector in Transitional Economies.* The World Bank, Washington, D.C.

Eggertsson, T. In press. The social science of wealth. *In* W. J. Samuels and S. G. Medema, eds. *How Should Economists Do Economics?* Edward Elgar, London.

Ensminger, J. 1992. *Making a Market. The Institutional Transformation of an African Society.* Cambridge University Press, Cambridge, UK.

Field, B. C. 1986. *Induced Changes in Property Rights Institutions* (Research paper). University of Massachusetts, Department of Agriculture, Amherst.

Field, B. C. 1989. The evolution of property rights. *Kyklos* 42:319–345.

Furubotn, E. G. and R. Richter, eds. 1991. *The New Institutional Economics.* J. C. Mohr, Tübingen.

Furubotn, E. G. and R. Richter, eds. 1993. The new institutional economics. Recent progress; expanding frontiers. Special issue: *Journal of Institutional and Theoretical Economics,* Vol. 149.

Galenson, D. W. 1989. *Markets in History. Economic Studies of the Past.* Cambridge University Press, Cambridge, UK.

Goldberg, V. P. 1976a. Toward an expanded theory of contract. *Journal of Economic Issues* 10:45–61.

Goldberg, V. P. 1976b. Regulation and administered contracts. *Bell Journal of Economics* 7:426–441.

Gordon, H. S. 1954. The economic theory of a common property resource: The fishery. *Journal of Political Economy* 62:124–142.

Granovetter, M. 1992. Economic institutions as social constructions: A framework for analysis. *Acta Sociologica* 35:3–12.

Klein, B., R. G. Crawford, and A. A. Alchian 1978. Vertical integration, appropriable rents, and the competitive contracting process. *Journal of Law and Economics* 21:297–326.

Landa, J. T. 1994. *Trust, Ethnicity and Identity. Beyond the New Institutional Economics of Ethnic Trading. Networks, Contract Law and Gift Exchange.* University of Michigan Press, Ann Arbor.

Libecap, G. D. 1989. *Contracting for Property Rights.* Cambridge University Press, Cambridge, UK.

Lueck, D. 1993. Contracting into the commons. Pages 43–60 *in* T. L. Anderson and R. T. Simmons, eds. *The Political Economy of Custom and Culture.* Rowman and Littlefield, Lanham, MD.

McCloskey, D. N. 1989. The open fields of England: Rent, risk, and the rate of interest, 1300–1815. Pages 5–51 *in* D. W. Galenson ed. *Markets in History. Economic Studies of the Past.* Cambridge University Press, Cambridge, UK.

Milgrom, P. and J. Roberts 1992. *Economics, Organization and Management.* Prentice-Hall, Englewood Cliffs, NJ.

North, D. C. 1981. *Structure and Change in Economic History.* Cambridge University Press, Cambridge, UK.

North, D. C. 1990. *Institutions, Institutional Change and Economic Performance.* Cambridge University Press, Cambridge, UK.

North, D. C. 1993. Institutions and credible commitment. *Journal of Institutional and Theoretical Economics* 149:11–23.

North, D. C. and B. R. Weingast. 1989. Constitutions and credible commitments: The evolution of the institutions of public choice in 17th century England. *Journal of Economic History* 49:803–832.

Olson, M. 1965. *The Logic of Collective Action.* Harvard University Press, Cambridge, MA.

Ostrom, E. 1990. *Governing the Commons: The Evolution of Institutions for Collective Actions.* Cambridge University Press, Cambridge, UK.

Ostrom, E., J. Walker, and R. Gardner. 1993. Covenants with and without a sword: Self-governance is possible. Pages 127–156 *in* T. L. Anderson and R. T. Simmons, eds. *The Political Economy of Custom and Culture. Informal Solutions to the Commons Problem.* Rowman and Littlefield, Lanham, MD.

Ostrom, E., J. Walker, and R. Gardner 1994. *Rules, Games, and Common-Pool Resources.* University of Michigan Press, Ann Arbor.

Schlager, E. and E. Ostrom. 1993. Property rights regimes and coastal fisheries: An empirical analysis. Pages 13–42 *in* T. L. Anderson and R. T. Simmons, eds. *The Political Economy of Custom and Culture. Informal Solutions to the Commons Problem.* Rowman and Littlefield, Lanham, MD.

Warming, J. 1911. Om "grundrente" af fiskegrunde. *Nationalökonomisk Tidsskrift:*495–506. Also see P. Andersen, 1983. On rent of fishing grounds: A translation of J. Warming's 1911 Article, with an introduction. *History of Political Economy* 15:391–396.

Weingast, B. R. 1984. The congressional–bureaucratic system: A principal–agent perspective. *Public Choice* 44:147–192.

Weingast, B. R. 1993. Constitutions as governance structures: The political foundations of secure markets. *Journal of Institutional and Theoretical Economics* 149:286–311.

Weingast, B. R. and W. J. Marshall 1988. The industrial organization of congress; or, why legislatures, like firms, are not organized as markets. *Journal of Political Economy* 96:132–163.

Werin, L. and H. Wijkander, eds. 1992. *Contract Economics.* Basil Blackwell, Oxford, UK.

Williamson, O. E. 1971. The vertical integration of production: Market failure consideration. *American Economic Review* 61:112–123.

Williamson, O. E. 1985. *The Economic Institutions of Capitalism.* Free Press, New York.

Williamson, O. E. 1993. The evolving science of organization. Pages 36–63 *in* E. G. Furubotn, and R. Richter, eds. *The New Institutional Economics.* J. C. Mohr, Tübingen.

PART III

Culture, Economic Development, and Property Rights

CHAPTER 9

Culture and Property Rights

JEAN ENSMINGER

Introduction

The structure of property rights always has distributional consequences. In any given society those who find such distribution culturally acceptable, that is, consistent with their values concerning the
just distribution of rewards, may voluntarily comply with the norms
that enforce such institutions. In other words, they self-enforce, or
comply with rules even when they could get away with breaking
them. Voluntary compliance with social norms forms the backbone
of society. Others who do not find the existing property rights structure ideologically acceptable or sufficiently materially rewarding may
still comply due to fear of community reprisals in the form of
informal sanctions. Such informal sanctions may play out in the
inability of a young man or woman to find a marriage partner willing
to marry into his or her family, or the failure of other households to
come to the rescue in times of need. The power of informal sanctioning, especially in less developed small-scale societies, points to the
extreme degree of interlocking values and institutions within societies. Cross-cutting ties through kinship and the social organization
of production and consumption serve as extremely effective mechanisms for maintenance of social order and social norms. Finally,
formal third-party enforcement may exist to deter those who are
most reluctant to cooperate with institutional norms.

The relative dependence upon the three forms of enforcement
varies tremendously across developed and developing societies, large
and small-scale. It also varies depending upon the degree of cultural
homogeneity in the society and the degree of stability in institutions
such as property rights. It may vary depending upon the absolute
level of inequality generated by the property rights, but systems of

gross inequality have the capacity to be ideologically enforced even by those they most disadvantage.

The relationship between culture and property rights becomes most exaggerated under conditions of change. When property rights are changed in such a way that they violate preconceived notions of fair distribution (at least for some significant portion of the population) we can predict a move away from self-enforcement of property rights to more dependence upon community and third-party formal sanctioning. Under these conditions, the costs of negotiating, monitoring, and enforcing new rights (the transaction costs) may undermine whatever efficiency benefits have been anticipated by a change in property rights. Should this be the case, a likely result will be the failure of new property rights. This chapter argues that this is the outcome witnessed all across the African continent, as new property rights have been formally imposed upon African societies. In particular, Kenya has been at the vanguard of national movements toward privatization of land in Africa, and its experiences have been replicated over much of the continent.

Policy planners in Africa confront an intriguing puzzle. At the same time that many Africa societies are changing social norms and indigenous rights in property to more individualistic systems approaching privatization, we find increasing numbers of societies backing away from government-sponsored formal systems of freehold land tenure. Even more curious, we often find the very same societies that evolved indigenous privatization, shunning government programs. Obviously something about the supply of formal rights imposed by governments is not meeting the demand for property right change at the local level. Some simple economic explanations provide partial answers: the transaction costs of the registration process are high, and undeveloped markets in essential complementary factors of production (particularly capital) may be constraining growth rather than property rights in land. But these explanations are not the whole story. Most agricultural production in Africa is still kin-based and highly risky. Lineages are not just kinfolk, they share some of the characteristics of corporations: they cooperate in labor, risk management, and investment. Fundamental to the high level of trust and cooperation that such systems enjoy are basic guarantees of subsistence in the short run, through access to land, and the long run, through inheritance of that land. Property right changes that violate this cultural complex of complementary interdependencies are doomed to fail. In deciding whether to comply with new property rights, a farmer will weigh the costs and benefits of compliance, and these will include the costs kinfolk might inflict for violation of prevailing ideology concerning just distribution. These costs also include loss of reciprocal support and cooperation from those who desire or feel the need to sanction norm violations. Thus, the fit between formal and informal institutions and values is key to the former's success.

New institutional economists have long appreciated the significance of the role of institutions in economic performance (North 1981; Eggertson 1990). Over the years, the challenge to be all-inclusive has moved further from the domain of institutions with obvious bearing upon economics, such as property rights (North and Thomas 1973), into the realm of informal social institutions (North 1990), and finally culture itself (Denzau and North 1994; Greif 1994; Putnam 1993). Anthropologists should applaud this trend, as it not only highlights the significance of their comparative advantage in the stock of knowledge but also reiterates the position taken by many of them. North (1990) brought informal institutions to the fore because they are important constraints on economic behavior—they both determine the calculus through which the all important incentives of formal rules will affect choice, and they provide for much of the enforcement that is essential to any economy. In North's words (1990:36):

> ... formal rules, in even the most developed economy, make up a small (although very important) part of the sum of constraints that shape choices; a moment's reflection should suggest to us the pervasiveness of informal constraints. In our daily interaction with others, whether within the family, in external social relations, or in business activities, the governing structure is overwhelmingly defined by codes of conduct, norms of behavior, and conventions. Underlying these informal constraints are formal rules, but these are seldom the obvious and immediate source of choice in daily interactions.

The need to better understand informal constraints is highlighted by the fact that, "the informal constraints that are culturally derived will not change immediately in reaction to changes in the formal rules. As a result the tension between altered formal rules and the persisting informal constraints produces outcomes that have important implications for the way economies change. . ." (North 1990:45). This last point is beautifully illustrated by the evidence of formally imposed private property rights in African land. An examination of the process of land tenure change in Africa clearly reveals the importance of *complementarity* between informal and formal institutions. When formal systems are imposed upon a society with which they are out of accord, self-enforcement may erode and externally engineered incentives may fail to yield the predicted results.

Africa provides a fascinating laboratory for testing theories of property rights. The vast majority of the continent still recognizes customary rights to land (generally in the form of commons in pastoral areas and control by the lineage or chief in farming areas), but there is also no shortage of experiments in government and locally initiated privatization. Yet at the same time that new government initiatives furthering privatization are underway, there is increasing evidence from anthropologists and other Africanists (Fleuret 1988; Haugerud 1983, 1989; Okoth-Ogendo 1986; Shipton 1988) that even the longest running national privatization efforts are unraveling, reverting to customary rights, and show few if any investment and productivity benefits over indigenous systems (Bruce and Migot-Adholla 1994). Does this mean, as one might conclude by reading between the lines of the anthropologists' reports, that Africans are communitarian and privatization is just inconsistent with their values, social norms, and social organization? Perhaps to a degree, but this ignores the forces of demographic and economic change which have driven changes in those very same values and social norms and have led to indigenous movement toward greater privatization in the absence of state programs. But the alternative is not to conclude that freehold property rights can be simply transplanted in Africa. As many anthropologists have noted and new institutional economists have accepted, "Property rights are always embedded in the institutional structure of a society, and the creation of new property rights demands new institutional arrangements to define and specify the way by which economic units can co-operate and compete" (North and Thomas 1973:5). As a consequence, when not properly embedded, new property rights become unimplementable and unenforceable. As Eggertson (1994:19) puts it, "The weakness of property rights analysis is its limited understanding of informal institutions, how they evolve and how they relate to formal institutions."

We know a great deal about African land tenure in the colonial, postcolonial, and contemporary eras. The cases are sufficiently numerous and detailed for us to make some real headway in understanding the place of property rights in African development, and even to make some suggestions for policy implications. A recent volume (Bruce and Migot-Adholla 1994) of quantitative studies on the effects of tenure security upon agricultural performance also provides us with much needed cross-cultural work from a unified and rigorous framework. I shall argue in this chapter that the basic assumptions of property rights theory (Demsetz 1967:350; North and Thomas 1973) are correct—as relative prices change (perhaps through demographic pressure, expanded commercial opportunities or new technologies—all of which may increase the value of land) new social norms and property rights emerge to internalize the beneficial and harmful effects and adjust to the new cost–benefit position. There is strong evidence that under these conditions of changing relative prices (especially an increase in the value of land relative to other commodities), African societies have moved toward increasing exclusivity of land rights since before colonialism.[1] Some even go so far as to see a convergence in this direction (Bruce, Migot-Adholla and Atherton 1994:262). But Demsetz (1967:350) also reminds us that the gains from property right change must exceed the costs in order to justify change. Further (p. 347), for new property rights to exist, the owner must possess "the consent of fellow men to allow him to act in particular ways. An owner expects the community to prevent others from interfering with his actions, provided that these actions are not prohibited in the specification of his rights." Increasing evidence from Africa is calling into question both of these conditions: (1) whether the gains of new property rights justify the transaction costs, and (2) whether the fit between customary tenure, social norms, and the new property rights is sufficient to lend legitimacy to their enforcement. If these conditions are not met, then privatization and titling does not necessarily yield more secure property rights. To understand why this is the case, we must examine the cost–benefit structure of property rights and the incentives they provide in the social context.

Imposed property rights are not endogenous, and as a consequence, they may fail to "connect" with other complementary indigenous norms and institutions. This is evidenced in Africa today in the most extreme case—where people with title deeds place so little value on them they do not bother to update their own titles—thus yielding a failure of self-enforcement.

In this chapter I begin with a brief sketch of customary land tenure in Africa. Next I turn to the Kenyan case, where we find evidence that formal titling in Kenya, the country with the first and most comprehensive government titling program, is unraveling. Although many Kenyan societies were well into the process of increasing privatization prior to the national government's efforts, the latter have been far less successful than might be expected. Evidence indicates that part of the failure can be attributed to the transaction costs of maintaining the titling system and lagging factor markets in capital and labor. But I shall argue that there is equally compelling evidence that the formal system is conflicting with the needs and interests of farmers as defined by their current production strategies based upon largely lineage-based systems. In short, there has been a failure of the formal system to properly interface with the informal.

Customary Land Tenure in Africa

One of the most interesting findings from a survey of indigenous systems of land tenure in Africa is the degree of similarity one finds in land tenure across comparable agro-climatic zones on the continent (Migot-Adholla and Bruce 1994:5; Migot-Adholla et al. 1994a:99).[2] One can capture the underlying principles of a few general types relatively simply, which is surprising on a continent made up of thousands of ethnic groups with autonomous institutions. A common characteristic in almost all African customary systems is for use rights to be assigned at the household level, while transfer rights are assigned at a higher level, such as by the lineage, clan, or chiefdom (Matlon 1994:65).

The major types of land tenure in Africa can be crudely lumped into common property (managed either by all members of the ethnic group or some recognized large subset), lineage controlled, and chief-controlled. Typically one finds common property where land is used by hunters and gatherers or pastoralists. Such areas are generally arid and have low population density, rendering more restrictive control costly due to the high transaction costs of negotiating, monitoring, and enforcing controls.

Lineage or clan control is especially prevalent in Africa. Generally the person who cleared the land first is entitled to use it and pass it down to his descendants (through the male line in patrilineal systems and through the sister's son in matrilineal systems). Over time, such lineages become large, as do the areas of land that they control. Generally, the head of the lineage has authority to allocate land to those with need, thus there is a tendency for land to be relatively efficiently matched in people–land ratios.[3] This system also affords the easy accommodation of newly married wives without necessarily having to deprive existing wives in a polygynous household. Typically a husband allocates each wife (or son's wife) separate parcels over which she has nearly complete control in farm management decisions. Upon the death of the father it was typical for the land to be subdivided among sons or for the eldest or youngest son to inherit the father's land, while the lineage allocated unoccupied land to the other sons. Until relatively recently, and still in many parts of Africa, land was not scarce. Once lineage lands became inadequate, sons set out to the frontier to break new ground and begin the process once again. The lineage system puts a premium upon *use* of the land rather than transfer rights. Those who fail to use the land risk losing it.[4] In some areas this provided people with an incentive to plant cocoa and coffee very sparsely over the plot, not for their economic value but in order to lay claim to the land (for Ivory Coast, see Koby 1979; Cameroon, see Levin 1976; Zanzibar, see Middleton 1961, cited in Feder and Noronha 1987:153). Once the frontier was gone social norms sometimes changed to allow for equal shares to sons, and this has necessitated the subdivision of parcels.

In more politically centralized African societies that had chiefs, paramount chiefs, and kings, all transfer rights in land ultimately rested with the central authority, who allocated use rights to households. When land failed to be used it reverted to the control of the centralized authority. Such systems shared many of the attributes of the lineage systems but were open to more widespread abuse by higher authorities once land became salable (see Firmin-Sellers, in press, for Ghana). One distinguishing characteristic of most of these systems is that prior to colonialism and the advent of cash cropping, land was rarely if ever recognized as a commodity over which individuals could sell their rights. But another general principle of such systems was enormous flexibility to respond to a wide range of shocks. Far from being conservatively timeless and unable to change, indigenous systems were dynamic and responded in quite predictable ways to the forces of demographic and economic change.

History of Kenyan Land Titling

Given the many endogenous efforts at privatization around the continent in the precolonial and early colonial days, it is not surprising that colonial governments, and later independent governments, experimented with nationalized tenure programs. In Kenya at least as long ago as 1933, the Carter land commission heard evidence arguing that communal tenure was retarding agricultural development and some advocated private tenure in the interests of development. Belief in the efficacy of fee-simple property rights was also shared by the African leaders of newly independent states. President Banda of

Malawi told the Parliament in 1967 that the absence of individual title was the main obstacle to development, "No-one is responsible for the uneconomic and wasted use of land because no-one holds land as an individual. Land is held in common. . ." (Malawi Parliamentary Debates 1967, cited in Chanock 1991:71).

Kenya was the first colony to initiate a nationwide effort to register land, and it was known as the Swynnerton plan (Swynnerton 1954).[5] Kenya has also experienced marked stability in government policy toward privatization, with the independent government of Kenya (since 1963) remaining deeply committed to land registration. As noted above, there were already areas in Kenya where customary tenure was moving in the direction of individualization and where land markets were developing. The Swynnerton plan attempted to speed up and formalize these efforts by imposing a system based upon 1925 English land law (Okoth-Ogendo 1986:79). The consolidation and registration began in the Kikuyu area in the 1950s and much of that area was registered by the end of the decade; Luo-land and Western Provinces were nearly completed by the mid-1970s. By 1981, over 6 million hectares had been registered nationally (Barrows and Roth 1990:269). Okoth-Ogendo estimated in 1993 that 90 percent of all land in farming districts had been privatized.

The goals of the Swynnerton plan (Swynnerton 1954) were to promote cash crop agriculture by consolidating scattered strips into units of "economic" size,[6] securing titles so as to encourage investment in the land, facilitate the extension of credit by use of title deeds to secure loans, reduce land disputes, and ease transfer. In fact, the planners consciously anticipated that titling would facilitate the concentration of land in the hands of farmers better able to farm more profitably. It was understood and accepted that this would create a landless class, who were expected to labor on the larger farms and in industry. The intention was that once consolidation, adjudication, and registration were complete, land would no longer be subject to customary law and would resemble English freehold tenure (Pedraza 1956; Sorrenson 1967).

Although Kenya's program is the best researched and most extensive in Africa, many other governments have attempted private titling, especially Ivory Coast and Malawi, but with variations: Botswana, Cameroon, Ghana, Lesotho, Liberia, Mali, Senegal, Sierra Leone, Somalia, South African reserves, Sudan, Swaziland, Uganda, and Zimbabwe (Feder and Noronha 1987:150; Shipton 1994:365). Meanwhile, socialist regimes have attempted collectivized land tenure in Ethiopia, Tanzania, and Mozambique with fairly disastrous results (see Shipton 1994:365 for case study references). Nigeria and the francophone countries proceeded by first declaring all lands as the property of the state, thus undermining lineage and chiefly claims and leaving the way open for outright land grabs by elites (Shipton 1994:365).

While those coming from a property rights tradition will easily discount the failures of socialized and nationalized efforts at land reform, explaining the unexpected consequences of the Kenya land reform and others like it (which most parallel the British system of freehold property rights) is more problematic. Not only have scholars failed to find strong evidence for the expected investment, productivity, and security effects from land titling (Bruce and Migot-Adholla 1994), but there is considerable evidence of reversion to customary tenure in titled areas, even those areas that prior to titling were experiencing indigenous shifts toward privatization.

Unraveling of Formal Title Systems in Kenya

Given that many African societies have been evolving systems of more privatized land tenure since the colonial days, one might expect the formalization of these changes at the national level to have been well received and effective. However, there is considerable evidence, much of it collected in detailed case studies by anthropologists, that things have not gone the way they were expected to go.

Data are mounting that what is occurring on the ground bears less and less resemblance to what is documented in land registries. Typically, parcels are subdivided among sons without them having legal title to the plots. What is more, even once the fathers die, the succession claims are often not registered. A government officer named Homan (1963, cited in Coldham 1979:618) reported that in the early 1960s "after about four years of full registration in Kiambu District [arguably the most developed in Kenya], over 3,000 titles are still registered in the names of deceased persons." Coldham (1979:618) himself observed that in East Kadianga (Luo-land in western Kenya) during 1966–1973, not more than 3.4 percent of successions (1 out of 29) had been registered, and in Gathinja during 1963–1974, not more than 21.4 percent (9 out of 42). Even more puzzling is the failure to register changes in title upon sale of the land. Coldham (1979:618) reports that in East Kadianga during 1966–1973, "at least 30 percent of all sales of land (13 out of 42) were unregistered, while in Gathinja during 1963–1974, the equivalent figure was 15 percent (2 out of 13). In Embu (Kenya), Haugerud (1983:73) also found similar evidence in 1979, twenty years after adjudication. Approximately 20 percent of her sample households occupied land registered in the name of an individual who was not a household member. Three-fifths of these (12 percent total) were living on land registered to a deceased person. She also found (1983:74) that refragmentation was common: 58 percent of sample households owned two or more pieces of land, 12 percent owned at least three parcels, and 6 percent owned at least four parcels. She noted that this degree of fragmentation approached that of the preconsolidation era.[7] In another study of a site in Luo-land, Migot-Adholla et al. (1994b:138) found that while 75 percent of the parcels in Kianjogu were titled, only 8 percent of the owners reported that they could be sold, thus implying that customary norms prevented them from doing so.

Mirroring many of North's (1990:45) statements about formal and informal institutions cited above, Coldham (1979:619) states the situation regarding customary versus formal land tenure clearly in the following passage:

> The fact that a title is registered, and that therefore the land ceases to be governed by customary law, is unlikely in itself to affect the behaviour of those concerned. Customary controls will continue to be exercised; customary institutions— like the 'redeemable sale' or the '*muhoi* tenancy' among the Kikuyu—will continue to exist; customary rules and procedures governing the transfer or inheritance of land will continue to be observed.

The literature leaves little doubt that formal land titling is not having the intended effects of increasing agricultural investment and productivity by providing greater security, or even, given its failure to replace customary norms of succession and transfer, of creating a land market. Why?

In my view the failure of formal land tenure change in Kenya is the result of the transaction costs of the registration process, the failure of complementary factor markets, and especially, incompatibility with the all-important social norms and organizations without which people cannot produce or enforce anything. I stop short of the position taken by some Africanists, however, whose tone sometimes suggests that customary systems are in equilibrium and suffer none of these limitations. Inheritance patterns are changing as land pressure intensifies, and these changes will drive further changes in customary land tenure. The real policy questions for Africa are when to leave customary systems to accommodate these changes and how to intervene if customary systems appear to no longer guarantee tenure security.

Economic Explanations for the Failure of Property Rights
Transaction Costs

The studies cited in Bruce and Migot-Adholla (1994), which fail to find compelling economic benefits as a result of land titling, certainly call into question whether the economic returns to society justify the transaction costs of the registration system. The costs from the point of view of Kenyan farmers themselves also appear to be prohibitive to some in both time and money.

Okoth-Ogendo (1986:88; see also Coldham 1979:618) describes the process of land registration as it related to succession, which under the original adjudication act was limited to five heirs. It should be borne in mind that in polygynous Kenya, which in the 1980s had the highest population growth rate in the world, men often had more than five heirs.

> The administration of this qualification [that only five heirs may succeed to any parcel of registered land], however, was turned over to local chiefs and courts rather than to the indigenous institutions or in consultation with them. As a result, the system turned out to be patently absurd, for *inter alia* its implementation depended very heavily on the active co-operation of potential heirs, particularly in the transmission of all relevant information relating to property left by intestate owners. For example, they were expected to report to their local chief the death of persons from whom they expected to inherit land. The chief was then required to transmit that information to the local court for the issuance of a certificate of succession. In that certificate, the court was required to indicate who the heirs and their respective shares were and, where the number exceeded five, to determine who among them would be allowed to succeed and how the rights of those excluded would be dealt with.
>
> To the extent that no provision was made for the participation of indigenous institutions, for example, family councils, clan elders, etc., in this procedure both at its reporting

and allocative stages, it remained to all intents and purposes a dead letter. Besides, to the extent that the procedure was patently inequitable, it became the cause of a great deal of *de facto* subdivision that was not reflected in the register. It is not surprising, therefore, that so very few applications for certificates of succession ever came up to the local courts.

This passage by Okoth-Ogendo captures both the cumbersome nature of the bureaucracy and also the unacceptable distributional consequences associated with disinheriting some of one's children.

Wangari (1990:70), writing on the land registration process in Embu, Kenya, also points to the inadequacy of the administrative structure and the simple logistical problems for rural families getting to towns in order to keep up their titles. Such trips can be extremely costly in time and money, and those who have lived in rural Africa will appreciate the fact that every trip to a government office does not necessarily result in finding the appropriate official, much less accomplishing the intended objective.

Many of the costs of land registration are the same regardless of the size of the parcel. It is not surprising, therefore, that the owners of larger parcels maintain their titles more often than do the owners of small parcels (Feder and Noronha 1987). From their Kenyan study, Migot-Adholla et al. (1994b:133) report that only 31.6 percent of households with less than $400 annual income have titles, while 87.9 percent of households with income above $2,250 per year have titles.[8] Time constraints, fees, and, in resettlement areas, the failure to have fully repaid purchase loans may explain the variation by wealth in use of titling. Haugerud (1989:84) for Embu, Blarel (1994:90) for Rwanda, Migot-Adholla et al. (1994a:102) for Ghana, and Ault and Rutman (1979:177) all suggest that the transaction costs of the registration process are not justified by the economic returns. The Land Tenure Center's comparative data (Bruce et al. 1994:256) estimate that survey and registration costs in smallholder agriculture run at least $50 to $100 per parcel, also calling into question the economics of this process from the point of view of African governments.

While transaction costs are clearly a relevant issue, they are not the whole story. Large landholders do appear to believe that titling is worth the expense, implying that there is some value (at least to some categories of farmer) in the process of registration. I turn next to the subject of lagging factor markets, which have also been suggested by many people as an explanation for the failure of titling to have positive economic effects.

Lagging Factor Markets in Capital and Labor

If land is not the constraining factor of production, it stands to reason that more formal property rights will accomplish little and probably not recoup their transaction costs. One can assume that the original architects of the Swynnerton plan in Kenya believed that title deeds must precede the widespread availability of credit because commercial lending institutions would require collateral. However, as innumerable researchers have noted, the development of capital markets in Africa, even in land-adjudicated countries like Kenya, has not lived up to expectations (Collier 1983). Barrows and Roth (1990:276) make the cogent point that when capital is limited by other factors, titling will merely *redistribute* the limited and nonexpanding (inelastic) supply.

Capital for agricultural investment is the key to the whole success of land registration. Titles were meant to provide sufficient collateral to open up commercial loans for investment in land improvement and purchase of necessary complementary inputs to raise agricultural productivity. The data on credit in Kenya are not altogether clear. Haugerud (1983:83) reports that only 15 percent of titles from one portion of the Embu coffee and cotton zones had current loans charged against them. Shipton (1992:374) reports a far lower rate of loans for Luo-land in Kenya. By 1991, sixteen years after land registration, only 6 percent of the registered parcels had ever been mortgaged to any financial institution. Okoth-Ogendo (1986:81) reports that in "Kisii and South Nyanza [Luo-land] districts, little more than 2 percent of registered smallholders were able to obtain secured or unsecured credit in any single year between 1970–1973." Migot-Adholla et al. (1994b:134) found a similar level of borrowing in their four Kenyan sites, where from 1987 to 1988 between 1 and 10.7 percent of households were currently borrowing. But of the 28 formal loans they recorded, only 12 were secured by land title. Citing Odingo's 1985 work, Barrows and Roth (1990:275) report that he, "found that farmers were reluctant to use land as collateral because of fear of losing it. About one-third of those sampled in Machakos had applied for credit, but very few had approached the commercial banks or used land as collateral. Only one percent had sought credit in Nakuru." In their quantitative Kenyan study in Njoro, Carter et al. (1994:159) found that capital was the limiting factor constraint for small farms, while labor was the limiting constraint for large farms. One of the most interesting questions raised by these findings is why titles have not led to an increase in the supply of credit. In order to address this question, we must delve more deeply into some norms and social practices in African societies. This brings us to the general question of the complementarity between informal institutions and formal land law.

Cultural Explanations for the Failure of Property Rights

Property rights in Africa are intimately wrapped up with kinship relations and rights over people. On the frontier, pioneers opened land as a means of attracting and controlling large numbers of dependents and followers (Kopytoff 1987). African agricultural production was and is lineage-based in most places. Formal land legislation conflicts with many of the social norms and relationships of production that are still crucial to agricultural success. We have seen the effects of these conflicts in a number of the studies cited above; they fall into the following domains: (1) consolidation was inconsistent with the ecological need for scattered strips and broke up cooperative work units, (2) the restrictions on the minimal allowable "economic unit" and the limit on heirs were inconsistent with indigenous norms of inheritance, (3) household composition was highly fluid over time, (4) asymmetries in information were great and meant that the educated were able to manipulate the system and gain what was perceived by others as illegitimate advantage, and finally, (5) the new property rights reduced the rights of many over the customary system, while enhancing those of the single titled "household head." To the extent that formal land tenure change failed to take account of these necessities of sound agricultural management, as well as "prevailing distributional norms," and the "vested interests they create" (Libecap 1989:116), it failed to take hold, and became mired in dispute, and worse yet, disuse.

Lack of Ecological Complementarity:
Fragmentation and Consolidation

As originally conceived, the Swynnerton plan put a great deal of emphasis upon the consolidation of fragments into one "economic unit" per household. A number of authors (including Bates 1989) have examined the political motivations of the colonial officials who promoted this practice. Although couched in the economic logic of efficiency and agrarian development, there is good reason to believe that consolidation also allowed the British to use land reform as a means of rewarding their friends, that is, the loyalists who fought against the Mau Mau during Kenya's war for independence, which also precipitated land reform. Although consolidation actually appears to have been welcomed later on in some politically less sensitive areas where it was also no longer an ecological liability (Fleuret 1988), the Embu experience is probably more typical. Haugerud (1983:74) found that much of the work of consolidation had been undone by the time of her survey in 1979, by which point 58 percent of households had more than one parcel. Embu is an area with high ecological diversity, ranging from the rich tea zone on the slopes of Mount Kenya, through the lucrative coffee area, to the far more arid cotton zone in the low-lying areas which is also good for cattle and where land is less scarce. Historically, households have split their holdings as a form of insurance. Given the re-creation of this pattern, one can only surmise that it still offers benefits that outweigh the costs of travel and dual maintenance.[9]

Fleuret (1988:149–152) notes that in the Msidunyi area of Taita, where they do not have irrigation, there is a high degree of fragmentation, with the mean number of parcels at 13. Fragmentation is a risk management strategy and there was much resistance to consolidation. In the nearby Iparenyi area of Taita, in contrast, the climate is much more favorable to cash crops such as coffee and there is water for irrigation. As a consequence, agriculture is less risky, farms are less fragmented, and consolidation (along with adjudication and registration) was complete by 1967, only four years after the start of the program in that area. Nevertheless, Fleuret (1988:149) notes an important problem associated with consolidation even in this area:

> [Traditional irrigation is] highly dependent on kinship relations and on the expression of those relations in landholding patterns for its success, in particular the proximity of close agnates [descendants of a common male ancestor] due to the partitioning of their father's holdings into individually held portions for each heir. But in Iparenyi, the act of consolidation has seriously disrupted the landownership pattern on which traditional water management rests. . . . Because the land reform program has as one of its consequences that close agnates no longer necessarily have holdings contiguous to one another, the basis for irrigation management has been transformed. Those who cooperate in such a system in Iparenyi now are business partners whose relationship is commercial rather than consanguine. Of the six existing systems, three are characterized by serious disagreements between the partners which inhibit the availability of water, and one has become privatized.

We see in this case a perfect instance of the trade-off between the economic rationale for consolidation (economies of scale) and the obvious increases in transaction costs due to the loss of kin connectedness that had benefited cooperation.

In a highly analogous situation, land adjudication among Masai pastoralists has also led to ecologically unviable units under management regimes that have no basis for traditional legitimacy (Coldham 1979:620–623). The Masai were the earliest pastoralists to be targeted with land tenure changes aimed at controlling overgrazing and the "tragedy of the commons." Coldham (1979:624) catalogs the disconnect with indigenous norms as follows:

> [The group ranch] introduces an alien system of land tenure: it creates boundaries which not only conflict with customary grazing patterns, but are the source of novel distinctions between members, invitees, and trespassers; and it establishes a new system of authority, and calls for the adoption of unfamiliar procedures based on election, representation, delegation, and the majority vote. In practice, as we have seen, the desired changes of behaviour have not occurred. The Masai continue their semi-nomadic existence in search of pasture regardless of ranch boundaries.

Lack of Complementarity with Social Organization: The Problem of Succession

The Swynnerton plan placed a great deal of import on the need to maintain economically viable units of land, and thus forbade the titling of units below a certain size (determined by local carrying capacity). The number of heirs was also limited to five to prevent rapid fragmentation of parcels through subdivision. As we have seen above, one response to these limitations was for families to subdivide the land anyway and merely fail to register the subdivisions, thus undermining the entire exercise (Okoth-Ogendo 1986:88). The conflict between the formal system and customary inheritance patterns was great. And in this instance, social institutions clearly outsurvived formal innovation. As Coldham (1979:617) notes, sometimes people were attracted to adjudication as a means to demarcate clear boundaries in areas where disputes were getting out of hand, but they did not intend to buy into a system that would also change their practices of conveyance.

Haugerud (1989:70) makes the important point that indigenous household composition was highly fluid and not well-suited to the inflexibility of title deeds. Only 20 percent of the households in her sample were nuclear families, which fit best with land registration, while about a quarter of the sample households had considerable changes in membership over her 20 months of fieldwork. Domestic conflict changed the composition of 27 percent of the sample households by one or more members. One of the advantages of customary tenure systems, where transfer rights were retained by the lineage, was the ability to respond quickly and frequently to needs for the reallocation of land.

Lack of Complementarity in Distribution:
The Problem of Asymmetries of Information

In the early days of land adjudication in Kikuyu (Sorrenson 1967) and Embu (Brokensha and Glazier 1973; Glazier 1985), there is considerable evidence that the educated elite took advantage of their position to secure far better and larger holdings than their less sophisticated kin. As Bates (1989:30–31) puts it, the educated had strong incentives for changes in property rights, they faced lower costs in pushing legal claims, they spoke the language of the colonizers, and the colonizers were dependent upon them for insight into local law and custom. Haugerud (1983:79) describes how mere knowledge of the implications of land registration and what was to come were used by the well-informed to gain advantage. In the early days, before most people understood what was happening, an assistant chief, his father, and other elders of his clan staked out claims in lowland Embu where the population density was relatively low and rights to land more ambiguous than in the tea and coffee zones. Because of his office, the assistant chief knew what evidence the land boards would consider legitimate for land claims, and the men were able to stake claim to much land prior to adjudication. These men wound up with parcels five to ten times the average size for that zone and also retained large claims in the richer zones.

As Libecap (1989:28) warns, "Distributional conflicts will be intensified if there are known serious information asymmetries among the competing parties regarding the evaluation of individual claims." This was certainly the case in Kenya's past, and quite likely in the present. While the population of Kenya is today quite literate by African standards, there are still large numbers of illiterate farmers (more of whom are women than men), who are vulnerable in the

courts as a consequence of their lack of familiarity with legal procedures and their lack of literacy. This is one argument for keeping as
many adjudication decisions regarding land as possible closer to the
village and out of the courts; in the village, information regarding
claims will be greater and the playing field more level (all other things
being equal).

Lack of Complementarity in the Distribution: Rights within the Household

When property rights are changed there are always winners and
losers. But it stands to reason that the closer the fit between the new
and old system, the less the injustice to prevailing distributions.
Libecap (1989:3–4) suggests that the net social gains from changes in
property rights will be modest specifically because the difficulty
involved in resolving the distribution conflicts that result is so great.
There is ample evidence from the Kenyan situation to support his
argument.

We have already noted above that the limitation on the number of
heirs resulted in disinheritance. So abhorrent was this perceived mis-
carriage of social justice, that households merely let titles lapse rather
than disinherit family members. But there were other mismatches of
rights between customary tenure systems and formal registration.
Most notably, women do much of the farming in Africa, and under
customary tenure were granted considerable control over farmland in
the form of usufruct rights and managerial control over the plots allocated to them by the household head. In the absence of a land market,
women's access to and control of property was considerable. With
land adjudication this changed markedly. Land was now registered
solely in one person's name and this was almost always the male
household head. Only 5 percent of parcels in Kenya are registered in
women's names, and rarely do sons have registered land while their
father is still living. With the development of a commercial credit
market and a land market, the potential now exists for titled heads of
households to sell their land (or lose it through loan default) and thus
extinguish all of the usufruct rights of women and the traditional lineage inheritance rights of sons.

Although the Kenyan registration process has always provided
some protection for the interests of others against sale of land, the
potential for mortgage foreclosure was not guarded against in the
original law. The protection against sale was built into the law in that
the land boards, which had to approve land sales, were specifically
entrusted to act paternalistically to look out for the best interests of

the landowner and his or her family (Okoth-Ogendo 1986:84). This meant that they had the authority to reject sales (and frequently did) if they deemed them not to be in the interest of the family, on the grounds that the land was the sole source of support for the family or that the remaining holding would be too small a parcel to sustain the family. The boards were also supposed to consult with other interested family members (especially wives and sons) prior to granting sale approval.[10] However, no such control upon loss of land due to loan default was built into the system (Okoth-Ogendo 1986:85).

I would argue that mortgage foreclosure, while it is an emotive issue anywhere, has been especially so in Kenya because of the failure of formal land law to adequately capture the full range of customary rights in land held by other parties. The fact that one member of a family can unilaterally extinguish those claims has caused enormous outrage. This is but one of the many examples in Africa where an inappropriate model based upon the assumption of uniform household preferences has led to unexpected consequences (cf. Guyer 1981). Although it may be the most extreme case, the Luo are worth considering in this context, as it is the best documented case of mortgage foreclosure.

Under customary tenure, Luo households were free to use the land, but a man could not transfer the rights of the lineage or his heirs by sale or gift to a stranger (Coldham 1978:94). Although Luo-land was one of the areas in Kenya that moved to greater privatization before land reform, land sales were rare and usually to clansmen. Shipton (1992:380) explains that the Luo have a segmentary lineage system, and that each genealogy is literally reflected in the landscape by the pattern of burials on local farms. Like many African peoples, the Luo revere their ancestors, who are buried on the family plot. To the Luo, (p. 375) "mortgaging the land is mortgaging the ancestors." Bank efforts to foreclose on land consistently meet with resistance or violence. People suspect that witchcraft is used against those buyers who try to settle, but eventually leave (p. 377). As one woman commented, "If you want to make an enemy for life, mess with a dead Luo" (p. 377). Land auctions have often been canceled for fear of violence or political repercussion, and for 13 months the AFC suspended its loan recovery program altogether (p. 378).

Under these circumstances, it is not surprising that banks place relatively little value upon title deeds as collateral for loans. They have learned that the prospects of foreclosure, at least in some areas, are too low to warrant the risk. Obviously this must affect the supply of credit and account at least in part for the failure of the anticipated increase in credit that was expected to flow from land registration. Thus, we see that what might appear as a "lagging factor market," has its roots more deeply in a failure of social complementarity between formal and informal norms and social organization. But is the root of the problem here really the segmentary lineage system of the Luo (as Shipton suggests), or the failure to properly acknowledge and give legal authority to the rights of all vested parties—namely, wives, widows, and sons—who may have had greater tenure security under customary law? I would suggest that the problem here is less the deep attachment to an ideology of burial and more an outrage over unjust distribution of property rights.

Conclusions

Anthropologists talk of the need for "contextual fit," in policy development (Shipton 1992:381), sociologists talk about "embeddedness," (Granovetter 1985), and institutional economists talk about the need for formal institutions to build upon informal institutions (North 1990). I suspect all of these theorists are talking to some degree about the same thing, but the abstractness of this language can obscure a great deal. There are in fact significant similarities and differences in the theoretical positions of all of these authors. I believe that by applying the concepts and theory to empirical case studies we are better able to move the debate forward and clarify points of agreement and difference.

I have attempted in this chapter to show that "contextual fit," or what I refer to as the complementarity between formal and informal institutions, really is crucial to successful property right change. But in my analysis I do not abandon a rational choice framework in which farmers make calculated choices concerning property rights under the constraints of prevailing distributional norms and their production systems. It just so happens that in Africa a large number of these constraints are connected to social relationships and kin. Violation of distributional norms is also a powerful motivation, perhaps too often overlooked by economists (see Knight 1992). Equally, embeddedness does not for me mean resistance to change, as I believe is well brought out in the evidence of indigenous embrace of privatization in the face of rising land values. For me, embeddedness means synchrony in change. During periods of rapid and intense exogenous shock, such as prevails in much of contemporary Africa, such adjustments may best be left to indigenous local institutions. However, there is ample evidence that these same exogenous shocks lead to increasing inequality and local heterogeneity, which eventually erode "community" and the cooperation, low transaction costs, and high self-enforcement that it affords (Taylor and Singleton 1993). Once this occurs, indigenous institutions may no longer be able to cope effectively and could benefit from national formal institutions designed as carefully as possible to fit with prevailing relations of production and distributional norms. Identifying the proper point and means of intervention is obviously *the* challenge for policy planners, and will demand a deep understanding of indigenous norms and local institutions.

NOTES

1. See Feder and Noronha (1987:154) for Ghana, Leakey (1977) and Muriuki (1974:70) for the Kikuyu of Kenya, Fleuret (1988:14) for the Taita of Kenya, Brokensha and Glazier (1973) for the Mbeere of Kenya, Dobson (1954) for Tanzania and Hecht (1985) for Ivory Coast.

2. For a recent overview of African land tenure see Shipton (1994).

3. Matlon (1994:47) demonstrates that this by no means ensures equality even under customary tenure. He found that average holdings varied by fourfold per capita in Burkina Faso. This was a result of historical sequencing and political influence. On the other hand, despite high population density, Blarel (1994:78) found that in Rwanda the incidence of absolute landlessness was rare under customary tenure.

4. Matlon (1994:54) notes that, in Burkina Faso, as land pressure increases people fear to lend land for more than one season.

5. For a discussion of the Ugandan and Zimbabwe privatization efforts, see Barrows and Roth (1990).

6. "Economic" size was defined locally according to the carrying capacity of the land. Local committees seem also to have given some consideration to the potential numbers of people who would have been rendered landless if the size was set too high (Haugerud 1983:73).

7. Similarly, in Rwanda Blarel (1994:89) found evidence that even shortly after registration, land was being sold and subdivided without a record of the transaction being made or the "title" being updated.

8. In Somalia (Roth et al. 1994:225) also found that whereas *all* large farms had title deeds, the same was not true of smaller farms.

9. In the only quantitative study of which I am aware in Africa on the costs and benefits of fragmentation, Blarel (1994:91) finds in Rwanda that the labor loss of walking due to fragmentation is more than compensated by the gains; furthermore, analysis reveals that farm fragmentation is not related to yields.

10. It is not clear how much local variation there was in practice concerning this stipulation.

ACKNOWLEDGMENTS

This chapter draws from the author's chapter entitled, "Changing Property Rights: Reconciling Formal and Informal Rights to Land in Africa," forthcoming in J. V. C. Nye and J. N. Drobak, eds. *Frontiers of the New Institutional Economics.* Academic Press, New York. The author wishes to acknowledge the generous research support provided, for three periods of fieldwork on which this chapter is based, by the following institutions: Fulbright-Hays, the Ford Foundation, the National Science Foundation (BSN-7904273), the Rockefeller Foundation, the National Institutes of Health (SSP 5 R01 HD213427 DBS), and the Beijer Institute. Finally, the National Museums of Kenya and the Institute of Development Studies at the University of Nairobi provided much appreciated institutional support during the fieldwork, and the Office of the President kindly granted research clearance.

REFERENCES

Ault, D. and G. Rutman. 1979. The development of individual rights to property in tribal Africa. *Journal of Law and Economics* 22(1): 163–182.

Barrows, R. and M. Roth. 1990. Land tenure and investment in African agriculture: Theory and evidence. *The Journal of Modern African Studies* 28(2):265–297.

Bates, R. 1989. *Beyond the Miracle of the Market: The Political Economy of Agrarian Development in Kenya.* Cambridge University Press, New York.

Blarel, B. 1994. Tenure security and agricultural production under land security: The case of Rwanda. Pages 71–96 in J. Bruce and S. Migot-Adholla, eds. *Searching for Land Tenure Security in Africa.* Kendall/Hunt Publishing Company, Dubuque, IA.

Brokensha, D. and J. Glazier. 1973. Land reform among the Mbeere of Central Kenya. *Africa* 43(3):182–206.

Bruce, J. and S. Migot-Adholla, eds. 1994. *Searching for Land Tenure Security in Africa.* Kendall/Hunt Publishing Company, Dubuque, IA.

Bruce, J., S. Migot-Adholla, and J. Atherton. 1994. The findings and their policy implications: Institutional adaptation or replacement? Pages 251–266 in J. Bruce and S. Migot-Adholla, eds. *Searching for Land Tenure Security in Africa.* Kendall/Hunt Publishing Company, Dubuque, IA.

Carter, M., K. Wiebe, and B. Blarel. 1994. Tenure security for whom? Differential effects of land policy in Kenya. Pages 141–168 in J. Bruce and S. Migot-Adholla, eds. *Searching for Land Tenure Security in Africa.* Kendall/Hunt Publishing Company, Dubuque, IA.

Chanock, M. 1991. A Peculiar Sharpness: An essay on property in the history of customary law in colonial Africa. *Journal of African History* 32:65–88.

Coldham, S. 1978. The effect of registration of title upon customary land rights in Kenya. *Journal of African Law* 22:91–111.

Coldham, S. 1979. Land-tenure reform in Kenya: The limits of law. *The Journal of Modern African Studies* 17(4):615–627.

Collier, P. 1983. Malfunctioning of African rural factor markets: Theory and a Kenyan example. *Oxford Bulletin of Economics and Statistics* 45(2):141–172.

Demsetz, H. 1967. Toward a theory of property rights. *American Economic Review* 57(2):347–59.

Denzau, A. and D. North. 1994. Shared mental models: Ideology and institutions. *Kyklos* 47(1):1–31.

Dobson, E. B. 1954. Comparative land tenure of ten Tanganyika tribes. *Journal of African Administration* 80(6).

Eggertsson, T. 1990. *Economic Behavior and Institutions.* Cambridge University Press, Cambridge, UK.

Eggertsson, T. 1994. "Property Rights, Economic Analysis and the Information Problem." Workshop in Political Theory and Policy Analysis. Bloomington, IN.

Feder, G. and R. Noronha. 1987. Land rights systems and agricultural development in sub-Saharan Africa. *Research Observer* 2(2):143–169.

Firmin-Sellers, K. In press. The Transformation of Property Rights in the Gold Coast. Cambridge University Press, Cambridge, UK.

Fleuret, A. 1988. Some consequences of tenure and agrarian reform in Taita, Kenya. *In* R. E. Downs and S. P. Reyna, eds. *Land and Society in Contemporary Africa.* University Press of New England, Hanover, NH.

Glazier, J. 1985. *Land and the Use of Tradition Among the Mbeere of Kenya.* University Press of America, Lanham, MD.

Granovetter, M. 1985. Economic action and social structure: The problem of embeddedness. *American Journal of Sociology* 91(3):481–510.

Greif, A. 1994. Cultural beliefs and the organization of society. *Journal of Political Economy* 102(5):912–950.

Guyer, J. 1981. Household and community in African studies. *African Studies Review* 24:114.

Haugerud, A. 1983. The consequences of land tenure reform among smallholders in the Kenya highlands. *Rural Africana* 15/16:65–89.

Haugerud, A. 1989. Land tenure and agrarian change in Kenya. *Africa* 59(1):61–90.

Hecht, R. 1985. Immigration, land transfer and tenure changes in Divo, Ivory Coast, 1940–1980. *Africa* 55(3):319–336.

Homan, F. D. 1963. Succession to registered land in the African areas of Kenya. *Journal of Local Administration Overseas* (London) 2(1).

Knight, J. 1992. *Institutions and Social Conflict.* Cambridge University Press, Cambridge, UK.

Koby, A. T. 1979. Projection des formations sociales sur l'espace: Example du pays Odzukru en Cote D'Ivoire. in *Maitrise de l'Espace Agraire et Developpement en Afrique Tropical.* ORSTOM, Paris.

Kopytoff, I. 1987. *The African Frontier: The Reproduction of Traditional African Societies.* Indiana University Press, Bloomington, IN.

Leakey, L. 1977. *The Southern Kikuyu Before 1904*. Academic Press, New York.

Levin, M. 1976. "Family Structure in Bakosi: Social Change in an African Society." Ph.D. Dissertation, Princeton University, Princeton, NJ.

Libecap, G. D. 1989. *Contracting for Property Rights*. Cambridge University Press, New York.

Matlon, P. 1994. Indigenous land use systems and investments in soil fertility in Burkina Faso. Pages 41–69 *in* J. Bruce and S. Migot-Adholla, eds. *Searching for Land Tenure Security in Africa*. Kendall/Hunt Publishing Company. Dubuque, IA.

Middleton, J. 1961. *Land Tenure in Zanzibar*. Colonial Research Studies 33. Her Majesty's Stationery Office, London.

Migot-Adholla, S. and J. Bruce. 1994. Introduction: Are indigenous African tenure systems insecure? Pages 1–14 *in* J. Bruce and S. Migot-Adholla, eds. *Searching for Land Tenure Security in Africa*. Kendall/Hunt Publishing Company, Dubuque, IA.

Migot-Adholla, S. G. Benneh, F. Place, and S. Atsu. 1994a. Land, security of tenure, and productivity in Ghana. Pages 97–118 *in* J. Bruce and S. Migot-Adholla, eds. *Searching for Land Tenure Security in Africa*. Kendall/Hunt Publishing Company, Dubuque, IA.

Migot-Adholla, S., F. Place, and W. Oluoch-Kosura. 1994b. Security of tenure and land productivity in Kenya. Pages 119–140 *in* J. Bruce and S. Migot-Adholla, eds. *Searching for Land Tenure Security in Africa*. Kendall/Hunt Publishing Company, Dubuque, IA.

Muriuki, G. 1974. *A History of the Kikuyu 1500–1900*. Oxford University Press, New York.

North, D. 1981. *Structure and Change in Economic History*. W.W. Norton, New York.

North, D. 1990. *Institutions, Institutional Change and Economic Performance*. Cambridge University Press, Cambridge, UK.

North, D. and R. Thomas. 1973. *The Rise of the Western World: A New Economic History*. Cambridge University Press, New York.

Odingo, R. S. 1985. The dynamics of land tenure and of agrarian systems in Africa: Land tenure study in the Nakuru, Kericho and Machakos areas of the Kenya highlands. U.N. Food and Agriculture Organisation, Rome.

Okoth-Ogendo, H. W. O. 1986. The Perils of Land Tenure Reform: The Case of Kenya. In . J.W. Artzen, L.D. Ngcongco, and S.D. Turner, eds. *Land Policy and Agriculture in Eastern and Southern Africa*. The United Nations University, Tokyo, Japan.

Okoth-Ogendo, H. W. O. 1993. Agrarian reform in sub-Saharan Africa: An assessment of state responses to the African agrarian crisis and their implications for agricultural development. Pages 247–273 *in* T. Bassett and D. Crummy, eds. *Land in African Agrarian Systems*. University of Wisconsin Press, Madison.

Pedraza, G. J. W. 1956. Land consolidation in the Kikuyu areas of Kenya. *Journal of African Administration* 8:82–87.

Putnam, R. 1993. *Making Democracy Work: Civic Traditions in Modern Italy.* Princeton University Press, Princeton, NJ.

Roth, M., J. Unruh, and R. Barrows. 1994. Land registration, tenure security, credit use, and investment in the Shebelle region of Somalia. Pages 199–230 *in* J. Bruce and S. Migot-Adholla, eds. *Searching for Land Tenure Security in Africa.* Kendall/Hunt Publishing Company, Dubuque, IA.

Shipton, P. 1988. The Kenyan land tenure reform: Misunderstandings in the public creation of private property. Pages 91–135 *in* R.E. Downs and S. Reyna, eds. *Land and Society in Contemporary Africa.* University Press of New England, Hanover, NH.

Shipton, P. 1992. Debts and trespasses: Land, mortgages and the ancestors in western Kenya. *Africa* 62(3):357–388.

Shipton, P. 1994. Land and culture in tropical Africa: Soils, symbols, and the metaphysics of the mundane. *Annual Review of Anthropology* 23: 347–377.

Sorrenson, M. P. K. 1967. *Land Reform in the Kikuyu Country: A Study in Government Policy.* Oxford University Press, London.

Swynnerton, R. J. M. 1954. *A Plan to Intensify the Development of African Agriculture in Kenya.* Government Printer, Nairobi.

Taylor, M. and S. Singleton. 1993. The communal resource: Transaction costs and the solution of collective action problems. *Politics and Society* 21(2):195–214.

Wangari, E. 1990. "Effects of Land Registration on Small-Scale Farming in Kenya: The Case of Mbeere in Embu District." Ph.D. Dissertation. The New School for Social Research, New York.

CHAPTER 10

Property Rights and Development

NARPAT S. JODHA

Introduction

This chapter deals with the relation between property rights and rural development, as illustrated by changes in community control and management of common-pool resources in the dry tropical regions of India. Collective rights and obligations are central to the management and sustainable use of local natural resources (Bromley and Chapagain 1984; Schlager and Ostrom 1991). In the dry regions of India and most other parts of dry tropics as well, such rights and obligations had in the past been in the form of conventions and customary rules and practices, with very little formal codification in legal documents. The lack of formal law existed because common-property regimes represented institutional adaptations that evolved over time in village communities, in response to the strains and stresses of agro-climatic conditions in the dry tropics (Berkes 1989). Due to the absence of formal, legal codification and *de jure* rather than *de facto* nature of community rights for common-pool resources, it is much easier for the modern state to disregard them while extending its authority in areas that were the traditional mandate of local communities. The replacement of informal conventions for resource use with formal sets of imposed rules has happened in the dry regions of India. State interventions have disrupted the community management of common-pool resources, transforming them to *de facto* open access resources, with all the resource degradation and other associated consequences.

Land reforms introduced in the early 1950s recognized the need for village common-pool resources and gave them legal status, but also created possibilities for resource privatization. The land reforms replaced traditional community organizations as custodians of common-pool resources with formal institutions. The replacement has disrupted the traditional management system without providing an effective substitute. The increased social and economic differentiation in the rural community that resulted from the general pattern of rural development adversely affected group action within villages, and common-pool resources have been a major victim of this change.

Common-Pool Resources in the Dry Regions of India

Common-pool resources can be broadly described as those resources to which a group of people have a coequal use right, especially rights that exclude use of those resources by other people. Corresponding to the rights there are obligations, which are enforced by the collective authority of the group and exercised through the group or its agency (Magrath 1986; Runge 1986; McCay and Acheson 1987; Ostrom 1988; Bromley and Cernea 1989; McKean 1992). In the dry tropical regions of India, common-pool resources include community pastures, community forests, village wastelands, watershed drainages, river or rivulet beds and banks, village ponds and their catchments, dumping grounds, and threshing grounds. Pastures, forests, wastelands, drainages, and riverbanks/beds are the most important types of common-pool resources, despite intervillage differences in their area and importance to the village economy. In addition, private croplands owned by individual households are used as common-pool resources during the non-crop season, functioning as seasonal common-pool resources. Within the common-pool resources, some may be owned by government agencies.

For example, village wastelands legally belong to the revenue department of the government. Water ponds and their catchments may have private ownership, and some forest pieces may belong to the temple authority in the village. However, according to customary practices, seasonal common-pool resources are used and managed as are year-round common-pool resources. Traditionally, it is the gradually evolved customary practices and conventions on the one hand and the community's status as a *de facto* decisionmaker on the other, that represent the local community's rights to common-pool resources (McCay and Acheson 1987; Berkes 1989; Schlager and Ostrom 1991). Table 10.1 illustrates common-pool resource management practices in over 80 villages in 20 districts of 6 states belonging to dry tropical parts of India. The methodological details of the village studies that generated the information on management practices as well as on resource status and productivity are presented elsewhere (Jodha 1985a, 1985b, 1986, 1989, 1990a, 1990b, 1992).

Historically, community adaptations to environmental stresses played the key role in strengthening the provision of common-pool

Common-Pool Resource[a] Management Practices Manifested through Decisionmaking and Enforcement

Area/resource protection (54 cases)	Usage regulation (87 cases)	Development (63 cases)
Decisionmaking		
Control of access; prevention of encroachment (i.e., area grabbing); guarding against cutting trees, shrubs, silt removal without specific permission; protection of shelterbelts, protection of shrubs on pond catchments, river banks, etc.	Rotational grazing; periodic closures of areas; location of watering point in grazing space; restrictions on specific types of animals, cutting live trees, cutting shrubs from shelterbelts or riverbanks; catchment of ponds; premature lopping of trees; guarding against outsiders	Physical measures such as fencing, trenching, and planting; desilting ponds; financial investment; payments to watchmen; purchases of seedlings and fencing materials
Enforcement		
Collective body of village elders, permanent watchmen, physical restructions, entire village gathering on specific issues	Collective body of villagers to decide seasonal changes in provisions guiding usage, rituals guiding the resource use, provision of watchmen	Resource mobilization through obligatory contributions, volunteer help, auction of common-pool resource products (e.g., trees from pond catchments and river banks), taxes and penalties on violators of rules
Provision of penalties, physical punishment, and social boycott for violators; and collective litigation	Provision of graded penalties and punishment differentiated by category of animals and by type of common-pool resources	Investment needs assessed through actual observation, informal discussions, implementation through user groups
Under special circumstances, collective (locally publicized) decisions on curtailing area/auctioning trees, etc.	Drought period relaxations on use proceedings against violators of rules	Surplus resources saved for other collective actions (e.g., drought period help)

Source: Field studies by the author (Jodha 1986, 1989).

[a]Common-pool resources include: community pasture, community forestry, wasteland, watershed drainage, pond/catchment, river/rivulet bank/bed dumping harvesting ground.

resources in dry areas (Jodha 1993). These adaptations are reflected through a number of customary practices indicating a community's decisionmaking and enforcement powers. It should be noted that due to local agro-climatic and ethnic differences, these practices may have some variations among different villages, particularly with reference to specific types of common-pool resources (Jodha 1989). For instance, measures relating to a village pond and its catchment may be more important in arid parts of Rajasthan than in the high rainfall villages of Madhya Pradesh. The role of caste Panchayats (traditional informal councils of caste leaders that deal with caste affairs) in common-pool resource management may be much greater in villages with ethnic homogeneity than in more heterogenous villages. Protection of sources of biomass (trees and shrubs) may be emphasized more in areas with low natural regeneration capacities than in areas with high regeneration potential. In some practices, for example processes of collective decisionmaking, one may find differences between the villages formerly ruled by the British and those formerly under the princely rulers.

Conventional Rights and Customary Practices

As indicated by Table 10.1, customary rights can be represented through the community's decisionmaking and enforcement of rules and practices for common-pool resources. Table 10.1 also summarizes the mechanisms and methods of decisionmaking and enforcement that existed prior to the introduction of land reforms and the Panchayat system in the 1950s. The Panchayat system is a set of formally elected village councils for the management of village affairs, as opposed to the customary system of informal caste Panchayats or groups of village elder leaders. Table 10.1 also reports on the number of case histories on which the summary is based. The rules and practices may relate to several aspects of common-pool resources, such as area and resource protection, usage regulation, and development (Jodha 1989).

Area and Resource Protection

Traditionally, the village community had the power to prevent access to outsiders, prevent encroachment by its own members, establish restrictions on cutting trees, and prevent the destruction of shelterbelts in the watershed, riverbanks, or catchments of ponds. Village elders or caste Panchayats were key decisionmakers. Enforcement decisions required the cooperation of the whole community, but a watchman was provided for day-to-day monitoring of violations. In the villages belonging to former princely states, the feudal landlords' authority, again operated through leaders of different caste groups, was more important (Jodha 1985a).

There are a number of interesting examples of customary rules and practices. In the Telangana area of Andhra Pradesh there used to be an "ax rule," according to which wood collected from the common forests was judged by cutting into it with an ax. If the wood was found to be wet rather than dry deadwood, the offender was punished. In some villages of Rajasthan, a wood fuel gatherer was punished if his collected stock contained any root of a tree or shrub. Similarly, in the villages of Rajasthan, Gujarat, and Madhya Pradesh, people displaced by drought had to follow specific conditions before entering the common lands of other villages.

Violators of community rules and decisions had to pay a penalty, face social boycott, or face costly litigation, depending on the nature of the violation and on their attitude. Litigation involved repeated hearings within the village, during which violators were required to feed all villagers participating in the proceedings. In some cases the offender was physically assaulted. To meet any specific problems, a curtailment of the common-pool resource area or of the rate of resource use (e.g., tree cutting) was allowed after a collective decision of the villager elders.

Usage Regulation

Mechanisms to enforce rules of use were similar to those described above for protection and access control. To prevent overgrazing of common-pool resources, rotational grazing was enforced through the physical location of watering points and the seasonal closure of specific grazing areas. To prevent the rapid siltation of ponds, some types of animals (e.g., sheep or goats) were periodically banned from pond catchments. To maintain soil fertility, a periodic ban on dung collection from common-pool resources was enforced. Watchmen played an important role in enforcing use regulations. Regulations on use also involved decisions on the postharvest dates when private lands were declared open as seasonal common-pool resources. This practice reflected a complementarity of community rights and private rights in resources use (Jodha 1993).

Development

The development of common-pool resources involved activities such as fencing, planting, trenching in forest and pastures, and the desilting of ponds. Such activities required resources. A village community mobilized these resources through obligatory contributions of cash and kind by users, voluntary labor, penalty fees, and revenues from the auction of resource products such as timber, gum, and dung. The investment needs and the deployment of collected resources were also decided by the community, largely on the basis of observed and felt needs. Such needs might include trenching a piece of pasture land to raise productivity, the desilting of a pond, or the maintenance of a village bull.

Development Interventions and Customary Rights of Communities

The preceding discussion and Table 10.1 give some idea of the customary rules and rights of the community regarding the multiple activities surrounding common-pool resources. How these rights to protect and manage common-pool resources have been affected by recent development processes is discussed below and summarized in Table 10.2.

General development patterns in rural areas have released several new opportunities and constraints which tend to change peoples' approaches and attitudes toward each other as well as to their common natural resources. Historically, environmental stresses in the dry tropical regions of India created circumstance which offered neither enough incentives (e.g., high land prices, alternative private uses of land) nor strong compulsions (e.g., due to low population and physical and market isolation) which could induce privatization of common-pool resources (Jodha 1993). Common-pool resources became part of the collective strategies to manage natural resources and share risks. The communities evolved norms and practices to operationalize such strategies, which involved a variety of group actions for protection, upkeep, and regulated use.

However, as elaborated elsewhere (Jodha 1990c, 1993), the circumstances lately have rapidly changed. Rapid population growth combined with increased physical and market integration of dry regions with the mainstream economy, the increased commercialization of resource use, irrigation, and new crop technologies such as the widespread use of tractors are the key elements of the process of change (Jodha 1985a, 1985b, 1990b). These changes have marginalized the role of group action and customary practices that guided the community's actions against biophysical stresses in the past. Common-pool resources have been a key victim of this change.

Increased economic differentiation of rural communities has radically changed peoples' attitudes toward group action and collective strategies. This has further reduced the resilience of customary rules and practices to other effects of rural development processes. This general process of change has been greatly accentuated by some other development interventions which are more directly focused on common-pool resources and customary rights of communities. These interventions are the introduction of land reforms and the introduction of Panchayat systems for village administration.

Land Reform

The introduction of land reforms in the early 1950s was a major development designed to improve the welfare of rural people in different parts of the country. With some variation among states, land reforms focused on the abolition of intermediaries between the state and farmers, such as absentee landlords or feudal landlords. Reforms also created tenurial security to peasants, a ceiling on land holding size, and provided land to the landless. Without belittling the positive impacts of such actions, the purpose of this discussion is to highlight their negative impacts on common-pool resources.

The land ceiling laws were designed to provide surplus land for the landless. When their implementation failed to achieve that goal, the state's distribution of land to the landless took place mainly through privatization of common-pool resources (Ladejinsky 1972). Both through the legalization of illegal encroachments into common-pool lands and the formal distribution of private land rights, the state opened attractive opportunities for private ownership. During a thirty-year period from the 1950s to the 1980s, 31 to 55 percent of the common-pool resource area was privatized in different study villages (Jodha 1992). The conventional provisions regarding protection of common-pool resources and a community's customary rights to those resources were bypassed in the process.

The undeclared policy of privatization of common-pool resources reduced the quantity available and led to increased pressure, overexploitation, and degradation of the remaining common-pool resources. Privatization also encouraged the transfer of these largely fragile and submarginal lands to crop farming, for which they were unsuited (Blaikie et al. 1985; Iyengar 1988; Chen 1988). Very low crop yields at the cost of potential natural resource biomass was the final consequence. Furthermore, the intended objective of helping the landless poor was hardly achieved, as the bulk of the privatized common-pool resources went to the households who already owned

T A B L E 10.2

Development Interventions Affecting Customary Rules and Practices
and Their Consequences for Common-Pool Resources

Interventions involving common-pool resources	Customary rules and practices affected by interventions	Consequences of interventions and formal rules
1. _Land reforms in the 1950s_		
• Undeclared policy of privatization of common resources	• Erosion of social sanctions and community authority to protect common resources, regulate their use, and develop them	• Decline of common-pool resource area, overcrowding, overexploitation, and physical degradation
• Distribution of common lands for private cultivation		
• Government acquisition of common land for public purposes	• Legal status to common-pool resources without effective enforcement mechanism due to loss of customary communal arrangement	• Village Panchayats failed to ensure people's participation for common-resource management
• Legalization of illegal encroachments		• Common-pool resources became open access resources
2. _Introduction of Panchayat system and other measures for common-pool resources_		
• Provision of village Panchayats (elected councils) as custodians of common-pool resources	• Replacement of traditional decisionmakers (e.g., village elders' group) by Panchayats	• Few village level initiatives for common-pool resources
		• Default on the part of Panchayats
• Government grants and subsidies to manage and develop community lands	• Cessation of participatory management, local resource mobilization, and group action for common resources	• Common-pool resources became open access resources with expected degradation and depletion
• External, formal, administrative, and legal measures extended to village affairs	• Authority and knowledge of local community ignored	• Common-pool resources became legal entities instead of a collective asset, with no effective mechanisms to put legal provisions into practice
	• Failure to implement legal provisions for common resources	

3. *Formal production and resource upgrading programs*

- Research and technology application on pilot scale
- Pasture, forestry, and watershed development projects
- Projects conceived from outside, sustained by government subsidy, characterized by "technique dominance"

- Disregard of local knowledge and institutional factors, user needs, and perceptions
- Marginalization of participatory approach, local resource mobilization, and collective action
- Alienation of community from its resources

- Area decline due to the acquisition of common lands for pilot projects
- Reduced access to common-pool resource users
- Common-pool resource development as part of development projects decided by state agencies

4. *Other developments with negative side effects*

- Tractor purchases with state subsidies
- New agricultural technologies with anti-biomass bias
- Market integration and promotion of commercialization of production, leading to individualistic approach and reduced group action and collective approaches

- Weakened appeal of social sanctions and norms favoring group action and collective resource management as the use of tractors made it easy to cultivate vast areas, anti-biomass approach of technologies reduced needs for common resources, and market forces gave low priority to collective concerns and group action

- Reduction of the role and importance of common-pool resources as a source of biomass and a collective strategy to manage fragile resources
- Tendency to acquire common-pool resources as private property rather than use them collectively

Source: Author's field studies (Jodha 1985a, 1985b, 1986, 1989, 1990b).

relatively more land (Jodha 1986, 1990b). Thus what the landless people collectively lost through privatization of common-pool resources (on which they depended most) was not compensated by their private gains as landowners.

The land reform program did recognize the importance of village common resources and gave them legal status. It also provided for rules and laws to govern common resources, to be implemented by village Panchayats and state land revenue authorities at the village or district level. However, at the operational level mechanisms to replace the customary community arrangements could not be enforced. Moreover, in practice the policy of land distribution got priority over the legal concerns about common-pool resources. The introduction of a new form of village administration through village Panchayats led to the further marginalization of the informal authority of the community, which had maintained common-pool resources in the past. Group action and the system of collective rights and obligations disappeared in the process.

Panchayat System

The second major intervention that affected the community's customary rules, rights, and practices for common-pool resources was the introduction of the Panchayat system: elected village councils as custodians of village affairs, including the management of common-pool resources. Village councils replaced the traditional informal leadership of village elders and in some villages feudal rulers (Jodha 1985a). However, this step toward formal democratization of village administration could not acquire legitimacy, genuine approval, or effective involvement of the people, which had been the strong points of earlier informal agencies such as village elder councils or caste Panchayats. This was because the formally elected councils were treated by the villagers more as state agencies, created to implement programs conceived of by the state and supported by state grants. In most cases these councils covered more than one village and this led to the neglect of the concerns of the smaller villages. The new arrangements gave room for the government bureaucracy to interfere in matters relating to local communities. In due course, Panchayats acquired a political culture with the associated features of factionalism, patronage, wooing the voters, etc. Finally, in most areas Panchayat elections were repeatedly postponed, further disillusioning the people about these institutions.

Because they were formal bodies, Panchayats did not (or could not) favor all the informal arrangements, group actions, or collective concerns which characterized the traditional systems. Governed by calculations such as pleasing the voters, they more easily approved any request for privatization of common-pool resources and could not enforce any regulations on their use. The people's obligatory and voluntary contributions for common-pool resource development and maintenance were replaced by periodic grants or subsidies from the government, which were rarely invested in common-pool resources (Jodha 1985a, 1990a, 1990c, 1992).

Thus the customary rights of the communities got formal legal existence through Panchayat laws and land reform laws. But the creation of formal legal authorization eliminated the informal conventions under which common-pool resources had been managed. At the operational level in the absence of genuinely participatory arrangements, the legal provisions replaced *de facto* rights of the village. In practice, all these changes transformed common-pool resources into open-access resources and led to overexploitation and resource degradation.

Conclusions

The replacement of customary management systems by formal systems for common-pool resources had several impacts on resource management as illustrated in Table 10.3.

Under customary arrangements, common-pool resources and their associated biodiversity were better protected. The new arrangements, largely by default, encouraged their curtailment. The collective rights and obligation to regulate use as well as mechanisms to enforce regulations under customary arrangements were eliminated by the new system. Despite provisions for regulated use, it has virtually converted common-pool resources into open-access resources, leading to their overexploitation and depletion. The development and productivity promotion under the traditional systems through group actions and obligatory and voluntary resource contributions are things of the past. Under the current formal arrangements, common-pool resource development is a rather casual activity involving government grants but little participation in terms of community control. With the exception of a few NGO-supported initiatives in recent years, people rely more on their own resources than on collective arrangement for withstanding problems caused by drought and seasonality (Shah 1987; Oza 1989; Jodha 1990c, 1993).

Under the formal system, group action and local resource mobilization of the past has been replaced by state-patronized activities

T A B L E 10.3

The Impact of Replacing Customary Management with Formal Management

| | Situation Under | |
Variables	Customary management (with involvement)	Formal management (with involvement of state though village Panchayats)
1. Control of access and protection of CPR area	Effective prevention of encroachment and curtailment in area	Deliberate encouragement to privatization, rapid area decline
2. Usage regulation	Collective rights/obligation; regulations enforced through different devices/social sanctions/physical measures	Common-pool resources as open access resource, little enforcement of regulatory provisions
3. Development, productivity promotion	Group action, obligatory/voluntary contributions for resource maintenance/investment	Periodic activities depending on government grants, little people's participation
4. Miscellaneous items:		
• Group action/collective sharing	Functional and high extent of group activities, participatory	Periodical, formal, state-patronized activity, involving local wage labor
• Autonomy/flexibility	High degree of flexibility, location, and ethnic group-specificity	Generalized, uniform patterns imposed from above, insensitive to local conditions
• Local needs and perceptions	People's needs/means key guiding factors	Perception of outsiders (e.g., government agencies) a key element
• Opportunities for grabbing common resources	Very little encroachment	Privatization of common lands encouraged
• "Free rider" problem	Nonexistent	New type of noncontributing beneficiaries on the increase
• Practice of "exclusion"	Only outside villagers had no access	On political consideration even local villagers can be prevented
• CPR productivity regeneration, and biodiversity	Sufficient regrowth, biodiversity as permitted by the nature	Reduced regeneration and biodiversity due to depletion and use of narrowly focused technologies
• Resource mobilization/self-help	Participatory activities a key factor in sustainability of common-pool resources	Increased external dependence, cost-free use/misuse of common resources

Source: Author's field studies (Jodha, 1985a, 1985b, 1986, 1989, 1990b).

with little participation. Autonomy, flexibility, and the location specificity of arrangements has now been replaced by a more generalized formal set of provisions imposed from above. Local needs and perceptions—so important in the past—have been replaced by the perceptions of outsiders, especially those of lawmakers and government field agencies. The absence of opportunities for grabbing common-pool resources has been replaced by new attractive opportunities to privatize them. Finally, the scope for maintaining resource biodiversity, productivity, and regeneration that existed under customary management practices is hardly possible under the new arrangements, which directly or indirectly encourage the depletion of common-pool resources and the introduction of only limited plant species in pilot project areas in the name of rehabilitating them (Gupta 1987; Chambers et al. 1989).

On a conceptual level the well-known problems of common-pool resources have acquired new dimensions. Under the customary arrangements, the provision of various collective rights and obligations and preventive measures helped to avoid the "free rider" problem and facilitated the exclusion of nonmembers. Under the new arrangement, various forms of patronage involving subsidies and the use of common-pool resources are purposely extended to nonmembers and nonusers, including outsiders. This has created battalions of "free riders" of different types. Similarly, on factional and political grounds, exclusion is implemented even for genuine members of the community (Jodha 1989).

The modern state, especially in developing countries, has strong tendencies to usurp local mandates and initiatives in the name of development and the betterment of people's lives. Its job becomes easier when the local-level mandates are in the form of customary provisions with little formal codification in the country's legal system. This tendency is illustrated by the rapid erosion of a community's informal authority over common-pool resources in the dry region of India. However, the general picture presented above has certain exceptions.

Detailed investigations during field studies of common-pool resources (Jodha 1986, 1989, 1990a) found that despite legal, administrative, and fiscal interventions in common, the status of customary rights over common-pool resources may vary between villages, even within the same district. Despite the provision of formal and legal arrangements, customary rules and management systems still prevail in some villages. Depending on the level of community consciousness and group solidarity, villagers are able to maintain past arrangements

(Brara 1987; Kaul 1987; Shah 1987; Iyengar 1988; Jodha 1989, 1990a). This resilience can be explained in terms of several ecological, ethnic, and economic factors. Ecologically marginal and isolated villages with homogenous ethnic groups and few external interventions by the government or market are still able to maintain customary rules and practices. Such villages remain for the most part untouched by the present pattern of development. Their future will depend on the pace and pattern of development and on rural transformation.

On the other hand, there is yet another pattern that is slowly emerging. Some local NGO-supported initiatives are rehabilitating common-pool resources and the control of user groups, either by making full use of formal arrangements (e.g., Panchayat power, state subsidies, or new technologies) or by ignoring them. The recorded cases (Shah 1987; Chambers et al. 1989; Jodha 1989; Oza 1989) are few, but they do represent a new possibility of local people acquiring control over local resources and their management. The state's approval of such NGO-supported initiatives indicates the possibility of change that is more conducive to stability and to the productivity of community resources (Brara 1987; Mishra and Sarin 1987; Shah 1987; Chambers et al. 1989; Oza 1989; Agarwal and Narain 1990; Arnold and Stewart 1990).

REFERENCES

Agarwal, A. and S. Narain. 1990. *Towards Green Villages*. Centre for Science and Environment, New Delhi.

Arnold, J. E. M. and W. C. Stewart. 1990. *Common Property Resource Management in India. Tropical Forestry.* Paper 24. Oxford Forestry Institute. Oxford University Press, London.

Berkes, F., ed. 1989. Common Property Resources: Ecology and Community-Based Sustainable Development. Belhaven Press, London.

Blaikie, P. M., J. C. Harriss, and A. N. Pain 1985. "The Management and Use of Common Property Resources in Tamilnadu." Overseas Development Administration, London.

Brara, R. 1987. "Shifting Sands: A Study of Rights in Common Pastures." Institute of Development Studies, Jaipur.

Bromley, D. W. and M. M. Cernea. 1989. The management of common property natural resources: Some conceptual and operational fallacies. World Bank Discussion Paper 57. The World Bank, Washington, D.C.

Bromley, D. W. and D. Chapagain. 1984. The village against the centre: Resource depletion in South Asia. *American Journal of Agricultural Economics* 66:5.

Chambers, R., N. C. Saxena, and T. Shah. 1989. *To the Hands of the Poor: Water and Trees.* Oxford and IBH Publishing Co. Pvt. Ltd, New Delhi.

Chen, M. 1988. "Size, Status and Use of Common Property Resources: A Case Study of Dhevdholera Village in Ahmedabad District, Gujarat." Paper presented at Women and Agriculture Seminar. Centre for Development Studies, Trivendrum, Kerala.

Gupta, A. K. 1987. Why poor people do not cooperate? A study of traditional forms of cooperation with implications for modern organization. In G. C. Wanger, ed. *Politics and Practices of Social Research*. George Allen and Unwin, London.

Iyengar, S. 1988. "Common Property Land Resources in Gujarat: Some Findings About Their Size, Status and Use." Working Paper 18. The Gujarat Institute of Area Planning, Gota, Ahmedabad, Gujarat.

Jodha, N. S. 1985a. Population growth and the decline of common property resources in Rajasthan, India. *Population and Development Review* 11:2.

Jodha, N. S. 1985b. Market forces and erosion of common property resources. In Agricultural Markets in the Semi-arid Tropics, Proceedings of an International Workshop, October 24–28, 1983. International Crops Research Institute for Semi-Arid Tropics (ICRISAT), Patancheru (AP) India.

Jodha, N. S. 1986. Common property resources and rural poor in dry regions of India. *Economic and Political Weekly* 21:27.

Jodha, N. S. 1989. "Management of Common Property Resources in Selected Areas of India." Paper presented at the seminar on approach to participatory development and management of common property resources, March 10. Institute of Economic Growth, Delhi.

Jodha, N. S. 1990a. Depletion of common property resources in India: Micro-level evidence. Pages 261–283 in G. McNicoll and M. Cain, eds. *Rural Development and Population: Institutions and Policy*. Oxford University Press, New York (also Supplement to Vol. 15, *Population and Development Review*).

Jodha, N. S. 1990b. "Rural Common Property Resources: Contributions and Crisis." Foundation Day Lecture. Society for Promotion of Wasteland Development, New Delhi.

Jodha, N. S. 1990c. "Drought Management: The Farmer's Strategies and Their Policy Implications." IIED Dryland Network Programme, Issues Paper No. 21. International Institute for Environment and Development, London.

Jodha, N. S. 1992. "Rural Common Property Resources: The Missing Dimension of Development Strategies." World Bank Discussion Paper 169. The World Bank, Washington, D.C.

Jodha, N. S. 1993. "Common Property Resources in Stressed Environments: A Case from High Risk Environments, India." Paper presented at IV IASCP Conference, June 16–19. Manila, Philippines.

Kaul, M. 1987. "Common Land in Delhi: The Bisgama Cluster Report." New Delhi. (Limited circulation.)

Ladejinsky, W. 1972. Land ceilings and land reforms. *Economic and Political Weekly* 7:5–7.

Magrath, W. B. 1986. "The Challenge of the Commons: Non-exclusive Resources and Economic Development—Theoretical Issues." WRI Working Paper. World Resource Institute,Washington, D.C.

McCay, B. J. and J. A. Acheson, eds. 1987. *The Question of Commons: The Culture and Ecology of Communal Resources*. University of Arizona Press, Tucson.

McKean, M. A. 1992. Success on commons: A comparative examination of institutions for common property resources. *Journal of Theoretical Politics* 4:3.

Mishra, P. R. and M. Sarin. 1987. Sukhomajri-Nada : A new model of eco-development. *Business India* (November 16–29), Bombay.

Ostrom, E. 1988. Institutional arrangements and the commons dilemma. *In* E. Ostrom, D. Feeny, and, H. Picht, eds. *Rethinking Institutional Analysis and Development*. International Centre for Economic Growth, Institute for Contemporary Studies Press, San Francisco.

Oza, A. 1989. Availability of CPR lands at micro-level: Case studies of Junagadh programme area of AKRSP (India). In *Status of Common Property Land Resources in Gujarat and Problem of Their Development*. Gujarat Institute of Area Planning, Ahmedabad, Gujarat.

Runge, C. F. 1986. Common property and collective action in economic development. In *Proceedings of the Conference on Common Property Management*. BOSTID, National Research Council, Washington, D.C.

Schlager, E. and E. Ostrom. 1991. "Property-Rights Regimes and Natural Resources: A Conceptual Analysis." Paper presented at the conference on Political Economy of Customs and Culture: Informal Solutions to the Commons Problem, June, Bozeman, Montana.

Shah, T. 1987. "Profile of Collective Action on Common Property: Community Fodder Farm in Kheda District." Institute of Rural Management, Anand, Gujarat.

PART IV

Property Rights at Different Scales

CHAPTER II

Common-Property Regimes as a Solution to Problems of Scale and Linkage

MARGARET A. McKEAN

Introduction

Most of us would agree that efficient resource use enhances welfare and is environmentally desirable compared to less efficient resource use, because it means that we invest, get the most out of the least, and waste little. But this proposition creates a paradox between two very well accepted principles of economics: (1) private property rights and markets allow for more efficient use of resources than does government ownership (so yield desirable environmental results), and (2) private property systems and markets are chronic underproviders of public goods like environmental health (so yield inadequate environmental results). The paradox, I would submit, is a result of mismatch in scale between institutions and natural ecological systems. That is, private property rights and markets are socially and environmentally efficient only insofar as externalities are internalized: only when those who impose social costs are somehow forced to pay for these costs, giving them an incentive not to impose these costs on society in the first place.[1]

Virtually every environmental problem indicates a failure to create institutions that internalize externalities, giving those who impose environmental damage on society insufficient incentive to stop doing so. Polluters do not pay the full cost of cleanup themselves, so do not clean up, or resource users do not pay the long-term cost of depletion themselves, so do not exercise restraint in use. Often we have failed to define property rights at all. Or we have vested ownership in too large an entity (e.g., highly centralized governments or firms that are too large), creating severe problems when bureaucrats, owners, and managers can insulate themselves from the undesirable social consequences of their actions. It is often very difficult for those who suffer these consequences to complain and get corrective action if their appeals must travel upward through many layers of bureaucracy. Or, finally, we have parcelled up private ownership rights to resources into units that are smaller than ecological boundaries, thus guaranteeing negative spillover effects among units. What follows is a theoretical justification for using common-property regimes as a way to internalize environmental externalities and align property boundaries with ecological ones. Also provided is a historical example from Japan where communities arrived at a complex mapping of common-property rights to match ecological and geographic realities.

Full internalization of externalities—in which those who generate social benefit receive personal benefit from doing so, and those who generate social costs suffer personally from doing so—is probably impossible. But the severity of environmental problems today indicates that trying harder would not be a waste of time. We need to aim at more complete capture of benefits, so that resource owners who invest in the productivity and environmental health of their resources can more fully capture returns from that effort. And we need to aim at more complete capture of costs, so that those who mismanage their resources or cause environmental harm suffer from their actions, not just a bit but more than anyone else, and to a degree approximating the damage they cause to others, so that they will therefore be interested in preventing or correcting that damage.

The creation of private property rights in resources has been advanced, understandably, as a way to internalize externalities, and in comparison to no property rights at all, private property rights win handily. But the enthusiasm for what is only crudely called "privatization" is too uncritical. It can become the justification for awarding ownership of an entire resource system to a single individual without regard to the political consequences of enraging all other former users of the resource, who then become poachers and degraders of a resource no longer theirs to protect. Or it can be used to justify parcellization of a resource system, creating externalities among competing parcels and exacerbating the very environmental damage that it was meant to prevent. The campaign for privatization is being conducted without sufficient consideration of such issues as these:

(1) In whom (to how many persons, to which persons, with what distributional consequences) should property rights be vested?
(2) Which rights in resources should be allocated to whom? Should use rights and rights of transfer be vested in the same entity? Should all rights to a resource be bundled together as has traditionally been argued?

(3) What kinds of resources should be privatized or parcelled? Are all objects equally able to be divided up? Should ecosystem boundaries matter?

Definitions

I am convinced that part of our problem is semantic: we use the same pair of adjectives, "public" and "private," as labels for three different pairs of things. We use them to distinguish between two different kinds of goods (public goods and private goods), between two different kinds of rights (public rights and private rights), and between two different kinds of bodies that may own things (public entities or governments, and private entities or individuals). The privateness of a *good* is a physical given having to do with the excludability and subtractibility of the good (see Table 11.1).[2] The privateness of a *right* refers to the clarity, security, and especially the exclusivity of the right: a fully private right specifies clearly what the rights-holder is entitled to do, is secure so that the holder of the right is protected from confiscation by others, and is exclusively vested in the holder of the right and definitely not in nonholders of the right. It is important to note here that the privateness of a right has to do with the right, and not the entity holding it; there is no requirement that this entity be a single individual. Finally, the privateness of a *body* has to do with its representational claims, in that a *public body* claims to represent the general population and not just one interest within that population, whereas a private body represents only itself.[3]

TABLE 11.1
Type of Good by Physical Characteristics

Type	Exclusion easy	Exclusion difficult or costly
Subtractible (rival in consumption)	*Private goods* Trees, sheep, fish, chocolate cake	*Common-pool goods* Forest, pasture, fishery, any environmental sink over time[a]
Nonsubtractible (nonrival in consumption)	*Club or toll goods* Kiwanis club camaraderie	*Pure public goods* Defense, TV broadcasts, lighthouse beams, an environmental sink at a given instant, a given level of public health, a given level of inflation

[a]An environmental "sink" is an air, water, or soil basin into which we dump pollutants. Thus any ecosystem receiving pollutants becomes such a "sink."

This confusion of goods (a natural given), rights (an institutional invention), and owners of rights (actors with varying claims to represent others) has led to serious errors. First, we fall very easily into the habit of thinking (a) that public entities own and produce public goods while private entities own and produce private goods; (b) that anything produced by government is a public good and anything produced by private parties is a private good; and finally (c) that we have established private rights to private goods and public rights to public goods. In fact, of course, there is no intellectual reason for this simple pairing off. Public entities are perfectly capable of owning and producing private goods (think of government-printed pamphlets, and the products and services from many nationalized industries and utilities). And private entities occasionally produce public goods, though not often intentionally, that range from loud noise to attractive landscaping visible to passersby. Similarly, we often attempt to create public rights in subtractible goods and private rights in pure public goods or common-pool goods, with tragicomic effects. We sometimes award an infinite amount of rights to an exhaustible resource, as in coastal zones with unlimited public access and use. Or we award exclusive rights to resources that cannot be exclusively held, as in the Anglo-American common law principle that owners of land also own all of the air space above their land. This results from another error, which is to think too often of only two types of goods (public and private) and to ignore the crucial differences between pure public goods and common-pool goods.

Pure public goods are those whose consumption does not reduce the quantity available to others to consume; they are therefore ubiquitous and cannot be depleted. That's the good news. The chief problem with pure public goods is not depletion, then, but provision—who has the incentive to produce them and how will they get produced? But common-pool goods pose both challenges for provision or supply and the risk of depletion. Not only is it difficult to get them produced, but it is easy to deplete the supply of whatever does get produced. And in spite of the enormous literature describing environmental quality as a public good, we are slowly discovering that many of the goods we thought were pure public goods are in fact finite in supply and subject to crowding: they are really common-pool goods, difficult to supply and easy to deplete. That's the bad news.

Given the distinctions among privateness of goods, rights, and rights-holders, it is theoretically possible to conceive of most of the possible combinations and permutations of resource types, property rights types, and rights holders. Surprisingly, there is very little agreement about which of these combinations and permutations are efficient. There is overwhelming consensus on only two points: (1) that private goods are best held as private property, and (2) that private property rights are an inadequate arrangement for public goods. There is also consensus, though weaker, on the inefficiencies that can arise when we vest ownership in any entity other than a single individual with a central nervous system. Hence the great concern in the theory of the firm with "principal–agent" problems, those that arise when owners, managers, and employees all have different incentives and there is a risk of shirking on the job, failure to cooperate in team production, and even corruption. Thus there is considerable controversy over when it improves matters to vest ownership in public entities, or collectivities (groups of individuals that can range from natural social communities to partnerships of individuals with shared interests to joint-stock corporations). And we are left with a gnawing problem: what kind of property rights arrangement should we design when we *know* that simple individual private property is inadequate or impossible?

Advantages of Common-Property Regimes

I view common property as a form of *shared* private property in that individuals jointly own some or all of the property rights to a resource system (just as individuals might share ownership of an unnatural system like an office coffee pool), and I argue here that common-property regimes offer certain efficiencies in the management of common-pool resources. Common-property regimes can reduce enforcement costs, make resource-protectors out of potential resource-destroyers, and offer us a way to reap the advantages of private property rights in resources without parcelling resources that are most productive when kept intact. First, sharing rights can help resource users economize on enforcement costs through collective enforcement of restraints on use and users. Users can patrol each other's use, and they can band together to patrol the entire resource system and protect it from invasion by persons outside of their group. Solving the exclusion problem then begins to solve the problem of provision or maintenance.

Second, vesting these shared rights in those who live nearest the resource enhances the incentive to protect the resource among those who face the lowest enforcement costs and who could, given inappropriate incentives, destroy the resource most easily. It follows that we can achieve the greatest improvement in incentive structures — reducing incentives to destroy and enhancing incentives to protect — by making sure that all, or at least primary, rights in a resource go to the community living nearest the resource. Where people still live near such resources and depend upon them, they have a built-in strategic advantage over other people in that whatever the arrangement of rights, they still possess the physical opportunity to use (and to destroy) these resources. They also have the strategic advantage in monitoring access by others who might have destructive intentions, though without enforceable property rights to the resources, they will have little incentive to do that monitoring. If the people who live nearest such resources and have ample opportunity to use them then lose property rights in the resource to others, they also lose any incentive they might have felt to manage these resources for their own maximum long-term benefit. Now they might as well—indeed must!—compete with each other and new users and claimants in a race to extract as much short-term benefit from the resource as possible. Vesting property rights in a resource's nearest neighbors strengthens the incentive of those most capable of enforcing rules about access to the resource to design rules that protect and enhance it. Vesting those rights in others instead destroys these incentives and converts those nearest the resource into likely poachers. Any rights scheme needs to consider the strategic importance of vesting resource rights in the communities living closest to the resource.

Finally, common-property rights can operate as a way of privatizing *rights* to *things* without dividing the things into pieces. If two people want to share a typewriter or a chain saw or an automobile, they would be foolish to chop it in half and try to use their halves separately. Natural resource systems are often similar to complex machines: they can be far more productive when left intact than when sliced up. Common-property regimes offer a way to parcel the flow of harvestable "income" (interest) from an interactive resource system without parcelling the stock (principal, the resource system) itself. There are several reasons why we cannot or should not chop a resource system into individual parcels the way unthinking "privatizers" might recommend.

Sometimes the common-pool resource is physically indivisible or unboundable (the high seas, the atmosphere) so we cannot parcel up the system or stock no matter how hard we try. Sometimes the location of the productive portions of the system is highly mobile and variable (tuna), and sometimes unpredictable as well (grazing or water supply in arid lands), so resource users may prefer to share the entire area and decide jointly where to concentrate use at a particular time, rather than parcel the system and thereby impose terrible risks on some individuals. Sometimes the administrative infrastructure that would be needed to support individual property rights may not exist—no cheap fencing, no courts—so a community finds that sharing rights to a large resource system is an economical way to provide enforcement of the group's rights.

But another reason for using common-property regimes is that they permit the internalization of externalities over a large resource system, and can improve the "fit" between institutional and ecological boundaries. In many resource systems, hilly ones for instance, uses in one zone immediately affect uses and productivity in another: deforesting the hillside ruins the water supply, uphill productivity, and downhill soil quality. If this ecological zone or resource system is divided into individually owned parcels, then different persons may own the uphill forests and the downhill fields—or for that matter small adjacent patches of forest and pasture—and make their decisions about resource use independently and separately. But in doing so, they may well cause harm to each other. If these externalities are substantial, they will want to negotiate contracts among themselves that will improve circumstances for all parties and increase social efficiency as a result (Coase 1960). Either the downhill farmers would pay uphill forest-owners not to cut all the trees they might want to, or uphill forest-owners would cut all the trees they want to and instead compensate downhill farmers for damaged fields with the extra earnings from timber sales. According to the Coase theorem, which stipulates the conditions under which these contracts can be negotiated, Coaseian bargains assume that all parties know and can eventually agree on who is suffering, who is causing harm, what the harm causing activity is that needs to be remedied, what the value of the losses due to damage is, and what the cost of preventing the damage would be. As Coase himself acknowledged, these bargains become impossible as transaction and information costs mount.

An institutional alternative to this series of bilateral exchanges is to create a common-property regime to make resource management decisions jointly, acknowledging and internalizing the multiple negative externalities that are likely to result from individual use of parcelled resources. Thus, for example, instead of having numerous individual owners of upland forest parcels, people could instead devise a common-property regime to manage their uphill forests, in which they all share ownership of the upland forests, restrain timbering to prevent soil erosion and damage to fields below, and earn more from their individual downhill farms than they sacrifice by not cutting as much uphill timber. Just as a Coaseian contract permits people to enhance their joint efficiency by dealing directly with an externality, so joint resource management through common-property regimes may enhance efficiency by internalizing externalities. Common-property regimes may become desirable when more intensive resource use multiplies the externalities between parcels, or when individuals face insurmountable transaction and information costs in Coaseian contracting. Coordinated management, prudent use, and prevention of externalities may well be possible even where bilateral contracting to compensate victims for externalities after they occur is not. There is probably some point at which economies of scale in negotiating take over, and collective decisionmaking, collective agreement on fairly restrictive use rules, and collective enforcement of those rules become easier (less time, lower transaction costs for the owners) than endless one-on-one deals.

Because natural resource systems are fundamentally interactive — forests provide watershed control, species are interdependent in ways we are often unaware of, etc. — many will be more productive in large units than in small ones. There are two kinds of "largeness" at stake here: first is the size of the natural ecosystem, and second is the size of the management units that human beings devise to harvest resources from that ecosystem. For some products, ecosystems that are too small drive production down to near zero, and production can rise considerably from larger ones. The need for large acreage is critical in the protection of wild species: it is common knowledge that the Chinese panda is dying out because the available acreage of bamboo forest, though probably adequate in total quantity to support a panda population, is fragmented rather than contiguous. For other products, both the ecosystem and the management units human beings devise must be immense. This is particularly true of tropical forests from which we extract numerous economically valuable products that we cannot cultivate on plantations. Here, the management units must be huge in order to permit proper rotation over a multi-year period of the zones to be harvested each year (on extraction of xate palm, allspice, and particularly chicle latex from the Peten in Guatemala, see Dugelby 1995). By offering coordination rather than fragmentation to keep ecosystems large and to keep management systems large enough to match those ecosystems, common-property arrangements may be useful in maintaining both kinds of largeness.

Finally, common-property regimes for very large ecological systems can be nested, so that small collectivities manage subsections of the resource but federations of these collectivities can be called into action if externalities among subsections arise. We might call this "resource federalism," an arrangement in which small units operate independently as long as they don't affect each other, but the units amalgamate into larger wholes to cope with problems that are physically larger than any single unit can handle. This explicitly federalist arrangement is the conventional method of grouping resource users in complex irrigation systems, and it could be reasonably applied to large forests and grazing lands as well (Ostrom 1990; Tang 1992).

Even where resource systems seem eminently divisible, where risk and uncertainty are low and uniform across the resource system, where many of the externalities that arise seem minor or manageable through individual contracting, and where administrative support for individually owned parcels is ample, major environmental externalities may be reasons to maintain common property at least at some level. In order to optimize the productivity of their own parcel, owners of individual parcels may want to guarantee that owners of adjacent parcels stick to compatible and complementary uses on their parcels, maintain intact wildlife habitat and vegetative cover, allow wildlife transit, refrain from introducing certain "problem" species, and so on. In effect, owners of individual but contiguous parcels may have an interest in mutual regulation of land use—the equivalent of zoning. An example might be individual owners of ordinary farms who want to use organic techniques: the larger the area on which the use of synthetic pesticides and herbicides is prohibited, the better. Short of owning an impossibly enormous farm on their own, they can only achieve this prohibition through mutual regulation of farming techniques with neighboring farms. In fact, zoning and urban planning are actually the creation of common or shared property rights in choices over land use, and the vesting of those rights in the citizens of a municipality. Just as zoning in a frontier area where population density is low would be an absurdly unnecessary effort, but it is increasingly desirable to control externalities in more densely populated areas, so common property becomes *more* desirable, not less, with more intense resource use.

To review then: a common-property regime consists of joint management of a resource system by its co-owners and is increasingly desirable when the behavior of individual resource users imposes high costs on other resource users—that is, where mutual negative externalities multiply, and where resource use intensifies and approaches the productive limits of the resource system. The more completely people depend on extracting as much out of a resource system as the system can sustain, the more essential careful mutual fine-tuning of resource use becomes. This means that we should expect to see common-property arrangements—careful coordination of potentially conflicting resource uses—*increasing*, not decreasing, in frequency as population density and intensity of resource use increase. Collective governance is not always easy, but if the cost of resource degradation is greater still, then we simply have to put up with the inconvenience of negotiating environmental externalities: before the fact in common-property regimes or after the fact otherwise. This is the price of living on a small planet.

A Japanese Example

It is odd in a way that advocates of community resource management and community ownership of resources have to fight such a battle to win a hearing today, as if the "natural" or "inexorable" historical trend is toward ownership by governments or by individuals. In fact, there have been times and places in history when national governments—even harsh and dictatorial ones with burgeoning absolutist ambitions and a perverse interest in regulating some of the tiniest details of daily life—found community resource ownership obvious, "natural," and convenient. In parts of the world that we now call developed—in Europe, Britain, and Japan—community resource management and ownership were quite widespread from the medieval period through early industrialization. And in Japan, which I know best, community resource management was valued after the 17th century in large part for its environmental benefits—in effect, for its ability to create a good "fit" between institutional and ecological boundaries. Thus the upland commons needed to be kept under vegetative cover in perpetuity, not only as a source of kindling and fertilizer and occasional timber, along with many other forest products with agricultural and commercial value including game, but also to prevent soil erosion and to control water flow.

Community ownership of resources in Japan evolved in three stages. First, the notion emerged that groups or communities (as opposed to individuals and governments) may own resources. The phenomenon of community ownership and management probably appeared first among the self-governing villages (*sôson*) of the early 15th century in central Japan (Troost 1990). Later came the idea that resources are finite and need to be managed conservatively by their owners, accounting for the emergence of cautious management regimes in some of these communities. But other communities may well have seen no need to adopt conservative use rules themselves until they observed deterioration of their own resources.[4] Thus there was probably an era of poor commons management in many areas, and more cautious resource rules probably did not spread until after Japan's 17th century crisis with deforestation (see Chiba 1956; Chiba 1970; Totman 1989; and Wigen 1985). Third, the definitions and boundaries around particular forests changed over time continually as rival communities challenged one another. We may view these changes—at least in the instance cited below—as an effort to improve the fit between institutional arrangements and ecological realities.

The boundaries of particular community forests were continually shifting. Villages first laid claims to uncultivated lands nearest them, and thus emerged single-village commons. Villages also fought among themselves to settle claims on land between villages, and thus emerged multi-village commons. As Tokugawa Japan "filled up" with people and literally approached zero population growth rates— 0.03% per year from 1721 to 1846, a rate requiring 2,000 years for the population to double (Smith 1977:7)—forest resources from the commons became increasingly precious to their users, and fighting over ownership and boundaries also became more worthwhile. Partial parcellization of the commons became routine, and during the Tokugawa period (1600–1867) many previously established multi-village forests were renegotiated by the participating communities into single-village forests. This partial parcellization probably occurred where transactions costs for negotiating use rules were high and the ecological losses or efficiency losses due to partial parcellization were negligible. Instead of an entire valley being owned by all of the villages within it, each village ended up owning only the slope above it, up to the ridge or mountain summit.

However, compelling historical or ecological reasons created exceptions to this trend of parcellization, and a multi-village commons might persist even in the face of some conflict. I offer an example below of an area where individual households held rights to arable land, where single villages held shared rights to certain upland meadows and forests, but where groups of villages also retained rights to other commons rather than subdivide them into single-village units. I have written elsewhere about how these villages managed their communal resources and designed rules to discourage overharvesting and encourage contributions of labor to maintenance of the commons (McKean 1982, 1986, 1992a, 1992b). The quick review provided here focuses only on which village(s) owned which commons, and demonstrates that who owned what made enormous sense in terms of internalizing externalities and achieving "fit" between institutional arrangements and ecological boundaries.

At 3,776 meters, Mount Fuji is Japan's highest point, a nearly perfect volcanic cone rising alone above the shallowly scooped-out valleys below. During the Tokugawa period, nineteen villages occupied the valleys on one side of Mount Fuji, below the summit: eight western villages surrounding Lake Kawaguchi, eight northwestern villages straddling the wide pass that descends to Tokyo (then called Edo), and three northern villages surrounding Lake Yamanaka. The eight western villages (Asakawa, Ooishi, Nagahama, Kodachi, Katsuyama, Narisawa, Ooarashi, and Funazu) shared the commons in the Lake Kawaguchi watershed. The three northern villages (Yamanaka, Hirano, and Nagaike) shared the commons around three sides of Lake Yamanaka. But the eight northwestern villages (Niikura, Koakemi, Ooakemi, Matsuyama, Shimoyoshida, Kamiyo-shida, Shinogusa, and Shin'ya) and three northern villages jointly shared the fourth side of northern slope of Mount Fuji itself. Here we will examine the geographic layout of the various patches of common property on all four sides of Lake Yamanaka in order to determine why the three villages within the valley were able to monopolize three sides of their valley but had to share the fourth and largest side with eight other villages.

Documentary evidence from the late 1500s and early 1600s indicates that the principal users of the uncultivated uplands of this valley were people who resided in the valley, not people who lived further away (Hôjô 1979:35–38). Dwellings and individually owned cultivated fields are located near the lake's edge. Three sides of the valley slope upward a short distance to the ridges of the mountains that embrace the valley. The forests and meadows of these three sides are divided into patches that ring the lake; each patch runs from lakeshore to ridge line (see Fig. 11.1). Each village now has exclusive ownership of the patch that is essentially directly uphill from the village itself, and adjacent villages share the patches between them. In this way the community with the greatest stake in maintaining vegetative cover above it owns that forest, and forests between villages are jointly owned and managed by the two or three villages with the greatest stake in coordinating their uses.

But the fourth side of the valley is the north Fuji slope, much more extensive in area than the slopes on the other three sides of the valley (because Mount Fuji is so much higher than the mountains around it). This slope extends directly above the village of Yamanaka, so applying the implicit rule just discovered above we would expect to find that Yamanaka has exclusive use of this slope. However, this is not so. In spite of the Tokugawa trend of parcelling multi-village commons due to conflict between villages over how to manage the land, this

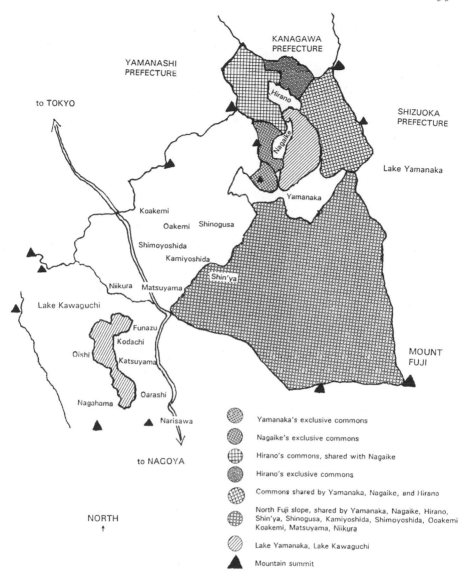

KANAGAWA
PREFECTURE

YAMANASHI
PREFECTURE

to TOKYO

Hirano

SHIZUOKA
PREFECTURE

Nagaike

Lake Yamanaka

Koakemi

Oakemi   Shinogusa

Yamanaka

Shimoyoshida

Kamiyoshida

Shin'ya

Niikura   Matsuyama

Lake Kawaguchi

Funazu

Kodachi

Oishi   Katsuyama

MOUNT
FUJI

Oarashi

Nagahama

Narisawa

to NAGOYA

NORTH

Yamanaka's exclusive commons

Nagaike's exclusive commons

Hirano's commons, shared with Nagaike

Hirano's exclusive commons

Commons shared by Yamanaka, Nagaike, and Hirano

North Fuji slope, shared by Yamanaka, Nagaike, Hirano,
Shin'ya, Shinogusa, Kamiyoshida, Shimoyoshida, Ooakemi
Koakemi, Matsuyama, Niikura

Lake Yamanaka, Lake Kawaguchi

Mountain summit

FIGURE 11.1. Common-property boundaries on the north Fuji slope.

slope survives today as a commons co-owned by eleven villages: by
the three northern villages within the valley of Lake Yamanaka
(Yamanaka, Hirano, and Nagaike), two (Shin'ya and Shinogusa)
located near the ridge line separating this valley from the northwestern zone, and the six northwestern villages beyond the valley
(Kamiyoshida, Shimoyoshida, Matsuyama, Niikura, Ooakemi, and

Koakemi). This arrangement was finalized in a series of lawsuits from 1709 to 1736, during which one or more of the six "outsider" villages sued one or more of the "inner" 3-plus-2 for attempting to block their traditional access to the large slope (Hôjô 1979, 39–332). Minor disputes also continued between the eleven northern and northwestern villages on the one hand and the eight western villages on the other until 1829, but we will focus on the delineation of rights among the eleven northwestern and northern villages.

In the 1736 settlement, the court declared that five of the villages had well-established senior rights to use the slope as they wished, including the right to extract products for sale to others: Yamanaka, Hirano, Nagaike, and the two villages on the adjacent ridge, Shinogusa and Shin'ya. Moreover, among these five, the two located closest to the slope itself, Yamanaka on the lakeshore and Shin'ya halfway up the slope but just over the western ridge of the valley, had the highest rights of all and were essentially allowed to enforce this settlement by excluding others. The entry and use rights of the remaining six villages, well beyond the western ridge and further away from the slope than Shin'ya, were more limited. They could take only grass and kindling for their own consumption and were not allowed to "work the mountain" (*yamakasegi*) for income-generating purposes (Hôjô 1979, 122–128).[5]

The three villages near the lake were the smallest of the eleven in terms of population and agricultural production; the two ridge villages had twice as many households but not much greater agricultural production (see Table 11.2). The power of these five in negotiations and the courts came from the fact that they were strategically located at the resource, and in the case of Yamanaka and Shin'ya, right on the routes most likely to be used by anyone entering the valley from its western entrance. For these geostrategic reasons they had been the earliest claimants, had the greatest incentive to enforce and patrol their claims (and relatively lower costs for this effort), and thus had the strongest legal claims.

These three villages, as well as Shin'ya, also made use of these areas in ways that also increased their incentive to pursue their claims. The villages in the valley did not have particularly good soils, or much flat land, on which to cultivate crops, and their agricultural production was low. But the hilly meadows made good grazing land for packhorses, and the forests provided important income in the form of fuel and useful materials, all fairly nearby. These mountain commons were somewhat less important as a contribution to livelihood for the more distant villages beyond the valley and at lower altitudes, which had much more arable land, fewer animals (only those needed to

TABLE 11.2

The Eleven Villages Sharing the North Fuji Slope (circa 1814)

Villages	Assessed agricultural yields [sondaka][a]	Households	Population	Horses
Northern				
1. Yamanaka	26.5.4.9	76	360	75
2. Hirano	24.6.1.5	62	250	30
3. Nagaike	3.1.0.4	34	172	30
Ridge				
4. Shinogusa	30.2.3.6	123	429	79
5. Shin'ya	56.4.8.3	135	529	30
Northwestern				
6. Kamiyoshida	628.5.1.1	335	1,304	26
7. Shimoyoshida	898.1.8.6	508	2,025	60
8. Matsuyama	35.8.8.6	111	451	25
9. Niikura	285.7.5.5	229	944	40
10. Ooakemi	155.8.2.9	149	604	52
11. Koakemi	205.9.7.0.8	249	871	71

[a]Yields are measured in the classic Tokugawa agricultural (decimal) units of
koku.to.shô.gô (10 gô equal 1 shô, 10 shô equal 1 to, and 10 to equal 1 koku).
One koku equals 180 liters or 5 U.S. bushels.

Source: Hôjô 1979:58.

work the soil), and a greater distance to cover in bringing back any
cumbersome high-bulk items from the mountain. Thus the three-
plus-two villages closest to the north slope of Mount Fuji had
the greatest incentive to preserve senior if not exclusive access to the
slope. The six junior villages outside of the valley had less need for the
slope and found it more troublesome to use. Moreover, because of
their location beyond the immediate watershed of Lake Yamanaka,
they would suffer somewhat less than the northern valley villages if
the slope were depleted, and hardly at all if poor management elsewhere around the valley caused environmental problems *within* the
valley. These six were powerful enough to demand some official participation and junior rights, but were not interested enough to fight
for more than that. Yamanaka needed their cooperation and did not
want an invasion by these villages. Thus a bargaining "space" existed
for compromise on hierarchically layered rights, all to the benefit of
the environmental health of the North Fuji slope.

The common-property arrangements for this valley offer a near-
perfect "fit" with both ecological and institutional considerations.
First and most obviously, the commons in question occupy one

complete watershed basin, and the principal rights-holders are the villages that lie in the basin or near the strategic access to that basin. Second, the uphill areas within the basin are owned and managed by the communities immediately below, which would be those with the greatest stake in the environmental quality of those areas *and* the greatest ability to enforce their will. Thus the patches of commons ringing the lake on three of its sides consisted, in order and proceeding clockwise, of Yamanaka's exclusive commons, Nagaike's exclusive commons, a commons shared by Nagaike and Hirano, Hirano's exclusive commons, and a commons shared by Hirano (including Nagaike, a village originally founded by Hirano residents) and Yamanaka.

The fourth (southern) side of the valley was the North Fuji slope, a huge expanse of forest and meadow. There are two puzzles to solve about its ownership: why was it owned by eleven villages rather than solely by Yamanaka, and why did these eleven villages *not* decide to parcel the slope into eleven pieces? As to the first, the slope was obviously too large for the single village below it, Yamanaka, to patrol alone, since it was so frequently subject to invasion. The 1736 court decision essentially acknowledged this geostrategic fact: Yamanaka would have to share rights with others as a side-payment to ensure that others, even those with smaller stakes, would cooperate in the healthful management of the slope.

These eleven co-owning villages might have opted to parcel this huge slope into eleven pieces. Had they followed the pattern we see on the other three sides of Lake Yamanaka, they would have sliced the slope into eleven village-sized portions. To insure that the owner of each section would have a stake in the environmental health of the lowlands, each section would be a strip running vertically from lakeshore to the Fuji summit, after the manner of the patches around the other three sides of the lake. But this did not happen. However, unlike the rest of the valley, which undulated around corners and had obvious subravines and subsections, parcelling the Fuji slope would have been ridiculous in ecological terms. Even to the untrained eye, the slope is one smooth unit with a broad swath of meadow running horizontally across it. This meadow requires annual burning, so the eleven co-owning villages would have to coordinate their actions anyway—parcelling would not reduce negotiations or transactions costs, and could reduce productivity.

So instead of further parcelling, a system of nested and layered rights shared by multiple villages emerged on this particular portion of the valley. Yamanaka and Shin'ya, strategically located so as to be able to control the access of others to the slope, had the highest or most senior rights to the slope. Hirano, Nagaike, and Shinogusa (somewhat further beyond the western ridge than Shin'ya) held "medium" rights in the slope. They were closer to the slope than any other villages outside of the valley, but their members still had to pass through the village of Yamanaka to reach it and thus had to defer to Yamanaka to some extent in their use of the slope. Finally, the six "outside" villages were able to hold on to junior rights to the slope. They were powerful enough (in terms of population and economic strength) to invade the slope if they wanted to, and this fact made it necessary for the higher rights-holders to strike a bargain with them. In return for junior co-ownership rights and judicious use of the North Fuji slope, the six junior rights-holders cooperated with resource management rules agreed upon by all eleven villages (as confirmed by the 1736 court), rather than invade and destroy the slope.

Thus these communities struggled to define shared or common-property rights in their commons over several hundred years. During this process they resorted to local and national (Tokugawa) courts to pursue their grievances and claims, and the courts relied on documentary evidence and legal precedent (and perhaps a bit on political reality) to determine which community(ies) owned which rights to which commons. But at no point before 1867 did the national government display any interest in asserting any claims of its own over this much-contested land. Rather, the national government's principal interest was in collecting taxes, and regardless of lawsuits over the commons, at any given instant there was an owner who could be taxed. In contrast to the land-hungry regimes in developing countries today, the national government in Tokugawa Japan (then also going through proto-industrial development) considered community resource management an appropriate and convenient way to insure productivity and thus availability of tax revenue from uncultivated lands. Communities like those in the Fuji basin negotiated among themselves and took each other to court. They eventually arrived at an arrangement that took both ecological and strategic political realities into account and lodged property rights in ascending order in the greatest stakeholders, those who would suffer most from environmental deterioration if it occurred, and those who also had the greatest advantage in enforcement. In the end, the choices of communities like these helped the Japanese archipelago recover from deforestation.[6]

Conclusion

This Japanese example illustrates that the government of this very early developing country had no objection to acknowledging and vesting property rights to resources in communities, as opposed to grabbing those rights for itself or transferring them to individuals. I argued at the outset that common-property rights are a form of shared private property, and indeed, in Japanese legal tradition common-property rights (*iriaiken*) are regarded as falling within the rubric of private property [*shi*] rather than state [*kan*] or public [*kô*] property). The North Fuji example also illustrates how common-property regimes could be used to create fit between institutional boundaries and ecological ones, using the watershed basin principle a couple of centuries before we developed folks thought we invented it. The eight villages around Lake Kawaguchi took care of the Kawaguchi uplands, the three villages around Lake Yamanaka took care of three sides of the Yamanaka uplands, and those three-plus-eight more took care of the vast North Fuji slope that descended in one direction toward Yamanaka village and in a more westerly direction toward the other eight villages.

The pattern of which villages owned which commons, and how many villages owned each commons together, was clearly based on the implicit principles of economizing on enforcement costs and internalizing the environmental externalities that could be imposed and suffered. Downhill villages owned their immediate uphill commons, and if several villages might together suffer damage from uphill destruction then several villages retained ownership of those uphill commons. Within multi-village commons, the villages that were likely to suffer more and the villages with a comparative advantage in monitoring, possessed higher rights and entitlements to the resource than villages likely to suffer much less (by reason of distance or topography).

And finally, the Tokugawa government, obsessed with tax revenue and public order but totally uninterested in civil liberties or democracy, nonetheless backed up these property-rights arrangements with enforcement through the courts, to which communities with rival claims could appeal. We must realize that if this legal backup system had operated whimsically or had been missing altogether, then the only villages able to protect the commons in which they had a stake would have been those capable of mounting extralegal vigilante squads. The long-run consequence of fighting by these means would not only have been extremely costly, but the uncertainty and short time horizons created by such conflict would have led to rampant resource destruction, much as we see in the developing world today. The lessons here for developing countries today are obvious: get the common-property rights right, make them match ecological consid- erations, vest resource rights in the communities nearest the resource, and defend those rights by offering access to courts (warning: these courts will have to use fair and predictable reasoning in their deci- sions). As a result, nations should get improved environmental con- ditions and better economic results, and governments should get higher tax revenue. Somebody ought to try it!

NOTES

1. The paper upon which this chapter is based was originally presented at the Fifth Meeting of the International Association for the Study of Common Property, Bodø, Norway, 24–28 May 1995.

2. The nature of a good can change with technology. Thus TV broadcasts from satellites are pure public goods when the satellite signals are unscram- bled. The advent of scramblers, cable services, and purchasable descrambler boxes converts TV broadcasts into excludable and nonsubtractible goods (thus toll goods or club goods). The advent of cheap illegal descramblers converts TV broadcasts back into nearly public goods again. But at any par- ticular technological moment, the nature of a good is indeed a given.

3. This definition obviously does not include all governments. Many auto- cratic governments neither intend nor accomplish the representation of the general public, and would be better described as private government.

4. I see no reason to argue that precapitalists are innately or self-con- sciously conservationist. Some precapitalist cultures espouse the notion that the natural world is infinitely abundant (see Berkes 1987 and Brightman 1987). But even such societies may produce conservationist outcomes in their resource use simply through practices that optimize yield per effort (see Hames 1987 and Stocks 1987).

5. The 1736 decision did not settle all conflicts of course. Disputes con- tinued over how to divide income from the North Fuji commons, over the invasion of the five "senior" villages' rice fields by the six "junior" villages, over the division of cultivable portions of the commons into arable fields, and so on. Occasionally villagers were overcome by irresistible urges to invade others' commons to steal birch bark or fodder, and they risked having vandals from the offended village come to raid their sheds, confiscate the contraband, and destroy their farm tools in return. Matters might be fur- ther confused when farmers with rights hired persons from villages without rights as their assistants for a harvesting trip to a particular commons. See Hôjô (1979), passim.

6. Chiba (1956, 1970) and Totman (1989) suggest that community man- agement was part of the problem during 17th century deforestation, and I agree that communities with either direct or vicarious experience with poor

management are much more likely than others to go to the trouble of developing prudent sustainable management. But I have argued elsewhere that whatever role community management played in contributing to the deforestation of 17th century Japan, surviving commons were part of the recovery (McKean 1988). In addition, it is vital to acknowledge that perhaps the greatest contribution to recovery was the development, by feudal lords for use on their own domain forests, of scientific silviculture (Totman 1989).

REFERENCES

Berkes, F. 1987. Common-property resource management and Cree Indian fisheries in subarctic Canada. Pages 66–91 *in* B. J. McCay and J. M. Acheson, eds. *The Question of the Commons: The Culture and Ecology of Communal Resources*. University of Arizona Press, Tucson.

Brightman, R. A. 1987. Conservation and resource depletion: The case of the boreal forest Algonquians. Pages 121–141 *in* B. J. McCay and J. M. Acheson, eds. *The Question of the Commons: The Culture and Ecology of Communal Resources*. University of Arizona Press, Tucson.

Chiba, T. 1956. Hageyama no kenkyû [*Research on Bald Mountains*]. Nôrin kyôkai, Tokyo.

Chiba, T. 1970. Hageyama no bunka [*The Culture of Bald Mountains*]. Gakuseisha, Tokyo.

Coase, R. 1960. The problem of social cost. *Journal of Law and Economics* 3:1–44.

Dugelby, B. 1995. Ph.D. Dissertation in Tropical Ecology. School of the Environment. Duke University, Durham, NC.

Hames, R. 1987. Game conservation or efficient hunting? Pages 92–107 *in* B. J. McCay and J. M. Acheson, eds. *The Question of the Commons: The Culture and Ecology of Communal Resources*. University of Arizona Press, Tucson.

Hôjô, H. 1979. Kinsei ni okeru rin'ya iriai no shokeitai [*The Various Forms of Common Access to Forest and Meadow in the Early Modern Period*]. Sonraku shakai kôzôshi kenkyû series #5. Ochanomizu shobô, Tokyo.

McKean, M. A. 1982. The Japanese experience with scarcity: Management of traditional common lands. *Environmental Review* 6(2):63–88.

McKean, M. A. 1986. Management of traditional common lands [*iriaichi*] in Japan. Pages 533–589 *in* D. W. Bromley, D. Feeny, J. L. Gilles, M. A. McKean, R. J. Oakerson, E. Ostrom, P. Peters, C. F. Runge, and J. T. Thomson, eds. *Proceedings of the Conference on Common Property Resource Management*, April 21–26, 1985, Annapolis, Maryland. National Academy of Sciences, Washington, D.C.

McKean, M. A. 1988. "Collective Action and the Environment in Tokugawa Japan: Success and Failure in Management of the Commons." Paper presented at the Association of Asian Studies, San Francisco.

McKean, M. A. 1992a. Management of traditional common lands [*iriaichi*] in Japan. Pages 63–98 *in* D. W. Bromley, D. Feeny, M. A. McKean, P.

Peters, J. L. Gilles, R. J. Oakerson, C. F. Runge, and J. T. Thomson, eds. *Making the Commons Work: Theory, Practice and Policy.* Institute for Contemporary Studies Press, San Francisco.

McKean, M. A. 1992b. Success on the commons: A comparative examination of institutions for common property resource management. *Journal of Theoretical Politics* 4(3):247–282.

Ostrom, E. 1990. *Governing the Commons: The Evolution of Institutions for Collective Action.* Cambridge University Press, Cambridge, UK.

Smith, T. C. 1977. *Nakahara: Family Farming and Population in a Japanese Village, 1717–1830.* Stanford University Press, Stanford, CA.

Stocks, A. 1987. Resource management in an Amazon *Varzea* lake ecosystem: The Cocamilla case. Pages 108–120 *in* B. J. McCay and J. M. Acheson, eds. *The Question of the Commons: The Culture and Ecology of Communal Resources.* University of Arizona Press, Tucson.

Tang, S. Y. 1992. *Institutions and Collective Action: Self-Governance in Irrigation.* Institute for Contemporary Studies Press, San Francisco.

Totman, C. 1989. *The Green Archipelago: Forestry in Preindustrial Japan.* University of California Press, Berkeley.

Troost, K. K. 1990. "Common Property and Community Formation: Self-governing Villages in Late Medieval Japan, 1300–1600." Ph.D. Dissertation in History, Harvard University, Cambridge, MA.

Wigen L. K. 1985. "Common Losses: Transformations of Commonland and Peasant Livelihood in Tokugawa Japan, 1603–1868." M. A. Thesis in Geography. University of California, Berkeley.

CHAPTER 12

Rights, Rules, and Resources in International Society

ORAN R. YOUNG

Introduction

We have embarked on an era of dramatic and highly visible new challenges to our capacity to solve problems of governance at the international level. At the same time, we are currently witnessing a variety of experiments with promising new forms of governance in international society. Because the resultant governance systems have emerged *ad hoc* in connection with specific issues and because many of them reflect developments that are not easy to fit into our conventional view of international society as a decentralized system of sovereign states, we are much more conscious of the rising demand for international governance than of the range of new options for supplying governance in this social context. Yet the new options are exciting not only because they suggest novel ways of addressing specific problems at the international level but also because they may stimulate new insights about the nature of governance and governance systems that are of broader or more generic interest (Young 1994a).

Nowhere is this more apparent than in the realm of issues pertaining to natural resources and the environment. Whereas the cold war bred an intense effort to protect and preserve existing institutions, the environmental challenge prompts a sense that new arrangements are needed to achieve sustainability in human/environment relations. Especially notable in this connection is the growth of functionally specific regimes dealing with such matters as marine pollution, endangered species, transboundary fluxes of airborne pollutants, ozone depletion, and climate change. What is more, efforts to solve environmental problems both reflect and affect significant developments in international society (Lipschutz 1992; Princen and

Finger 1994). Although states remain central players in this issue area, nonstate actors have made particularly striking advances both in the creation of environmental regimes and in efforts to make these regimes effective once they are in place (Wapner 1995). As the environment and trade debate makes clear, moreover, dealing with environmental concerns has made us aware of the need to think more systematically about institutional linkages or the ways in which individual governance systems are embedded in larger institutional structures that impinge on each other in international society (Charnovitz 1995). None of this suggests that international society will undergo a sea change during the foreseeable future giving rise to some successor to the familiar states system. Rather, it emphasizes the need for a more sophisticated understanding of international society emphasizing the significance of new forms of governance in a setting in which states continue to serve as primary repositories of authority.

In this chapter, I sketch out the main contours of the new conception of governance that is arising among students of international relations with particular reference to issues relating to natural resources and the environment.[1] The first substantive section addresses the idea of governance at the most general level. This is followed by a section dealing with several conceptual matters that require attention in making the transition from generic ideas about governance to the specific setting of issues pertaining to natural resources and the environment at the international level. The next three sections take up matters relating to the formation of international governance systems, their effectiveness as determinants of collective outcomes in international society, and the processes through which they change over time. A final substantive section turns to the problem of scale and asks whether there are helpful comparisons to be drawn between international environmental governance systems and the small-scale systems that are the central focus of the burgeoning literature on governing the commons (Ostrom 1990).

The Idea of Governance

Governance arises as a matter of public concern whenever the members of a social group find that they are interdependent in the sense that the actions of each individual member impinge on the welfare of the others. Interdependence gives rise to conflict when the efforts of individuals to achieve their goals interfere with or thwart the efforts of others to pursue their own ends. It emerges as a basis for cooperation, on the other hand, when opportunities arise to enhance social welfare by acting to coordinate the activities of the individual members of the group. More generally, interdependence leads to interactive decisionmaking and generates the potential for collective-action problems in the sense that individual actors, left to their own devices in an interdependent world, frequently suffer joint losses as a result of conflict or fail to reap joint gains due to an inability to cooperate (Olson 1965; Schelling 1978; Hardin 1982; Young 1989). The higher the level of interdependence among the members of the group, moreover, the more pervasive and complex these collective-action problems become.

At the most general level, governance involves the establishment and operation of social institutions or, in other words, sets of roles, rules, decisionmaking procedures, and programs that serve to define social practices and to guide the interactions of those participating in these practices (North 1990). Such institutions may address a wide range of issues. But politically significant institutions or governance systems are arrangements designed to resolve social conflicts, enhance social welfare, and, more generally, alleviate collective-action problems in a world of interdependent actors (Young 1994a). Governance, on this account, does not presuppose the need to create material entities or organizations—"governments"—to administer the social practices that arise to handle the function of governance (Ellickson 1991). The burden of proof may actually reside with those who maintain that the establishment of governments is necessary to achieve these ends. This is so because the operation of any government or organized public authority is costly, both in material terms (for example, the revenues required to run government agencies) and in terms of more intangible values (for instance, the bureaucratic inefficiencies and the restrictions on individual liberties imposed by even the most enlightened governments).

Approached in this way, the initially counterintuitive distinction between governance and government and the growing interest in the idea of "governance without government" become clear (Rosenau and Czempiel 1992). The key issue for those of us interested in this distinction concerns the role that social institutions or governance systems, in contrast to organizations or governments, play in ameliorating or resolving collective-action problems currently rising to the top of the political agenda in a variety of settings. The general proposition that groups of interdependent actors can and often do succeed in handling the function of governance without resorting to the creation of governments in the conventional sense is now well established. The literature on common property arrangements in small-scale stateless societies, growing rapidly as a counter to the intuitively appealing but empirically tenuous notion of the "tragedy of the commons" (Hardin 1968), bears this out (McCay and Acheson 1987, Bromley 1992). Today, leading students of governance are busy pinning down the conditions under which "governance without government" can succeed rather than prolonging unproductive debates about the need to establish centralized organizations to solve an array of collective-action problems (Ostrom 1990; McKean 1992).

The point of drawing a clear distinction between governance and government, however, is not to abandon the idea that organized public authorities can and often do play important roles in coming to terms with the agenda of governance problems arising in the world today. On the contrary, the introduction of the distinction opens up a major new research agenda for students of governance (Young 1994a). What roles can organizations perform in establishing institutional arrangements designed to allow groups to avoid or alleviate collective-action problems? Under what conditions can the resultant institutions operate successfully without the aid of organizations to administer their provisions? When administrative arrangements are needed, how can we design appropriate organizations well-tailored to the roles they are expected to play in connection with specific institutions? Answers to these questions will carry us a long way toward developing the intellectual capital needed to meet the challenges to our capacity to solve problems of governance likely to arise during the foreseeable future.

International Governance

Recent work on governance in international society centers on the study of regimes or social institutions consisting of agreed-upon principles, norms, procedures, and programs that govern the interactions of actors in specific issue areas (Levy et al. 1995). For the most part, the formal or official members of these regimes are states, although it is increasingly apparent that a variety of nonstate actors have influential roles to play in both the formation and the operation of international governance systems. Thus, we speak of the international trade regime resting on the General Agreement on Tariffs and Trade (GATT) together with the more recent agreement establishing the World Trade Organization (WTO), the regime for Antarctica and the Southern Ocean comprising the several components of the Antarctic Treaty System, and the ozone regime consisting of the 1985 Vienna

Convention together with the 1987 Montreal Protocol as amended in London in 1990 and in Copenhagen in 1992. As these examples suggest, international regimes can and often do vary substantially in terms of membership, functional scope, geographical domain, degree of formalization, and stage of development. Yet most regimes rest on one or more (not necessarily legally binding) constitutive documents, and all successful regimes produce a convergence of expectations on the part of their members.

Approached in this way, international governance systems are not about property rights in the ordinary sense of the term. The essential point, in this connection, flows from the distinction between *imperium* and *dominium.* States—like other collective or corporate entities—can and often do become owners of real property, including land and natural resources. In some countries, the state holds title to the great majority of the land and associated natural resources. Even in the United States, where the political culture emphasizes the virtues of private property, the federal government owns about a third of the country's land and associated resources (Public Land Law Review Commission 1970; Brubaker 1984). In their role as the principal members of international society, however, states are concerned primarily with the entitlements of political authority or, in other words, sovereign rights (that is, *imperium*) in contrast to the entitlements of ownership or property rights (that is, *dominium*). By exercising sovereign rights, states can place restrictions on the activities of holders of property rights and, in extreme cases, act to rearrange the bundles of rights available to property owners. For the most part, by contrast, holders of property rights have no such capacity to influence the exercise of sovereign rights. It follows that international regimes, like those established under the convention on long-range transboundary air pollution (LRTAP) and its protocols, or the convention on international trade in endangered species of fauna and flora (CITES), are properly understood as systems of rights, rules, and relationships designed to bring order into the interactions of sovereign states and other actors in international society rather than as systems of property rights intended to bring order into the interactions of property owners. Even so, the similarities between resource regimes in international society and property regimes in other social settings are sufficiently strong to make it illuminating to compare and contrast these institutional arrangements systematically (Young 1994b).

Although it is obviously desirable to begin a discussion of governance systems with propositions framed at the most general level, there are often good reasons to partition the universe of issues involving natural resources and the environment at the international level into subcategories or classes. Many criteria are available for use in subdividing this universe of cases; none is objectively correct. In thinking about the formation and operation of governance systems, however, I have found it particularly helpful to focus on the jurisdictional characteristics of the problems at stake and to differentiate among international commons, shared natural resources, and transboundary externalities.

International commons are physical or biological systems that lie wholly or largely outside the jurisdiction of any of the individual members of international society but that are of interest to a number of members—or their nationals—as valued resources. Examples of current interest include high seas fisheries, deep seabed minerals, the electromagnetic spectrum, the stratospheric ozone layer, the global climate system, the global hydrological system, and outer space (Brown et al. 1977). Three broad options are available to those concerned with the governance of international commons: enclosure through the extension of national jurisdiction, the creation of a supranational or world government, and the introduction of codes of conduct analogous to common property arrangements in small-scale stateless societies. Although the attention of students of international relations has long focused on the first two of these options, the rise of the idea of governance without government has stimulated a rapid growth of interest in the third option.

Shared natural resources, by contrast, are physical or biological systems that extend into or across the jurisdictions of two or more members of international society. They may involve renewable resources (for example, migratory stocks of wild animals or straddling stocks of fish), nonrenewable resources (for example, pools of oil and gas that underlie areas subject to the jurisdiction of two or more states), or complex ecosystems that transcend the boundaries of national jurisdictions (for example, river basins or regional seas). As these examples suggest, there may be significant asymmetries among the states concerned with shared natural resources. The circumstances of upstream states differ from those of downstream states, and fish stocks that are economically important to one state may be of little interest to another. But in all cases, the fundamental problem in dealing with shared natural resources is to establish joint management regimes or arrangements analogous to unitization schemes among property owners in domestic society (Bernauer 1994; Richardson 1988).

For their part, transboundary externalities arise when activities occurring wholly within the jurisdiction of one state nevertheless produce results affecting the welfare of those residing in other jurisdictions. The classic cases involve tangible impacts, like the acidification of Swedish lakes arising from emissions of airborne pollutants on the European continent or the loss of biological diversity associated with the destruction of moist tropical forests in the Amazon Basin. But transboundary externalities may also involve intangible concerns, as in the case of the destruction of a world heritage site (for instance, the city of Dubrovnik) as a result of civil war. As these examples suggest, transboundary externalities can and often do give rise to asymmetries between victims and perpetrators of environmental harms. This accounts for the widespread interest in devising comprehensive liability rules covering transboundary impacts of actions occurring within individual jurisdictions as well as promulgating general rules covering such situations (for example, the "polluter pays" principle). But experience suggests that actual cases raise complex issues concerning the rights of outsiders to intervene in the domestic affairs of individual states as well as the benefits to victims of offering to assist perpetrators to change their ways (Lyons and Mastanduno 1995).

The Formation of Governance Systems

It is undoubtedly accurate to say that students of international governance systems have accorded top priority over the last 10 to 15 years to the study of regime formation—the effort to understand why specific regimes emerge to deal with some problems but not others (Haggard and Simmons 1987; Rittberger 1990; Young and Osherenko 1993). The resultant stream of research offers a broad range of perspectives on the process of regime formation. But even in this brief account, it will help to differentiate four distinct concerns that have surfaced in the literature on the formation of governance systems: the nature of the problem, processes of regime formation, stages of regime formation, and social driving forces.

An intuitively appealing argument suggests that the "properties of issues . . . (pre)determine the ways in which they are dealt with" (Rittberger and Zuern 1991:171). This idea has generated an effort to introduce theoretically grounded distinctions among types of issues and to show the links between the type of issue under consideration and the prospects for success in efforts to form international regimes. Volker Rittberger and Michael Zuern, for example, argue that issues involving value conflicts will be harder to deal with from the perspective of regime formation than issues featuring conflicts of interest about relatively assessed goods and that both of these types of issues will be more difficult to handle than issues featuring conflicts of interest about absolutely assessed goods (Rittberger and Zuern 1991). Others have turned to game-theoretic ideas suggesting, for example, that coordination problems (that is, interactive relationships featuring at least one equilibrium outcome) will be easier to deal with than collaboration problems when it comes to the formation of regimes (Martin 1994). The problem with this suggestive line of analysis is that it is difficult to characterize real-world problems in terms of distinctions of this sort either because actual problems exhibit elements of several analytically different types of issues or because they are not sufficiently well-specified in the thinking of the participants to allow for this type of categorization. Under the circumstances, this approach to the study of regime formation has not yet contributed much to our efforts to explain successes and failures in connection with the creation of international resource regimes.

Another approach that has received attention among students of regime formation focuses on processes and features a distinction among spontaneous or self-generating regimes, imposed regimes, and negotiated regimes (Young 1989). While most regimes are sooner or later articulated in treaties, conventions, or other explicit agreements, there are cases in which such agreements are largely matters of codifying informal rights and rules that have evolved over time through a process of converging expectations or tacit bargaining (Downs and Rocke 1990). These are spontaneous regimes. In other cases, a dominant actor or hegemon (in the language of recent analyses of regime formation) plays the central role in the process of forming governance systems either by coercing others into accepting its preferred institutional arrangements or by making it attractive for others to accede to its preferences (Keohane 1984). Negotiated regimes, by contrast, are products of an explicit bargaining process in which a number of actors possessing significant, though not necessarily symmetrical, bargaining strength reach agreement on the constitutive provisions of an international regime (Young 1989). This approach has proven quite helpful to those endeavoring to reconstruct and understand the processes involved in the formation of specific regimes, although it is now apparent that the central distinction is analytic in nature in the sense that two or more of the processes may play some role in connection with a single case of regime formation.

Additionally, it now seems helpful to subdivide the overall process of forming governance systems into at least three stages: agenda formation, negotiation, and operationalization. Recent studies have tended to emphasize the negotiation stage, which covers the period starting with the initiation of explicit bargaining over the terms of an agreement and ends with the signing of the agreement itself. In the case of climate change, for example, the negotiation stage began with the first meeting of the Intergovernmental Negotiating Committee (INC) in February 1991 and ended with the signing of the Climate Change Convention in the course of the United Nations Conference on Environment and Development (UNCED) during June 1992 (Bodansky 1993). On this account, agenda formation and operationalization bracket the central stage of negotiation. Agenda formation covers the processes through which an issue initially makes it way onto the international political agenda, is framed for purposes of consideration in international forums, and rises to a sufficiently prominent place on the international agenda to justify the expenditure of time and political capital required to move it to the negotiation stage (Stein 1989). Operationalization, by contrast, encompasses the processes involved in moving from the negotiation of an agreement to the establishment of a governance system—from paper to practice (Mitchell 1994). This includes not only the ratification process but also the setting up of international machinery and the initiation of programmatic activities within the jurisdictions of individual members (Spector and Korula 1992). Although this line of analysis is just developing, it is already clear that the distinction among stages crosscuts the distinction among processes so that different processes are more or less central during different stages of regime formation.

All of this has given rise to a lively debate about the relative importance of various driving social forces in determining success and failure in efforts to form international governance systems and to shape the substantive content of the regimes that are established. Recent studies of regime formation have directed attention to the exercise of power (for example, the role of hegemons) (Keohane 1984; Snidal 1985), the impact of ideas (for instance, the significance of epistemic communities) (Haas 1992), and the interplay of interests (for example, the dynamics of institutional bargaining) (Young 1989, 1994a). The debate about the relative weight of these drivers as determinants of regime formation taps into larger debates about the roles of material conditions, cognitive factors, and interactive decision-making as determinants of the course of human affairs. It is hardly surprising, under the circumstances, that we are nowhere near a definitive resolution of this debate with respect to the formation of international governance systems. What is clear at this stage, however, is that different driving forces are more or less prominent in different cases of regime formation and, perhaps more importantly, that power, ideas, and interests often interact in complex ways as determinants of outcomes in specific cases of regime formation (Young and Osherenko 1993).

Regime Effectiveness

Those who study institutions operative in international society have become increasingly concerned with the question of whether and how international governance systems matter in the sense of impacting the flow of collective outcomes. Ultimately, the study of institutions in any social setting rests on the premise that some significant proportion of the variance in the collective outcomes occurring in that setting can be explained or accounted for in terms of the operation of institutions in contrast to material conditions or ideas (Cox 1986). Although the idea that institutions are important in this sense is generally accepted without debate among students of domestic societies, it is a contentious matter in the field of international relations, which has long been dominated by the views of realists and neorealists who tend to view institutions as epiphenomena that reflect deeper forces like the distribution of power in international society (Strange 1983). To meet this challenge, students of international environmental regimes and international governance systems more generally have now embarked on a rapidly growing program of research dealing with the implementation of international accords, compliance with the provisions of governance systems, and, more generally, the behavioral impacts of international regimes (Chayes and Chayes 1995; Haas et al. 1993; Levy et al. 1991; Wettestad 1995). In this connection, four clusters of issues have emerged as central to the debate about effectiveness: the meaning of effectiveness, causal links between institutions and outcomes, behavioral pathways, and broader consequences.

Intuitively, it makes sense to regard international regimes as successful or effective when they serve to solve or alleviate the problems that motivate their founders to create them. As it turns out, however, it is extremely difficult to evaluate such effectiveness empirically. This has led to a variety of other perspectives on effectiveness that emphasize things like goal attainment, implementation and compliance, behavioral change, social learning, and the initiation of new social practices (Young 1994a). It is apparent that there is some relationship between these different measures of effectiveness. Achieving the goal of a 30 percent reduction of sulfur dioxide emissions under LRTAP, for example, has something to do with solving the problems caused by transboundary fluxes of airborne pollutants. But as this example makes clear, these different measures of effectiveness are by no means perfect substitutes for one another. Beyond this, some analysts are equally, if not more, interested in evaluative considerations, like the extent to which the outcomes produced by institutions are efficient, equitable, or sustainable, in contrast to the simple question of whether or not governance systems make a difference. Students of regime effectiveness therefore have a sizable agenda of conceptual issues to deal with in coming to terms with the consequences of international governance systems.

The issue of causal links turns on the problem of separating spurious correlations from real connections. In general, it is not sufficient to observe that a governance system is created and that the problem that led to its creation subsequently subsides. The danger of ending up with spurious correlations in the sense that both the problem and its solution are attributable to other causes is too great for that. Several methodological procedures have emerged as potentially helpful solutions. These include: natural experiments, thought experiments, and laboratory experiments. It is sometimes possible to conduct natural experiments, for example, by finding cases that resemble each other closely except in terms of the character of the institutional arrangements that are present and then looking for systematic effects of the institutional variance. With respect to thought experiments, attention has focused recently on the exploration of counterfactuals and the use of process tracing and thick description as means of thinking about them (Fearon 1991; Biersteker 1993). Finally, laboratory experiments can be helpful sources of insights that can be formulated subsequently as hypotheses to be tested through an examination of real-world cases.

Useful as these techniques are in weeding out spurious relationships, they are no substitute for exploring the behavioral pathways or causal mechanisms that link institutions to behavior and ultimately determine the extent to which they succeed in solving the problems that motivate their creation. Among other things, an understanding of such behavioral pathways will prove invaluable to those charged with designing new governance systems to deal with problems like climate change and the loss of biological diversity. Two major studies have opened up this stream of work among students of international resource regimes. One emphasizes the roles that regimes play in increasing concern about relevant problems, improving the contractual environment among participants, and enhancing the capacity of individual members to implement the provisions of regimes (Haas et al. 1993). An even more ambitious project starts by spelling out a series of distinct behavioral models that seem relevant on theoretical grounds and proceeds to investigate the extent to which these models can account for variance in the behavior of regime members in actual cases (Levy et al. 1995). Thus, regimes may be thought of as (i) utility modifiers, (ii) enhancers of cooperation, (iii) bestowers of authority, (iv) learning facilitators, (v) role definers, and (vi) agents of internal realignments. What differentiates these models from one another is the assumptions they make about the driving forces that govern behavior at the international level.

Whether or not specific regimes prove effective in solving the problems that motivate their creation, governance systems can and often do produce consequences that extend beyond the issue area in which they are located. These broader consequences may take the form of demonstration effects (where arrangements devised in one issue area are subsequently copied in other issue areas) or of cognitive effects (where efforts to solve one problem lead to the development of new ways of thinking that influence the analysis of other problems). At the same time, broader consequences may be more overtly political. Regimes can establish social practices whose operation alters the distribution of power among key actors over time or fosters developments that have important implications for international society as a whole (for example, the growing role of nonstate actors). For the most part, these broader effects are unintended and unforeseen by those who labor to create international governance systems in the first place. But this does nothing to diminish the significance of these consequences (Levy et al. 1995).

Institutional Change

Once formed, international regimes rarely become static, unchanging institutional structures. On the contrary, they give rise to highly dynamic social practices that change continually. As the case of whales and whaling suggests, profound changes can follow shifts in the size and composition of a governance system's membership. The case of ozone depletion, by contrast, illustrates how institutional change can flow from altered understandings of the nature of the problem to be solved. Or to turn to the case of Antarctica, changes can involve a broadening of functional scope resulting from the addition of new elements that enlarge the range of substantive issues a regime covers. These collectively merely illustrate the wide array of institutional changes that occur in connection with most international governance systems on a regular basis. It is probably accurate to say that regime change has received less attention from students of international affairs than issues relating to regime effectiveness and, especially, regime formation. But any systematic treatment of change in international governance systems must deal with at least four concerns: types of change, forms of change, processes of change, and sources of change.

Institutional changes come in many varieties. At the simplest level, regimes may undergo changes affecting their functional scope, geographical domain, or membership. But many other types of change are common and may occur in conjunction with such simple changes. Changes can lead to alterations in decisionmaking procedures, compliance mechanisms, or revenue sources. In other cases, organizations emerge to administer the provisions of governance systems where none existed in the original design of the regimes in question. The recurrent debate about whether to create a standing organization to operate the Antarctic Treaty System centers on this type of change. Even more fundamentally, governance systems may experience transformations of defining principles or norms, merge with other institutional arrangements to form new institutions, or go out of existence altogether. This has led some observers to ask whether international resource regimes exhibit an identifiable life cycle, which features a process of growth toward maturity and subsequent decline. Of course, a number of different types of change are apt to occur simultaneously in real-world situations so that characterizing the dynamics of any given governance system can become a tricky business.

Regardless of type, institutional change may assume any of a number of forms. Two central dichotomies will help to organize thinking in this area. Thus, change may be endogenous (or developmental) or exogenous (or environmental). Endogenous changes are those that take place as a result of the operation of a regime itself. The addition of new consultative parties to the Antarctic Treaty System as a result of explicit actions on the part of the Antarctic Treaty Consultative Meetings is a case in point. Exogenous changes, by contrast, are results of forces external to the regime itself (for example, major alterations of a marine ecosystem due to changes in water temperature). At the same time, institutional change may be incremental (gradual) or discontinuous (nonlinear). Although the dividing line is sometimes arbitrary, incremental change takes place step-by-step (for example, the addition of new members to a regime one by one over a period of years), whereas discontinuous change involves a sharp break with the past (for example, a wholesale change in membership all at once).

Obviously, it is possible to combine these dichotomies to form a matrix in which the cells represent incremental endogenous change, incremental exogenous change, discontinuous endogenous change, and discontinuous exogenous change. All these forms of change occur with considerable regularity in the realm of international resource regimes, and any of these forms of change may affect any of the types of change identified in the preceding paragraph.

Turning now to processes of change, several additional aspects of regime dynamics come into focus. Changes may take the form of intentional or planned alterations in institutional arrangements or unintentional or *de facto* alterations. To make matters more complex, some changes are ardently pursued by some of the participants in a governance system, while others are just as vigorously opposed. Consider the debate over the introduction of the so-called Revised Management Procedures for whaling or the negotiation of substantive protocols pertaining to the emission of greenhouse gases as cases in point (Victor and Salt 1994). Beyond this, changes may be sought through the use of procedures spelled out in the regime itself or through processes that are not recognized, much less accepted as legitimate, under the provisions of the relevant governance system. To make this issue more complex, governance systems vary greatly both in the extent to which they prescribe procedures for changing their provisions and in the stringency of the relevant transformation rules in cases where they do set forth explicit procedures to be followed by those advocating change. What is more, real-world cases may turn out to be difficult to sort out with respect to these questions of process. Determined advocates of change are apt to pursue their goals through all available channels both within the rules and outside the rules. Moreover, changes that are ultimately attributable to pressure brought to bear outside the confines of a governance system itself are often ratified through the use of formal procedures prescribed by the regime.

As these observations suggest, we must also examine the sources of institutional change or the driving forces leading to alterations in international resource regimes. Surprisingly little effort has been devoted to answering such questions. An early attempt on the part of Robert Keohane and Joseph Nye seeks to explain institutional changes in terms of factors relating to economic processes, overall power structure, issue structure, and international organizations (Keohane and Nye 1977). Although this analysis constitutes a good beginning, it leaves much to be desired as a theory of institutional change. It overemphasizes material conditions in contrast to evolving ideas or shifting configurations of interests; reflects a preoccupation with power, which is common among students of politics but which is misplaced in the study of international governance systems; and leaves no place for changes in the physical and biological systems with which social institutions interact and which are often highly dynamic in their own right. Understanding the driving forces is critical to any effort to explain or predict patterns of change in international resource regimes. This is an area that deserves much more attention than it has received so far among students of international governance.

The Problem of Scale

The mainstream of the rapidly growing literature on human/ environment relations deals with small-scale stateless societies and centers on the issue of governing the commons (Ostrom 1990). Although some writers have raised questions about the impact of outside forces on these local systems (Jodha 1993), the bulk of the existing literature treats local systems as largely self-contained entities and focuses on the dynamics of endogenous forces. At the same time, a second, largely unrelated, stream of analysis deals with international resource regimes or governance systems operating at the international level. In this connection, the problem of scale turns on the extent to which findings derived from the study of small-scale societies can be scaled up to apply to international society and, conversely, the extent to which findings resulting from the study of international institutions can be scaled down to apply to small-scale societies (Young 1994b). The problem revolves around the transferability of propositions and models from one level to another in the dimensions of space and time.

As it turns out, the two bodies of literature have a number of things in common, including a focus on interactive decisionmaking, a concern with collective-action problems, and an interest in the role of social institutions as devices for solving these problems (Keohane and Ostrom 1995). Clearly, macroscale systems are not merely small-scale systems writ large, and microscale systems are not mere microcosms of large-scale systems. It follows that we cannot simply assume that the mechanisms at work at the two levels are the same and that any effort to transfer propositions from one level to another—to scale up and scale down—should be treated with a healthy sense of skepticism. Yet the similarities between the two bodies of literature are striking. It is therefore important to think carefully about both common themes that unite the two and analytic disparities that divide them. The observation that transparency is an important determinant of compliant behavior at both scales, for example, is a significant finding (Ostrom 1990; Chayes and Chayes 1993). By contrast, the differences between systems based on property rights (*dominium*) and arrangements based on sovereign rights (*imperium*) are surely significant. The evaluation of similarities and differences between the two levels, however, is less important than the insights about both to be gleaned from an effort to sort out what is transferable across scales and what is peculiar to microscale or macroscale systems in the realm of human/environment relations.

Conclusion

The study of international regimes or governance systems has accelerated among students of international relations over the last two decades. This is particularly apparent in the realm of issues pertaining to natural resources and the environment and has contributed significantly to our understanding of international society by drawing a clear distinction between governance and government and by providing an alternative to the traditional emphasis on intergovernmental organizations (e.g., the United Nations) in solving problems of governance at the international level. Will this research program yield cumulative insights and make a lasting contribution to our understanding of international governance? The answer to this question depends on answers to several more specific questions. Has regime analysis produced a distinctive conception of governance that offers a viable alternative to preexisting conceptions? Will international regimes prove effective as problem solvers in at least some important areas, and can we identify conditions that might guarantee success in this realm? Does the operation of specific regimes in a variety of issue areas have broader consequences for the future of international society? Are these consequences likely to serve the interests of conservatives (seeking to maintain the states system) or of reformers (seeking to modify that system)? The jury is currently out regarding these questions; it may remain out for some time. Yet early (favorable) responses to these questions justify an investment of additional resources to flesh out this approach to governance in international society.

NOTE

1. An essay prepared under the auspices of the Research Program on Property Rights and the Performance of Natural Resource Systems of the Beijer Institute in Stockholm formed the basis of this chapter.

REFERENCES

Bernauer, T. 1994. *Protecting the River Rhine Against Chloride Pollution.* Harvard Center for International Affairs, Cambridge, MA.

Biersteker, T. J. 1993. Constructing historical counterfactuals to assess the consequences of international regimes: The global debt regime and the course of the debt crisis of the 1980s. Pages 315–338 *in* V. Rittberger, ed. *Regime Theory and International Relations.* Clarendon Press, Oxford, UK.

Bodansky, D. 1993. The United Nations framework convention on climate change: A commentary. *Yale Journal of International Law* 18:453–558.

Bromley, D. W., ed. 1992. *Making the Commons Work: Theory, Practice, and Policy.* ICS Press, San Francisco.

Brown, S., N. W. Cornell, L. L. Fabian, and E. Brown Weiss. 1977. *Regimes for the Oceans, Outer Space, and Weather.* Brookings Institution, Washington, D.C.

Brubaker, S., ed. 1984. *Rethinking the Federal Lands.* Resources for the Future, Washington, D.C.

Charnovitz, S. 1995. Improving environmental and trade governance. *International Environmental Affairs* 7:59–91.

Chayes, A. and A. Handler Chayes. 1993. On compliance. *International Organization* 47:175–205

Chayes, A. and A. Handler Chayes. 1995. *The New Sovereignty: Compliance with Treaties in International Regulatory Regimes.* Harvard University Press, Cambridge, MA.

Cox, R. W. 1986. Social forces, states, and world orders: Beyond international relations theory. Pages 204–254 *in* R. O. Keohane, ed. *Neorealism and Its Critics.* Columbia University Press, New York.

Downs, G. W. and D. M. Rocke. 1990. *Tacit Bargaining, Arms Races and Arms Control.* University of Michigan Press, Ann Arbor.

Ellickson, R. 1991. *Order Without Law: How Neighbors Settle Disputes.* Harvard University Press, Cambridge, MA.

Fearon, J. 1991. Counterfactuals and hypothesis testing in political science. *World Politics* 43:169–185.

Haas, P. M., ed. 1992. Knowledge, power, and international policy coordination. *International Organization* 46:1–390.

Haas, P. M., R. O. Keohane, and M. A. Levy, eds. 1993. *Institutions for the Earth: Sources of Effective International Environmental Protection.* MIT Press, Cambridge, MA.

Haggard, S. and B. A. Simmons. 1987. Theories of international regimes. *International Organization* 41:491–517.

Hardin, G. 1968. The tragedy of the commons. *Science* 162 (Dec.):1343–1348.

Hardin, R. 1982. *Collective Action.* Johns Hopkins University Press, Baltimore.

Jodha, N.S. 1993. *Property Rights and Development.* Paper available from the Beijer International Institute of Ecological Economics, Stockholm.

Keohane, R. O. 1984. *After Hegemony: Cooperation and Discord in the World Political Economy*. Princeton University Press, Princeton, NJ.

Keohane, R. O. and J. S. Nye. 1977. *Power and Interdependence: World Politics in Transition*. Little Brown, Boston.

Keohane, R. O. and E. Ostrom, eds. 1995. *Local Commons and Global Interdependence: Heterogeneity and Cooperation in Two Domains*. Sage Publications, London.

Levy, M. A., G. Osherenko, and O. R. Young. 1991. *The Effectiveness of International Regimes: A Design for Large-scale Collaborative Research*. Paper available from the Institute on International Environmental Governance at Dartmouth College.

Levy, M. A., O. R. Young, and M. Zuern. 1995. The study of international regimes. *European Journal of International Relations* 1:267–330.

Lipschutz, R. 1992. Restructuring world politics: The emergence of global civil society. *Millennium* 21:389–420.

Lyons, G. M. and M. Mastanduno, eds. 1995. *Beyond Westphalia: State Sovereignty and International Intervention*. Johns Hopkins University Press, Baltimore.

Martin, L. L. 1994. Heterogeneity, linkage and commons problems. *Journal of Theoretical Politics* 6:473–493.

McCay, B. J. and J. M. Acheson, eds. 1987. *The Question of the Commons: The Culture and Ecology of Communal Resources*. University of Arizona Press, Tucson.

McKean, M. A. 1992. Success on the commons: A comparative examination of institutions for common property resource management. *Journal of Theoretical Politics* 4:247–281

Mitchell, R. B. 1994. *Intentional Oil Pollution at Sea: Environmental Policy and Treaty Compliance*. MIT Press, Cambridge, MA.

North, D. C. 1990. *Institutions, Institutional Change and Economic Performance*. Cambridge University Press, Cambridge, UK.

Olson, M. Jr. 1965. *The Logic of Collective Action*. Harvard University Press, Cambridge, MA.

Ostrom, E. 1990. *Governing the Commons: The Evolution of Institutions for Collective Action*. Cambridge University Press, Cambridge, UK.

Princen, T. and M. Finger. 1994. *Environmental NGOs in World Politics: Linking the Local and the Global*. Routledge, London.

Public Land Law Review Commission. 1970. *One Third of the Nation's Land*. U.S. Government Printing Office, Washington, D.C.

Richardson, E. 1988. Jan Mayen in perspective. *American Journal of International Law* 82:443–458.

Rittberger, V., ed. 1990. *International Regimes in East–West Politics*. Pinter, London.

Rittberger, V. and M. Zuern. 1991. Regime theory: Findings from the study of 'east–west' regimes. *Cooperation and Conflict* 26:165–183.

Rosenau, J. N. and E.-O. Czempiel, eds. 1992. *Governance Without Government: Order and Change in World Politics.* Cambridge University Press, Cambridge, UK.

Schelling, T. C. 1978. *Micromotives and Macrobehavior.* W.W. Norton, New York.

Snidal, D. 1985. The limits of hegemonic stability theory. *International Organization* 39:579–614.

Spector, B. and A. Korula. 1992. "The Post-Agreement Negotiation Process: The Problems of Ratifying International Environmental Agreements." IIASA Working Paper WP-92-90.

Stein, J. G., ed. 1989. *Getting to the Table: The Processes of International Prenegotiation.* Johns Hopkins University Press, Baltimore.

Strange, S. 1983. *Cave! hic dragones:* a critique of regime analysis. Pages 337–354 in S. D. Krasner, ed. *International Regimes.* Cornell University Press, Ithaca, NY.

Victor, D. G. and J. E. Salt. 1994. From Rio to Berlin: Managing climate change. *Environment* 36 (Dec.):6–15 and 25–32.

Wapner, P. 1995. Politics beyond the state: Environmental activism and world civic politics. *World Politics* 47: 311–340.

Wettestad, J. 1995. *'Nuts and Bolts for Environmental Negotiators?' Designing Effective International Regimes.* Fridtjof Nansen Institute, Oslo.

Young, O. R. 1989. *International Cooperation: Building Regimes for Natural Resources and the Environment.* Cornell University Press, Ithaca, NY.

Young, O. R. 1994a. *International Governance: Protecting the Environment in a Stateless Society.* Cornell University Press, Ithaca, NY.

Young, O. R. 1994b. The problem of scale in human/environment relationships. *Journal of Theoretical Politics* 6:429–447.

Young, O. R. and G. Osherenko, eds. 1993. *Polar Politics: Creating International Environmental Regimes.* Cornell University Press, Ithaca, NY.

CHAPTER 13

Building Property Rights for Transboundary Resources

SCOTT BARRETT

Missing Markets and Transboundary Resources

A striking feature of many resources is that rights to them are difficult to define and enforce, with the consequence that markets for such resources do not exist (or, if they do exist, function badly). For example, though fossil fuels are bought and sold routinely, atmospheric concentrations of greenhouse gases are not traded. Markets are also missing for stratospheric ozone, whales in the high seas, biodiversity in protected rainforests, and many other resources.

Where markets do not exist, resources will not be allocated efficiently; it will be possible to identify an alternative (feasible) allocation in which at least one party is made better off and no party is made worse off. Users of a resource may, by their actions, affect the set of outcomes attainable by other parties, but they will have no incentive to take these effects into account when they act. For example, when a country emits greenhouse gases into the atmosphere, global concentrations of these gases increase, with the expected consequence that the future climate of all countries will be changed. Countries emitting greenhouse gases do not do so with the intention of altering the climate of other countries. Potential climate change is largely an unintended consequence of the emission of greenhouse gases by all countries. Every country has an incentive to take into account the effect its own actions have on itself, but where markets are missing, no country has any incentive to take into account the effect its own actions have on others. The outcome is an inefficient allocation of atmospheric resources: though each country may be behaving in a manner which most advances its own interests, the consequence is an outcome which is likely to be unattractive to all countries. In short, atmospheric concentrations of greenhouse gases are likely to be "too great." Likewise, stocks of ozone in the stratosphere, whales in the sea, and biodiversity in protected rainforests are likely to be "too small."

The atmosphere, stratosphere, and whales in the high seas are "transboundary" resources in the sense that they are not confined within the jurisdiction of any one party. Biodiversity is a transboundary resource in a different sense: its existence is valued outside the boundary in which it is protected.[1] Both types of transboundary resource, however, are victims of missing markets.

The boundaries which are relevant to the allocation of environmental resources are those which delineate zones of control over resources, including the authority to define rights to resources and to enforce those rights. Such authority is almost invariably accorded to nation states, and only to nation states. As an example, the United States Constitution provides that: "No state shall, without the consent of Congress . . . enter into any agreement or compact with another state or with a foreign power." Furthermore, the federal government may itself impose an allocation upon states if they fail to reach an agreement themselves on the allocation of a resource. For example, the Boulder Canyon Project Act of 1928 conferred upon the Secretary of the Interior the authority to apportion the waters of the Colorado River at Hoover Dam and below among the three affected states (California, Arizona, and Nevada) in the event that the three states could not agree to a tristate compact. Similarly, when the province of British Columbia threatened to enter into an agreement with the United States over the development of the Columbia River, the Canadian federal government passed the International Rivers Improvement Act, which required that works on rivers that flowed into the United States be approved first by the federal government. This allowed the federal government to veto a proposal by British Columbia which would have sacrificed wider Canadian interests (see Krutilla 1966, LeMarquand 1977).

While every nation can potentially control the resources confined within its own borders, and hence ensure that these resources are allocated efficiently, there is no world government which can control transboundary resources. This is because states have chosen not to recognize such an authority but to acknowledge instead the sovereign equality of all states. Not all countries are members of the United Nations but, more importantly, resolutions by the General Assembly are not even binding on those states which are members. Furthermore, an agreement between countries cannot be enforced by a third party (Barrett 1990). One country may take another to the International Court of Justice, the principal judicial organ of the United

Nations, for violating an agreement, but the court will not hear the case without the prospective defendant's consent. Even if the case is heard, the parties cannot be compelled to comply with the court's decision. Agreements between countries over the use of a resource must be negotiated by the parties themselves and be *self-enforcing*. It is for this reason that transboundary resources are particularly difficult to manage efficiently.

How can transboundary resources be better managed? One possibility is to redraw boundaries such that these resources are brought within the jurisdiction of individual nations. Of course borders do change, and they sometimes change for this reason—a good example being the expansion of national jurisdiction over the oceans' 200-mile Exclusive Economic Zones. But borders change for other reasons, too, even if at the expense of the efficient management of resources. For example, the Indian subcontinent was partitioned in 1947 even though the division of the Indus basin between India and Pakistan meant foregoing the advantages of joint use and development of the basin (indeed, diversion of the waters by India in 1948 almost led to a war with Pakistan). Furthermore, nationalization is not always feasible. While rights to airspace can be delineated along geographic lines, concentrations of greenhouse gases are mixed in the atmosphere and cannot be nationalized.

More typically, transboundary resources are managed by agreements between nations which specify the rights and obligations of signatories (including, in some cases, the way in which signatories should behave toward nonsignatories). Such institutions have a surprisingly long history; the oldest that I have been able to trace is a unilateral declaration by Emperor Charlemagne in 805 A.D., which granted freedom of navigation to a monastery. International environmental agreements are also remarkably common; well over 100 multilateral agreements, and many more bilateral agreements, are in force today. But the fact that such agreements exist tells us nothing about whether they are able to allocate transboundary resources efficiently. The constraint of sovereignty could well prevent them from doing so. This chapter sketches a theory that explains how property rights to transboundary resources are defined and enforced and that predicts the consequences of such property-rights regimes for efficiency.[2]

Coase's Theorem and Customary Law

Coase's (1960) famous theorem tells us that, in a dispute between two parties over the use of a resource, provided the rights to the resource are allocated to one of the parties (it doesn't matter which one) and provided those rights can be enforced, the resulting allocation of resources will be efficient if (see Mäler 1990): (i) both countries know the payoff functions for each party, (ii) there are no transaction costs, (iii) the question of the allocation of a resource can be seen in isolation of other relations between the parties, and (iv) the payoffs are independent of the initial allocation of rights. The theorem thus tells us that the assignment of property rights affects the distribution of net benefits, but not the total sum of net benefits, which through trade will always be maximized.

But do the assumptions behind the theorem hold? As we have seen, one important feature of transboundary resources is that the initial allocation is not given and cannot be assigned by a supernational authority. The case of transboundary resources is thus quite different from the one analyzed by Coase. Coase assumed that a third party could allocate rights to the resource and enforce those rights. State sovereignty means that this assumption will be violated in the case of transboundary resources.

If rights cannot be allocated by a third party, then an allocation will have to be negotiated by the countries which are affected by the use of the resource. The alternative is conflict, and conflict is something which states would normally prefer to avoid (see below). In particular cases, the allocation of rights to transboundary resources is articulated in treaties. These will be discussed later. Treaties, however, are negotiated against the background of international custom, and to understand the law of treaties one needs first to understand the law of custom.

Customary law is important in international relations precisely because there is no world lawmaking body. Customary law serves to coordinate expectations about how other states will behave, and it also prescribes how each state should behave itself. Custom is therefore an equilibrium behavior: when other countries consent to the custom, it is in each state's own interest to consent to the custom as well. To fail to comply with custom is to be in breach of international law, and this is something which, like conflict, states prefer to avoid.[3]

Nation states tend to support a custom or to negotiate an allocation of rights in treaties because disputes over a resource cannot be seen in isolation of other relations between states. Assumption (iii) of the Coase theorem does not apply in the case of international relations.[4] States wish to agree to an allocation and consent to a custom because there is some penalty for failing to agree and consent. The penalty could be armed aggression, but it could just as well be a threat to reciprocate in the case of another issue where the tables are turned, or to reciprocate in the management of the same resource at some future time.

Coase considered allocating rights to one or the other party. In international law, these allocations are defined by the principles of *unlimited territorial sovereignty* and *unlimited territorial integrity*. The former states that a country has exclusive rights to the use of resources within its territory, while the latter states that the quantity and quality of resources available to a country cannot be altered by another country. If the externality involves an upstream state polluting a river which is shared by a downstream riparian system, then the former allocation would assign the right to pollute to the upstream state while the second principle would assign the right to an undisturbed flow of the river to the downstream state.

While these allocations accord with Coase's analysis, neither is endorsed by custom. To take an example, the doctrine of unlimited territorial sovereignty was famously invoked by the Attorney General of the United States in 1895 when Mexico protested against U.S. plans to divert water from the Rio Grande for irrigation. But only 11 years later, the United States signed an agreement with Mexico on the Equitable Distribution of the Waters of the Rio Grande for Irrigation Purposes. Numerous other agreements have established equitable utilization as the customary allocation of international water resources in international law (Birnie and Boyle 1992). This principle recognizes that rights to resources are shared.

A good example of the application of the principle is the Convention on the Protection of the Rhine Against Pollution by Chlorides, which came into force in 1985. Salt pollution of the Rhine has been particularly harmful to the Netherlands, which is the farthest downstream nation. The cheapest way to reduce emissions into the Rhine was to reduce emissions from a single source, a French potash mine, Les Mines de Potasse d'Alsace. Yet Germany and Switzerland also polluted the Rhine, and it was the combined emissions of all three countries which ultimately polluted the Rhine downstream. If rights to the resource had been allocated under the doctrine of unlimited territorial sovereignty, efficient trade would have resulted in the Netherlands bearing all of the costs of reducing emissions from the French mine. By contrast, if rights had been prescribed by the doctrine of unlimited territorial integrity, the Netherlands would have borne none of this cost. The agreement actually reached involved sharing the costs: France and Germany each paid 30% of the cost; the Netherlands paid 34%; and Switzerland paid 6%.

The principle of equitable utilization (or variations of it) has also been employed in allocating rights to other types of transboundary resources, including resources which are "shared" by two or more nations with overlapping jurisdictions (such as rivers and lakes which serve as borders, air sheds, or migratory species) and resources which do not fall under the jurisdiction of any one country or group of countries (like fish and mammals in the high seas, the atmosphere, or the stratospheric ozone layer).

An example of an agreement governing the use of this last type of resource is the 1911 North Pacific Fur Seal Treaty. As a consequence of excessive harvesting over a number of years, the fur seal nearly became extinct at the turn of the century. Different breeding populations existed on American, Russian, and Japanese soils, but seals spend much of their time at sea (including beyond territorial limits), and Canada and Japan hunted the seals at sea under an open-access regime. Pelagic sealing is inefficient; selective harvesting is difficult at sea, and many seals are killed but never recovered. Furthermore, open access invites entry by additional sealing vessels until all economic rents are exhausted. It was harvesting at sea under an open-access regime which threatened extinction of the species. The agreement reached in 1911 banned pelagic sealing, and hence effectively assigned property rights to the nations with breeding populations. In doing so, the agreement enabled capable management of the resource. The two pelagic sealing nations (Canada and Japan) were compensated for conceding their right to harvest seals at sea by being given a share (15%) of the annual catch taken by Russia and the United States. In addition, the United States paid Canada (actually Britain, on behalf of Canada) and Japan $200,000 each to compensate their private sealers for immediate losses (see Gay 1987).

The Montreal Protocol on Substances that Deplete the Ozone Layer (negotiated in 1987) and its associated amendments is similarly structured, although it is a more complicated agreement, not the least because ozone depletion is a global problem.[5] While the agreement could not assign rights to the ozone layer itself, it did assign rights to produce and consume ozone-depleting substances (consumption is defined as production plus imports minus exports) for each signatory country. A distinction is made in the agreement between developed and developing countries (the latter are referred to in the agreement as "Article 5" countries). Under the agreement, developed country parties must reduce their production and consumption from current levels according to a schedule which eventually phases out a number of substances. Article 5 countries which consume less than 0.3 kilograms per capita of certain controlled substances are entitled to delay their compliance with the phase-out schedule for ten years. Developing countries are also entitled to be compensated by the developed countries for the "agreed incremental costs" of complying with the treaty. Effectively, developed countries bear the full costs of phasing out the controlled substances, while all countries share the benefits.

Unlike the Rhine convention and the North Pacific Fur Seal Treaty, the Montreal Protocol does not assign a final allocation of rights. As the agreement allows international trading in production and consumption rights, it prescribes instead an initial allocation. However, the extent of trading has been predictably small as: (1) trade in production and consumption rights is restricted (in some instances) by the treaty; (2) the rights are allocated to developed country parties on the basis of historical usage; and (3) since ozone-depleting substances are to be phased out, trading could only be temporary.

Bargaining over Rights to Transboundary Resources

The problem of allocating rights to transboundary resources can be seen as a bargaining problem. But it is an unusual bargaining problem in that there exists no clear status quo point. While international law may prescribe that transboundary resources be allocated according to the principle of equitable utilization, it is not clear exactly what this implies, except that the allocation "will generally entail a balance of interests which accommodates the needs and uses of each state" (Birnie and Boyle 1992:220). We can be pretty sure that equitable utilization is not the same as unlimited territorial sovereignty or unlimited territorial integrity, but we cannot be any more precise than this (e.g., Birnie and Boyle 1992) note that equitable utilization is not the same as equal utilization). We can, however, expect that the final allocation will be efficient; otherwise, by definition, one party could be made better off without any other party being made worse off. My purpose in this section is to sketch a possible solution to a particular bargaining problem, which is loosely based on the Rhine negotiations.

A river runs through three countries.[6] It starts in country A, and then flows through countries B and C consecutively. Countries A and B each emit one unit of pollution into the river, and this pollution only harms countries that are downstream. The pollution can be abated, but abatement is costly. Abatement by each of the polluting countries must lie between zero and one (no country can abate more than it pollutes) and is denoted x_A and x_B, respectively. Each country's payoff (country i's payoff is denoted p_i) is the difference between the benefit it receives from abatement and the costs it incurs to effect this abatement, plus or minus any money transfers. The benefit of abatement is a monetary value, reflecting the environmental damage avoided by the abatement. This will depend on the amount of abatement undertaken by all upstream countries. The larger this abatement, the larger the benefit to downstream riparians. The cost of abatement by country i will depend on the abatement by i and (by assumption) not on the abatement undertaken by the other countries. This cost is also a monetary value, and will increase with the amount of abatement. Ignoring transfers for the moment, suppose that the payoffs are as follows: $p_A = -1.5x_A$, $p_B = x_A - 0.5x_B$, $p_C = x_A + x_B$. According to these payoffs, the benefit of abatement for each country is equal to the quantity of abatement undertaken upstream, while the unit cost of abatement is higher for country A than for country B. Obviously, every country prefers a larger payoff to a smaller one, and will act to maximize its own payoff.

Under the doctrine of unlimited territorial sovereignty, each country is free not to abate. Given the above payoff functions, country A will maximize its payoff by setting $x_A = 0$. Similarly, B can do no better than to set $x_B = 0$. Hence, given the initial allocation of rights, in the absence of trade, no abatement will be undertaken, and the payoffs (p_A, p_B, p_C) will be $(0, 0, 0)$.

This allocation is inefficient in the sense that the aggregate of net benefits can be increased if positive abatement is undertaken. Obviously, $p_A + p_B + p_C = 0.5x_A + 0.5x_B$. Under the full cooperative outcome—the outcome which maximizes collective net benefits—$x_A = x_B = 1$, and aggregate net benefits rise from 0 to 1. This is the potential gain from trade.

While aggregate net benefits are maximized when A and B abate all of their pollution, A is made worse off under this outcome compared with the initial allocation prescribed by the doctrine of unlimited territorial sovereignty, while B and C are made better off: the payoffs under the full cooperative outcome are $(-1.5, 0.5, 2)$. Notice, however, that while country B prefers the outcome where $x_A = x_B = 1$ to the outcome where $x_A = x_B = 0$, it prefers the outcome $x_A = 1$, $x_B = 0$ to the former outcome because the payoffs under the latter outcome are $(-1.5, 1, 1)$. The situation can therefore be summarized as follows: under unlimited territorial sovereignty, A and B have no incentive to abate their pollution unilaterally, but all countries could potentially be made better off if A and B abated all of their pollution.

Since A and B have a right to pollute as much as they like, it would not be rational for either country to abate its pollution without compensation. Similarly, it would not be rational for C to provide compensation in excess of the benefits it receives from upstream abatement. As each country's payoff is zero in the absence of trade, any negotiated outcome must therefore satisfy $p_A \geq 0$, $p_B \geq 0$, and $p_C \geq 0$. The highest aggregate payoff that the three countries can receive is 1. Hence, it would not be rational for all three countries to accept a negotiated agreement which did not also require $p_A + p_B + p_C = 1$.

These are not the only requirements that a treaty must satisfy, however, for it is possible that two countries will cooperate independently of the third. As there are three countries, there are three possible two-party coalitions: A and B, B and C, and A and C. Begin by considering the first case. If A and B cooperate independently of C, they could do no better than to maximize $p_A + p_B = -0.5x_A + -0.5x_B$. This expression is maximized if neither A nor B abate their emissions. To be acceptable to A and B, the negotiated agreement must therefore satisfy $p_A + p_B \geq 0$. However, this constraint is already satisfied by the requirement that $p_A \geq 0$ and $p_B \geq 0$. Suppose now that B and C cooperate independently of A. Then B and C will choose $x_B = 1$ to maximize $p_B + p_C = 2x_A + 0.5x_B$, while A will choose $x_A = 0$. Hence, the negotiated agreement must also satisfy $p_B + p_C \geq 0.5$. This constraint is different from the ones listed above and is therefore a further constraint that must be satisfied by any agreement. Finally, suppose A and C cooperate independently of B. They will choose $x_A = 0$ to maximize $p_A + p_C = -0.5x_A + x_B$, while B will choose $x_B = 0$ to maximize p_B. But the minimum payoffs implied by these choices are satisfied given our nonnegativity constraints. Taking all of these requirements together, the core set of outcomes must satisfy $p_A \geq 0$, $p_B \geq 0$, $p_C \geq 0$, $p_B + p_C \geq 0.5$, and $p_A + p_B + p_C = 1$. Provided the negotiated outcome lies within this set of core outcomes, it is not credible for any country to withdraw from the agreement, either unilaterally or in partnership with another country.

The problem with this set of outcomes is that it is large, and we cannot be sure what negotiated outcome will be agreed.[7] For example, the allocations (0.1, 0.4, 0.5) and (0.25, 0.5, 0.25) are both in the core. However, there is one core outcome which is compelling by virtue of its symmetry. This is the outcome where the gains from trade are shared equally by the three parties: (0.33, 0.33, 0.33). Under this outcome, A and B abate all their pollution and both B and C transfer funds to the farthest upstream country, A.

The allocation which would result under the doctrine of unlimited territorial integrity is much easier to analyze. By definition, countries A and B must abate all of their pollution in the status quo, yielding the payoffs (−1.5, 0.5, 2). Since the full cooperative outcome does not yield a higher aggregate payoff, the core is unique and consists of the initial allocation. Given that no party has a right to pollute and observing that, starting from this allocation, there are no gains from trade, the initial allocation is also the final allocation.

Under the doctrine of unlimited territorial integrity, the initial allocation is efficient (in this example), and the payoffs are (−1.5, 0.5, 2). Under the doctrine of unlimited territorial sovereignty, the initial allocation is not efficient (in this example), and the set of core bargaining outcomes is large. Let us suppose that the parties agree to implement the symmetric bargaining solution in this last case (that is, suppose that the final allocation under the doctrine of unlimited territorial sovereignty is (0.33, 0.33, 0.33)). Though we can only be sure that equitable utilization will result in an allocation somewhere between these two outcomes, let us assume that the parties agree to divide the two allocations evenly. Equitable utilization then implies the final allocation (−0.59, 0.42, 1.17). The farthest downstream country (C, or the Netherlands in the Rhine example) bears part of the cost of abatement, but it does not bear the full cost. The farthest upstream country (A, or Switzerland in the Rhine case) also contributes toward the cost of abatement, even though it does not benefit from the abatement.

In the Rhine Chlorides agreement, France and Germany agreed to contribute toward the total cost of abatement for reasons of equity (LeMarquand 1977). The Swiss contribution was based on the principle of "solidarity," defined by the OECD Principles on Transfrontier Pollution as seeking ". . . as far as possible an equitable balance of rights and obligations as regards the zones concerned by transfrontier pollution." LeMarquand (1977:119) argues that this position reflects the playing of a possible reciprocal and repeated game: "No doubt [the Swiss] also feel that solidarity on this issue could be advantageous to them on other subsequent issues." As mentioned before, it is because relations between states are reciprocal and different issues can be linked that states have incentives to agree to property rights allocations.

Compliance with International Agreements

The analysis of bargaining assumes that agreements are binding in the sense that they can be enforced by a third party. Countries decide whether or not to sign an agreement, but once they sign they have no opportunity to withdraw and no option but to comply with the agreement. We have seen, however, that binding agreements are not feasible under the rules of international law.

In fact, full compliance with international agreements is more a rule than an exception (Chayes and Chayes 1991). Where states do not comply, the reason is often that states do not have the means to comply rather than that they do not wish to comply. For example, four years after the Montreal Protocol was signed, only about half of the signatories had complied fully with the treaty's reporting requirements. But according to Chayes and Chayes (1993:194), "the great majority of the nonreporting states were developing countries that for the most part were simply *unable* (emphasis added) to comply without technical assistance from the treaty organization." The reason states comply with international agreements is by now familiar. It is not because agreements impose sanctions for noncompliance; such formal mechanisms are almost never used. The reason states comply with international agreements is that their relationships are reciprocal and linked to other issues. "It is inevitable that a state's defection from treaty rules will generate repercussions and linkages throughout the network of its relationships with others in the community" (Chayes and Chayes 1991:320). Hence, much the same forces which compel states to seek equitable but efficient allocations of rights also compel them to comply with agreements which articulate these rights. It would be odd if the situation were otherwise.

Compliance with an agreement, however, is only one prerequisite to sustaining an efficient outcome. A second prerequisite is that the parties to the agreement include all countries which have an interest in the outcome. It is one thing for a country not to fulfill a promise it has made to comply with an agreement. It is quite another for a country which has not made such a promise to behave contrary to the agreement, which it is quite entitled to do under international law. Reciprocity and linkage may not be enough to sustain full participation.

Participation in International Agreements

Consider the hypothetical example illustrated in Figure 13.1. Some 101 countries have an interest in the management of a global environmental resource, like the atmosphere or the stratospheric ozone layer. Each country is assumed to be identical, and each may choose to abate its pollution or to pollute. The payoff to any one country is P_S if the country plays Abate and P_N if the country plays Pollute. Any one country's payoff depends not only on whether it plays Abate or Pollute but also on whether the other 100 countries play Abate or

Pollute. The horizontal axis in Figure 13.1 represents the number of the other 100 countries which play Abate. The figure shows that the payoff to any one country increases with the number of other countries which play Abate, but it also shows that, irrespective of what the other 100 countries do, it is in each country's interest to play Pollute (P_N always exceeds P_S). Hence, the equilibrium to this game is unique: it involves each country playing Pollute. Each country therefore earns a payoff of 1. Notice, however, that if all countries played Abate, each would earn a payoff of 9. This is the maximum payoff that can be secured by all countries and it is denoted in Figure 13.1 by the open circle. The equilibrium, identified by the solid circle in Figure 13.1, is plainly inefficient.

The game depicted in Figure 13.1 is a version of the famous prisoners' dilemma game played by 101 players. Its essential features are that (1) in seeking to advance their self-interests, all players behave in a manner which is not in their joint interests; and (2) the strategy chosen by each player is independent of the choices made by the other players. The game is a caricature of international relations but it nicely illustrates the problem we are concerned with. If no country had a right to pollute and if this right could be enforced, the equilibrium to the game would involve each country playing Abate and earning a payoff of 9. The outcome would be efficient. The problem is thus reminiscent of the bargaining game considered earlier. However, the bargaining game assumed that binding agreements were

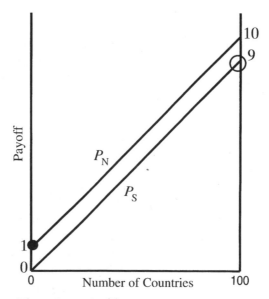

F I G U R E 13.1. The prisoner's dilemma.

feasible. In the prisoners' dilemma game, agreements cannot be enforced by a third party. This is why the game sustains an inefficient equilibrium.

However, the prisoners' dilemma is a caricature; it is not the game that countries actually play. One assumption of the prisoners' dilemma is that the choices which the countries can make are binary; they can play Abate or Pollute. For most problems of interest, choices will be continuous. For example, it would be reasonable to assume that countries could abate any quantity along the continuum from zero to the total quantity of emissions. It can be shown that allowing countries to choose from a continuum of feasible abatement levels changes the game. The prisoners' dilemma game is rather strange in that the best choice that any one country can make is independent of the behavior of the other 100 countries; play Pollute is therefore a *dominant strategy*. When choice sets are continuous, this will not generally be so, and allowing for continuous choice sets is one way in which each country's best choice can be shown to depend on the behavior of other countries. However, there is one important choice which is binary, and this is the choice of whether or not to be a signatory to an agreement. As this last choice is a more natural one, let P_N now denote the payoff to being a nonsignatory and P_S denote the payoff to being a signatory. Figure 13.1 then describes a situation in which no country accedes to a treaty but where all countries would be better off if all did accede.

In a model in which choice sets are continuous, I have shown that countries may be able to sustain partial cooperation as an equilibrium (Barrett 1994a). By specifying an agreement that prescribes the behavior of signatories, and by assuming that compliance with the agreement is full, it can be rational for some countries to cooperate, even while the rest do not. Countries which cooperate—the signatories—choose abatement levels so as to maximize their joint payoff (consistent with the bargaining analysis in the section above entitled "Bargaining over Rights to Transboundary Resources"), while perhaps also taking into account the abatement decisions by those countries which do not cooperate—the nonsignatories. Each nonsignatory, however, chooses its abatement level to maximize its own payoff, taking as given abatement by all other countries.

Two features of the agreement sustain cooperation. First, the model assumes full compliance. As noted in the section above entitled "Compliance with International Agreements," signatories do typically comply fully with their obligations. Second, the terms of the agreement allow signatories effectively to "punish" countries which withdraw from the agreement and "reward" those which accede. Use of the words "punish" and "reward" requires careful interpretation, because the game I am describing, like the prisoners' dilemma, is one-shot. Reactions are therefore infeasible. However, in having abatement by signatories be increasing in the number of signatories, the agreement specifies actions which have the effect of "punishing" defection and "rewarding" accession. The assumption that signatories maximize their joint payoffs, however, limits the magnitude of these "rewards" and "punishments," and for this reason the agreement can only have a limited effect.

Figure 13.2 illustrates this game. Unlike the prisoners' dilemma, illustrated in Figure 13.1, here each country's best choice depends on what the other countries choose to do. If the number of other signatories is "small," it is best to be a signatory. When that number is "large" it is best to be a nonsignatory. The equilibrium to this game is again unique; it involves some countries being signatories and some being nonsignatories. In the figure, about 60 countries are signatories and the remaining 40 are nonsignatories.[8] However, as in the prisoners' dilemma game, the equilibrium is not efficient; all countries would be better off if all were signatories.[9]

I find that the number of signatories that can be sustained by an agreement depends on the nature of the the costs and benefits of abatement. An agreement can sustain a large number of signatories,

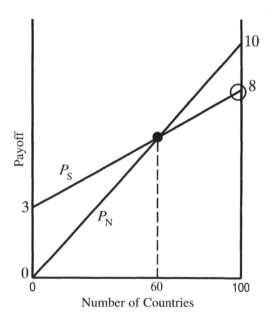

FIGURE 13.2. A self-enforcing, incomplete international agreement.

but only when the potential gains to cooperation are relatively small. When the gains to cooperation are relatively large, I find that an agreement cannot sustain a large number of signatories. Though not as bad as the equilibrium to the prisoners' dilemma game, the equilibrium for a self-enforcing international environmental agreement is still likely to be inefficient.

Reciprocity in International Agreements

The above model shows that the design of an international agreement can be important. However, the model's great weakness is that it does not explicitly acknowledge the reciprocal nature of international relations. Let us suppose, therefore, that the one-shot game described above is repeated infinitely often. It is well known that if the one-shot prisoners' dilemma game is repeated infinitely often, then the full cooperative outcome of the one-shot game can be sustained as a non-cooperative equilibrium of the infinitely repeated game provided countries do not discount the future too much (see, for example, Axelrod 1984). There is no guarantee that the full cooperative outcome will be the equilibrium to the repeated game; there are other equilibria. However, because the full cooperative outcome maximizes the joint payoffs of all countries, it seems likely that countries could coordinate in this equilibrium.

An example will make these points clearer. Suppose the game depicted in Figure 13.1 is repeated over and over again forever. Then the outcome where every country plays Nonsignatory in every period remains an equilibrium. It is an equilibrium because each player can do no better than to play Nonsignatory, given that the other players play Nonsignatory. What is different about (infinite) repetition is that this is no longer the only equilibrium.

Suppose the players play the following strategy: play Signatory in the first round and continue to play Signatory in every successive round provided the other players played Signatory in every previous round; if any other player played Nonsignatory in any previous round, play Nonsignatory. This is a "grim" strategy in that the punishment to cheating on an agreement to play Signatory is huge and unforgiving. Can the grim strategy sustain full cooperation as an equilibrium to the repeated game? We shall see that it can, provided the future is not discounted too heavily.

To be an equilibrium, it must be the case that it is in each country's interest to play "grim" when all other countries play "grim." If a country plays "grim" while all others play "grim," each country receives a payoff of 9 in each period. Let us suppose that in every round of the game up to round t, all players played Signatory. Would it be rational for a country to deviate in round t? If the player does not deviate in round t, the present value of the future stream of payoffs, from the perspective of time t, will be $9 + 9/r$, where r is the rate at which the future is discounted. If the player does deviate in round t, it gets a payoff of 10 in this round, which is 1 more than it would have received had it not cheated. However, in each successive round the player can do no better than to receive a payoff of 1. Hence, the present value sum of payoffs at the time of the deviation is $10 + 1/r$. Given that all other countries play "grim," it will only be rational for a player to deviate if the payoff to deviating exceeds the payoff to conforming; that is, if $10 + 1/r > 9 + 9/r$. This means that the "grim" strategy can be sustained as an equilibrium for a rate of discount less than 800%!

The real problem with this analysis is that it assumes that the parties choose their strategies at time 0 and then implement them. If a country does cheat, there is no opportunity to renegotiate. This is odd, because if a country did cheat, then it would make sense for the parties to let bygones be bygones and to try to cooperate again, just as they did in the initial period. That is, the rules of the game should allow the countries to renegotiate the agreement. But any agreement which countries would want to renegotiate cannot be self-enforcing.

I have analyzed this problem building on the type of game described above and have found that renegotiation does limit the extent to which the full cooperative outcome of the one-shot game can be sustained as a self-enforcing agreement. I find that, for an arbitrarily small discount rate, the full cooperative outcome can only be sustained as a self-enforcing agreement if the number of countries with an interest in the outcome is not "too large" (see Barrett 1994a, b). The meaning of "too large" here depends on the potential gains to cooperation. I find that, the larger the gains to cooperation, the smaller the number of countries which can sustain the full cooperative outcome. This is reminiscent of the results reported in the previous section.

Linkage in International Agreements

Repetition is not the only way in which cooperation can be sustained. We have also seen that it is important whether countries interact in other areas than the management of the transboundary resource. One important area of interaction is trade. In fact, trade is often linked to the transboundary resource automatically. For example, if signatories to a climate change agreement abate carbon dioxide emissions at home, this will raise the cost of emitting CO_2 at home and hence shift comparative advantage in CO_2-intensive production to nonsignatories. Emissions by nonsignatories will therefore increase as a consequence of abatement by signatories. This phenomenon is known as *leakage*. Leakage undermines attempts to manage transboundary resources efficiently.

To reduce leakage, some kind of policy will be required which reverses this shift in comparative advantage. Border tax adjustments could be used for this purpose, but here I shall focus on quantitative trade restrictions. This is because the latter may also be effective in encouraging participation in international agreements.

Suppose that we begin with a situation like that shown in Figure 13.1 but that the agreement specifies that signatories are not permitted to trade with nonsignatories. Then, if one country plays Signatory and all others play Nonsignatory, the signatory suffers large losses in the gains from trade. This will be enough to discourage any country from playing Signatory given that all other countries play Nonsignatory. Suppose instead that all other countries play Signatory. Then there is a huge penalty to playing Nonsignatory; the only nonsignatory loses all the gains from trade. This suggests that, with trade restrictions, it will sometimes be attractive for countries to be signatories provided the number of signatories exceeds a certain threshold. Such a game is illustrated in Figure 13.3. The threshold number of countries is about 60 and there are two equilibria. One is where all countries play Nonsignatory. The other is where all countries play Signatory. Though there exist two equilibria, only one is efficient. This is the equilibrium where all countries play Signatory.

The problem, then, is how to get countries to select the efficient equilibrium. This is quite easy. Suppose that the agreement specifies that it will only become "binding" (in the sense of international law) if signed by at least 60 countries. Then, if the number of signatories is less than 60, countries have nothing to lose by playing Signatory. However, once more than 60 countries play Signatory, all countries prefer to play Signatory. Hence, the *minimum participation clause* is a device which compels all countries to play Signatory.

Notice that, once all countries are signatories to the agreement, trade is never restricted. However, were it not for the threat of restricting trade, coupled with the minimum participation clause, all countries would not play Signatory. To be self-enforcing, however, the threat of trade restrictions must be credible; it must be in the interests of signatories to restrict trade in order for the threat of trade restrictions to sustain the full cooperative outcome. In a preliminary

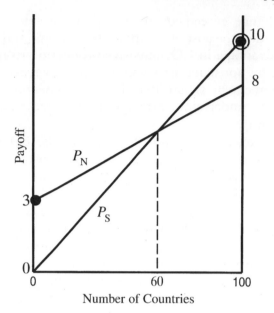

F I G U R E 13.3. A complete international agreement enforced by trade sanctions.

analysis of this problem, I find that trade restrictions are not always credible (Barrett 1994c).

Trade restrictions and a minimum participation clause are both employed in the Montreal Protocol. The agreement would not come into force until signed by at least 11 countries making up at least two-thirds of global consumption of ozone-depleting substances. Trade in these substances between signatories and nonsignatories is banned. Moreover, trade in products containing these substances or made using these substances is also subject to a ban. According to the chief U.S. negotiator at the Montreal Protocol talks, "These provisions were critical, since they constituted the only enforcement mechanism in the protocol" (Benedick 1991).

Conclusion

I began this chapter by noting that transboundary resources will be misallocated because markets for such resources are lacking. However, I have gone on to show how the allocation of transboundary environmental resources is affected by international institutions, including the laws of custom and treaties. These institutions are markets of a sort; they are "institutions which make available to affected parties the opportunity to negotiate courses of actions" (Dasgupta 1990:53). The problem with managing transboundary resources is thus not the absence of markets as such but rather the requirement that the actions negotiated through international law be self-enforcing. Self-enforcement is a severe constraint, but it need not render international institutions impotent. Reciprocal and linked relations coupled with inventiveness in the design of international agreements are enough to sustain efficient outcomes in some but perhaps not all instances.

NOTES

1. I concentrate here more on the former problem, but the latter is amenable to the same analysis. See Barrett (1994b).

2. Earlier versions of this chapter were presented at two Property Rights Workshops at the Beijer Institute, and the present version reflects what I learned from the participants of these workshops.

3. International custom and social norms are similar phenomena. For an analysis of the latter in the context of the environment, see Dasgupta (1990).

4. In fact, many if not all of the assumptions underlying the Coase theorem cannot be expected to hold, even in the case of intranational resources. I concentrate here only on the assumptions that are uniquely relevant to transboundary resources.

5. As of the end of 1994, the Montreal Protocol had been ratified by 146 countries.

6. It matters that there are more than two countries, but not that there are only three; nothing interesting would be learned by modeling this problem with four countries. The reason for considering bargaining among three countries is that this allows for the possibility that any two countries may form a coalition that excludes the third. Note that Coase considers two-party bargaining.

7. In some cases, a core outcome may not exist—the core may be empty; see Shubik's (1987:541–542) "garbage game."

8. In fact, the equilibrium in Figure 13.2 is not quite 60 signatories. To see this, recall that the horizontal axis is the number of *other* countries that are signatories. Denote the number of signatories by k. The payoffs depend on k, and we may therefore express them as a function of k. The two payoff curves cross where $P_N(60) = P_S(61)$. This is not the equilibrium. The equilibrium occurs where 59 countries are signatories. The payoff to being a nonsignatory when 59 other countries are signatories equals the payoff to being a signatory when 58 other countries are signatories; that is, $P_N(59) = P_S(59)$. This is an equilibrium because when the number of signatories is 59 no country can improve its payoff by deviating unilaterally—no signatory

can do better by becoming a nonsignatory and no nonsignatory can do better by becoming a signatory.

9. Since the horizontal axis represents the number of other countries that are signatories, when there are 60 signatories the payoff to being a signatory is the value of the payoff curve P_S when there are 59 other signatories. This is less than the payoff to being a nonsignatory when there are 60 signatories. Hence, nonsignatories receive a higher payoff than signatories. This is because nonsignatories experience a free ride on the additional abatement undertaken by signatories.

REFERENCES

Axelrod, R. 1984. *The Evolution of Cooperation.* Basic Books, New York.

Barrett, S. 1990. The problem of global environmental protection. *Oxford Review of Economic Policy* 6:68–79.

Barrett, S. 1994a. Self-enforcing international environmental agreements. *Oxford Economic Policy* 46:878–894.

Barrett, S. 1994b. The biodiversity supergame. *Environmental and Resource Economics* 4:111–122.

Barrett, S. 1994c. "Trade Restrictions in International Environmental Agreements." CSERGE Working Paper GEC 94–13. Centre for Social and Economic Research on the Global Environment. University College London.

Benedick, R. E. 1991. *Ozone Diplomacy: New Directions in Safeguarding the Planet.* Harvard University Press, Cambridge, MA.

Birnie, P. W. and A. E. Boyle. 1992. *International Law and the Environment.* Clarendon Press, Oxford, UK.

Chayes, A. and A. H. Chayes. 1991. Compliance without enforcement: State regulatory behavior under regulatory treaties. *Negotiation Journal* 7:311–331.

Chayes, A. and A. H. Chayes. 1993. On compliance. *International Organization* 47:175–205.

Coase, R. H. 1960. The problem of social cost. *Journal of Law and Economics* 3:1–44.

Dasgupta, P. 1990. The environment as a commodity. *Oxford Review of Economic Policy* 6:51–67.

Gay, J. T. 1987. *American Fur Seal Diplomacy: The Alaskan Fur Seal Controversy.* Peter Lang, New York.

Krutilla, J. V. 1966. The international Columbia river treaty: An economic evaluation. Pages 69–97 *in* A. V. Kneese and S. C. Smith, eds. *Water Research.* Johns Hopkins University Press, Baltimore.

LeMarquand, D. G. 1977. *International Rivers: The Politics of Cooperation.* Westwater Research Centre, University of British Columbia, Vancouver.

Mäler, K.-G. 1990. International environmental problems. *Oxford Review of Economic Policy* 6:80–108.

Shubik, M. 1987. *A Game-Theoretic Approach to Political Economy.* MIT Press, Cambridge, MA.

Index